Agnes C. P Watt

Twenty-Five Years' Mission Life on Tanna, New Hebrides

Biographical sketch and introd. by T. Watt Leggatt

Agnes C. P Watt

Twenty-Five Years' Mission Life on Tanna, New Hebrides
Biographical sketch and introd. by T. Watt Leggatt

ISBN/EAN: 9783337319007

Printed in Europe, USA, Canada, Australia, Japan

Cover: Foto ©Andreas Hilbeck / pixelio.de

More available books at **www.hansebooks.com**

TWENTY-FIVE YEARS' MISSION LIFE

ON

TANNA, NEW HEBRIDES.

BIOGRAPHICAL SKETCH AND INTRODUCTION BY

REV. T. WATT LEGGATT,
NEW HEBRIDES.

J. AND R. PARLANE, PAISLEY.
JOHN MENZIES AND CO., EDINBURGH AND GLASGOW.
HOULSTON AND SONS, LONDON.
1896.

PREFACE.

This book was undertaken at the request of many friends who had appreciated Mrs Watt's general letters and desired to have them in a permanent form. Although the New Hebrides has been a good deal written about of late, I believe that there is still room for the present work. These letters exhibit mission work from a somewhat unusual view-point; inasmuch as they record twenty-five years' faithful and incessant work with little apparent result. It is not difficult to be cheerful and enthusiastic in a flood-tide of success; but it is given to few to labour as Mrs Watt laboured, amid reverses and discouragement, for a quarter of a century, and meet the summons home with a heart as hopeful as on the first day she set foot on Tanna. Years of hope deferred, no doubt impressed her with a juster appreciation of the difficulties of the work, yet to the end disappointment failed to damp her ardour or sour her kindly disposition. She never despaired of Tanna, nor lost her faith that the gospel of Christ, which she offered to its people, was the power of God unto salvation to all who believe.

The materials at my command were far from being so full as I could have desired, and residence on a remote island, with unfrequent communication, has occasioned considerable delay in collecting them and completing the work.

I have endeavoured to let her tell the story of her life and work in her own letters and journals. Sometimes an explanatory note is appended, or passages from letters of different date are inserted, where the same subject is referred to; but in every case this has been indicated.

I can only hope that to some extent I have succeeded; and that this may not only be an addition to the literature of Missions, but also a source of comfort and inspiration to others who may be working for Christ in depressing and discouraging circumstances either at home or abroad.

T. WATT LEGGATT.

"AMY GERTRUDE RUSSELL" MISSION HOUSE,
    AULUA, MALEKULA,
        NEW HEBRIDES, *March, 1896.*

CONTENTS.

	PAGE
BIOGRAPHICAL SKETCH	17
TANNA AND ITS MISSIONARIES	47

Letters.

I.
MELBOURNE AND NEW ZEALAND ... 53
TO HER FATHER.

II.
FIRST SIGHT OF THE ISLANDS ... 62
GENERAL LETTER.

III.
BEGINNING WORK ON TANNA ... 77
1. TO HER FATHER.
2. TO THE FAMILY.
3. TO THE FAMILY.

IV.
MAN TANNA ... 104

V.
SETTLING NEW MISSIONARIES ... 114
TO THE FAMILY.

VI.
STREAKS OF DAWN ... 123
   1. TO THE GLASGOW FOUNDRY BOYS' RELIGIOUS SOCIETY.
   2. TO THE TREASURER OF THE GLASGOW FOUNDRY BOYS' RELIGIOUS SOCIETY.

VII.
HOW WE SPENT THE HOT SEASON OF 1870 ... 132

VIII.
FIRST EXPERIENCE OF A HURRICANE ... 142
   TO THE FAMILY.

IX.
A GLIMPSE OF CIVILISATION. THE MARTYRDOM OF TAUKA ... 152
   1. TO THE FAMILY.
   2. EXTRACTS FROM JOURNAL.
   3. TO THE FAMILY.

X.
"EARTHQUAKES, WARS, AND RUMOURS OF WARS" ... 164
   TO THE FAMILY.

XI.
RAIN-MAKING ... 178

XII.
THOUGHTS ABOUT HOME-GOING ... 185
   TO HER PARENTS.

XIII.
BACK TO TANNA ... 189
   TO HER FATHER.

XIV.
FORMATION OF THE CHURCH ON TANNA ... 200
TO THE FAMILY.

XV.
INCIDENTS—FOLKLORE 211
COMPILED FROM LETTERS IN 1882-83.

XVI.
IN PERILS BY SEA ... 217
GENERAL LETTER, 1884.

XVII.
ON ANIWA 226
COMPILED.

XVIII.
A MONOTONOUS SUMMER ... 239
GENERAL LETTER, 1885.

XIX.
AN ILLUSTRATED LETTER 252
GENERAL LETTER, 1886.

XX.
EXTENDING THE MISSION NORTHWARD ... 271
GENERAL LETTER, 1887.

XXI.
TOILING ON 282
GENERAL LETTERS, 1887-88.

XXII.
"AND THEY WENT FORTH AND PREACHED THAT MEN SHOULD REPENT" 294
GENERAL LETTER.

XXIII.
CLOUDS AND SUNSHINE — 307
GENERAL LETTER.

XXIV.
INTO HARNESS AGAIN — 320
GENERAL LETTER.

XXV.
SICKNESS AND WAR — 330
GENERAL LETTER.

XXVI.
THE CARE OF ALL THE CHURCHES — 337
TO MISS CROIL, MONTREAL, CANADA.

XXVII.
A COOL SEASON'S WORK — 352
GENERAL LETTER.

XXVIII.
"FAINT, YET PURSUING" — 360
GENERAL LETTER.

XXIX.
WAITING — 368
THE LAST GENERAL LETTER.

APPENDIX.
MEMORIAL MINUTES, ETC. — 381

ILLUSTRATIONS.

	PAGE
AGNES C. P. WATT	*Frontispiece*
MR AND MRS WATT—AT MARRIAGE	22
CHURCH, WITH MEMORIAL WINDOW	39
MRS WATT'S GRAVE	41
TABLET IN CHURCH	44
MEMORIAL WINDOW	45
GRAVES OF MRS PATON AND MR JOHNSTON	51
VOLCANO (YASOOR) AND LAKE	69
GRASS CHURCH, KWAMERA	75
KWAMERA FROM THE SEA	85
TANNA MEN—MODE OF DRESSING THEIR HAIR	107
KWAMERA NATIVES AND TEACHERS (NAHI-ABBA TO THE RIGHT)	165
WATERFALL, IFEFE, TANNA	175
YAM GARDEN	191
FIRST COMMUNICANTS AT KWAMERA	209
STREAM AT KWAMERA	213
OLD MISSION HOUSE, PORT RESOLUTION	221
MR AND MRS WATT	253
KWAMERA—CHURCH AND MISSION HOUSE	255
YEMEITAHAK AND NANCY	259
GIRLS IN MISSION HOUSE AT KWAMERA	261
TANNA MEN AND BOYS	263
HOUYE—FROM A PHOTO TAKEN IN MELBOURNE	265
TANNA WOMAN	267
BOYS WITH YAMS	273
PUBLIC SQUARE, MALEKULA	277
SYNOD OF 1889, HELD AT KWAMERA	313
SCHOOL-HOUSE, YANATUAN	317
CHURCH AND PEOPLE—PORT RESOLUTION	325
YECRIMU	339
LINE OF MARCH	341
PARTY AT CRATER, YASOOR	347
WATERFALL AT KWAMERA	375

AGNES C. P. WATT.

BIOGRAPHICAL SKETCH.

AGNES CRAIG, the eldest daughter of Robert Paterson, merchant, and his wife Agnes Campbell, was born in Tylefield Street, Glasgow, Scotland, on the 27th September, 1846.

In those days her birthplace was a quiet and almost rural locality, although somewhat less aristocratic than in the earlier years of the century. Even then the wealthy merchants had begun to leave their substantial mansions for more fashionable quarters. Over their quiet demesnes straggling streets of two-storey houses were rising, where douce weaver bodies, in apron and Kilmarnock nightcap, drove the shuttle, or in their leisure hours delved their kailyairds or discussed politics with their cronies. Now-a-days the mansion houses have been replaced by huge mills and foundries, whose workers and their families reside in the gaunt unlovely tenements which are fast displacing the picturesque dwellings of the decent hand-loom weavers.

Little Agnes Paterson was the child of many vows and prayers. Her two elder brothers had died in infancy, and her own health caused much anxiety to her parents. Referring to that time in a letter to herself after she had left home, her father says: "How earnest I was that you should be spared. Many a time the silent desire went up, that if God would spare you I would be willing that He should use you for His service in any way He chose."

While she was quite young the family removed to Carluke, where her father had a cottage, and there most of her early years were spent. During her residence there, the great Revival movement of 1859 swept over Scotland, into which Mr Paterson entered with his whole heart. He took an active part in organising and keeping up meetings in that village, and under his roof the speakers usually resided. One of the evangelists, who thus visited Carluke, was a Mr Robert Steel, a gentleman farmer, near Biggar; and Agnes ever regarded him as her spiritual father, and for many years corresponded with him on religious matters.

Another of those who came to help in the good work was a Mr William Veitch of Edinburgh; who also gave a daughter (Mrs Milne of Nguna) to mission work in the New Hebrides. The two fathers lost sight of each other for many years till the departure of Mr and Mrs Milne for these islands (where the Watts were already stationed) led to a renewal of intercourse.

About 1862 Mr Paterson and his family returned to town, and took up their abode in Pollok Road, Shawlands, on the south-side of Glasgow. Their residence was not very far from the ancient burgh of Pollokshaws, and in the vicinity of Langside, where in

1568 the battle between the forces of the Regent Moray and Mary Queen of Scots was fought—an encounter which finally shattered the fortunes of that beautiful but misguided sovereign.

While living at Pollok Road, Agnes found many opportunities for Christian work. Tract distribution, reading the Scriptures to aged and sick people, and teaching in the Sabbath School, were all taken up with characteristic heartiness. Being the eldest daughter, a good many domestic duties fell to her lot. Her special charge was the care of the younger children, who were as fondly attached to her as she to them.

Although the families of Patersons and Watts were closely related, it was not until they came to reside in Shawlands that Agnes became acquainted with her father's cousin, who was destined to become her husband. Mr William Watt was at that time attending his final session in Divinity at the Reformed Presbyterian Hall, with the intention of devoting himself to mission work in the New Hebrides, which the Reformed Presbyterian Church or "Cameronians," although few in numbers, had adopted as their Mission field with considerable ardour. Six missionaries from this historic church had already gone out there, in addition to which it may also be mentioned that it had also maintained for many years a Mission among the Jews in London.

Mr Watt's elder brother John, also a Divinity student, was residing with the Patersons at the time, and giving lessons to some of the family. While visiting him the two young people met. Their intimacy ripened into a very warm affection, which led her in due time to accept his invitation to share with him the trials and dangers of Mission life.

There are, probably, but few women who do not feel honoured by the esteem expressed in an offer of marriage; but when the offer comes, as in this case, from one who has devoted his life to the evangelising of a savage and degraded people, it calls for serious consideration. Some women have gone out to the foreign field in order that they may accompany and minister to their husbands. We honour them for the devotion which led them to share such trying work, even where they felt no call to it in itself. By Agnes Paterson, however, the offer of marriage was regarded as a direct summons to take part in the evangelisation of the heathen. In those days there were no other ways into the foreign field open to women save as the wives of missionaries. Zenana work, teaching in mission schools, and medical missions to women were as yet hardly thought of.

Notwithstanding her earnest desire to engage in the work abroad, the fact of her having to part from those she loved at home, with few opportunities of hearing from them, and but a remote possibility of ever seeing them again, gave her much anxiety. In a letter to her parents from the ship "White Star," shortly after leaving England, she says: "Both of you know that it was not without some anxious thought that I devoted my life to this cause. Wearisome nights, with my pillow soaked with tears, I spent, ere I could decide that most momentous question, Is it my duty to go or stay? Blessed be His name, He gave me grace to choose, what to some seems the evil, but, as I think, the path of duty. I do, indeed, rejoice to say that I have never been left, even for a moment, to regret the step I have taken."

Time amply proved the wisdom of her choice, for her decision brought blessing to herself and many others. Her father, who felt the parting very keenly, said himself in a letter to her two years afterwards, "Who can tell but what you may have more comfort and contentment, even in a temporal sense, where you are, than if you had remained at home?" And again, "It cheers my heart to think that you have never had a sad reflection since leaving home. I often think that if you had not gone away, I would not have so much comfort concerning you."

I would commend these words to some parents who are unwilling to let their children go out to Christ's service among the heathen. You may have your own way, but take care lest in so insisting upon it, you are thrusting from you much blessing and comfort for future years.

Mr Watt and Miss Paterson were married on the 29th of April, 1868, by the minister of the bride, the Rev. Dr Patterson of Hutchesontown Free Church, Glasgow. After a short honeymoon trip to Lochgilphead they returned to town to make preparations for departure. Mr Watt was ordained a missionary to the New Hebrides on the 7th of May. The service took place during the sittings of the Reformed Presbyterian Synod in Great Hamilton Street Church. The Rev. Dr Wm. Symington preached from 2 Cor. x. 15, 16 : " Having hope . . . to preach the gospel in the regions beyond," and Mr Watt's beloved Professor, Rev. Dr Binnie of Stirling, gave the " charge."

On the Sabbath after the ordination, they were asked by Mr William Strang, a friend of Mr Watt's, who was deeply interested in the New Hebrides, and one of the founders of the Glasgow Foundry Boys' Religious Society, to address the Branch with which he was connected, in Eglinton Street. They complied, and so interested the members and office-bearers, that they pledged themselves that very night to support a native

teacher on Tanna. Right nobly has this Society fulfilled its promise. Several teachers employed by Mr Watt on Tanna have been supported by it up to the present day. It has sent out annually boxes of cloth and other useful articles to the natives. Last, but by no means least, in 1874 it sent out a fine Printing Press, which it has also kept supplied with type and paper. This press has been a most valuable adjunct to the mission in the New Hebrides. Other islands as well as Tanna have been benefited by it, as lesson sheets, hymns, and portions of Scripture have been printed from it. This continued interest in mission work was, to a very great extent, due to Mrs Watt's frequent and interesting letters which were read at the meetings of the Society. These letters and her addresses while at home were the means of leading several connected with the Society to go out as missionaries to heathen lands.

On June 3rd, they left Glasgow for Liverpool to join the "White Star," a sailing vessel of 2500 tons, which was going out to Melbourne with a large number of emigrants.

Those who have gone through such an experience will thank me for passing over the parting in silence. It was borne on both sides with Christian fortitude. In Liverpool they were the guests of the Rev. Dr Symington of Birkenhead. From there Mrs Watt wrote home daily, one might almost say hourly, until the vessel sailed. In one letter referring to her railway journey, she says: "I may tell you I felt happy, although sorry, very sorry to part with you all. I had an inward joy, that it was in order to carry the gospel to the heathen I had gone. Thus far I have proved God to be a covenant-keeping God. 'As thy days, so shall thy strength be.' May He comfort and sustain you all in the hour of trial. 'Cast thy burden on the Lord, and He shall sustain thee.' Think of me not only as going from you, but also as under the special protection of God, who says: 'Touch not mine anointed, and do my prophets no harm.'"

Thus she is calm and resolved and hopeful—resting on the blessed promises which are all Yea and Amen in Christ Jesus. She has taken the first step in her missionary career. Resolutely she has put her hand to the plough, nor once looks back, for she has reckoned the cost. Together the devoted couple set their faces to "the regions beyond." For friends and home

"Some natural tears they dropp'd, but wiped them soon;
The world was all before them, . . .
And Providence their guide."

On June 8th they sailed from Liverpool. That day she took every opportunity of sending home farewell messages, even from such unlikely places as the quay while waiting on the tender to take them off to the vessel. The voyage to Melbourne took eighty-two days, and was on the whole very enjoyable. Their passages had been taken in the "Sulina" which left a week or two earlier, but owing to Mr Watt's having an attack of facial paralysis, they were transferred to the "White Star." As it turned out the delay was providential, for not only had they longer time at home before sailing, but reached the colonies before the steamer. The "White Star" having some six hundred emigrants on board, they were enabled to do much good among them. After obtaining permission from the authorities on board, Mr Watt conducted Divine Service on the poop-deck on Sabbaths. Along with Mrs Watt, he held weekly Bible Classes and Prayer Meetings on different evenings during the week, among the single men, single women, and married people; by all of whom their ministrations were much appreciated.

By the tug which accompanied them well down the channel she sent back the following letter: "We have much to encourage us with regard to weather. I have scarcely felt that the ship was moving, only I feel as if I were sitting on a spring-bottomed chair. We have good food; the only difference from home is that we have one accompaniment to every meal; we get potatoes twenty-one times a week for a rarity. If you ask me what I get to breakfast I would say 'taties'; what to dinner, 'taties'; what to supper, 'taties.' Now you are not to think that we get nothing but potatoes; there are plenty of other things; roast beef, boiled cabbage, smoked ham, fresh eggs, pies, tarts, and everything that is good. We have a splendid cabin and a large saloon."

Evidently the voyage was just beginning, for on the 10th she writes: "We were aroused this morning by the captain calling, 'Get your letters ready.' The tug is going off, and I have only one feeling of sorrow that I cannot send you letters by the way; but daily, nay, constantly, shall my prayer ascend to Jesus that we may be all one with Him. Then shall we soon meet and be an undivided family in heaven. It is vain to wish to meet on earth, if after we meet we have to part again."

After some kind messages to her brothers and sisters, she concludes: "Mother, this is for you, 'Because thou hast not withheld thy *child*, therefore in blessing I will bless thee'; and father, see in my mission to the heathen the result of faithful pious training and an answer to prayer."

They arrived at Melbourne on the 21st September, and were warmly received by friends of the mission.

With their wonted thoughtfulness the Rev. J. and Mrs Clark of Williamstown came off to the ship in a boat and took them ashore. They also stayed with the Rev. Dr Macdonald of Emerald Hill (South Melbourne), and the Smellies, who were old family friends. Their intention had been to proceed direct to the Islands by the first vessel which might be going in that direction; but in Melbourne they were strongly advised to go round by New Zealand. By so doing they would become acquainted with the church which was to support them, and embark for the New Hebrides in the mission vessel "Dayspring."

They reached Wellington in the end of September, and spent several months travelling through the country visiting the different congregations. To Mrs Watt, with her deep love of nature, the magnificent scenery of New Zealand was a source of great delight. Everywhere they met with kindness, and formed many lasting friendships, so that when they departed at last for their lonely outpost of duty they were cheered with the assurance that the church had them constantly in tender and prayerful remembrance. By some strange instinct Mrs Watt had always looked forward to settling on the island of Tanna; and was actually somewhat anxious lest they should be sent to Erakor Efate, from which Mr Morrison was retiring through ill health. Her mind was therefore set at rest by a letter from the Rev. J. Inglis of Aneityum, who took it for granted that Tanna was to be their destination; and they were cheered by the prospects of a favourable opening there. The letter also announced that the Rev. T. Neilson had been settled at Port Resolution, and that the Aneityumese at Aname were making cinet for the building of their house. The Assembly of the Presbyterian Church of New Zealand was held that year in Wellington, in the month of November, 1868 ; but on account of the unsettled state of the country, owing to the Maori war, only seven ministers were present. It was agreed to raise Mr Watt's salary to £150 per annum, instead of the modest £120 at which he was engaged. They were also granted a whale-boat, and £30 to purchase timber for a house.

When the meeting of Assembly was over the Watts proceeded to Dunedin, where they joined the " Dayspring," and after calling again at Wellington, they went on to Auckland, which port they left for the islands on March 31st, and arrived at Aneityum on the 18th of April. They then went round the group to see the several stations, and, so far as they could, the work of the Mission. At the Annual Meeting of the Missionaries (now called the Synod), they were designated to Kwamera at the south-east point of Tanna: and Messrs Inglis and Neilson were appointed to assist in their settlement. Kwamera was considered to be a very promising opening, and certainly the people gave them a very hearty welcome. It was not long, however, until they made it abundantly plain that the calico, knives, and other things which the missionary brought were much more valued by them than his teaching. Moreover, Kwamera was on the weather side of the island, exposed to the full force of the S.E. trade winds. It had no shelter whatever for the Mission vessel, and only a very narrow passage through the reef for landing. Frequently the

"Dayspring" had to lie off and on for days until the sea would moderate sufficiently to allow her boats to land their stores. Passengers embarking had many a long and dangerous passage from the shore to the ship. In those days difficulty of access was supposed to protect the natives from undesirable traders; but in this the advantage was very slight, while the discomfort and nervous strain of boating told severely on Mrs Watt's health.

The first break in their island life was a short visit to Sydney in 1874. Two years later they had a furlough of three months in New Zealand. In 1878 they left for a visit to Scotland, which they reached in March, 1879, when Mrs Watt had about eleven months at home, and greatly enjoyed the society of her loved ones. On that visit, she invariably refused to speak at public meetings, but by her vivid descriptions of native life and mission work in private gatherings she did much to stimulate fresh interest in the New Hebrides.

On the 6th February, 1880, they left England in the Orient steamer "Chimborazo." The weather was rough when they started, and increased in severity. On the second day out, a huge wave struck the vessel and heeled her over. The heavy steam launch and five boats, together with almost everything on the spar deck, were carried away. One of the passengers and two seamen were washed overboard, and another killed on board, while eighteen were more or less severely injured. It was indeed a very narrow escape, for the engine sky-light was carried away, and had another wave broken over them, the engine room would have been flooded and the fires put out. That afternoon the captain managed to get the vessel round and put back for Plymouth, where the passengers were sent ashore while the steamer returned to London for repairs. In ten days she was ready, and started out again in the teeth of another gale, which however moderated, and with the exception of a break-down of the engines for a few hours, they had a prosperous voyage, reaching Sydney in safety on the 8th of April. Two days later they left for the New Hebrides in the "Dayspring," which had been detained to pick them up.

Shortly before their arrival on Kwamera, a dreadful hurricane swept over the islands, which destroyed the natives' food and severely tried the Mission buildings. Their welcome back was on that account rather a sad one.

The exciting scenes through which they had passed, and the suspense occasioned by the news of the hurricane, had a very disturbing effect on Mrs Watt's nervous system, so that in 1881 she was compelled to go to Melbourne, in the "Dayspring," for medical advice, while Mr Watt remained on Tanna. Of Dr Macmillan, whom she consulted, she ever afterwards spoke with liveliest gratitude.

Soon after their return from Scotland, the Rev. J. G. Paton and family went up to Melbourne, and at his request the Mission Synod appointed Mr Watt to the oversight of the work in Aniwa. From that time until 1889, Aniwa and its concerns took up a considerable part of Mrs Watt's time and care. They were no strangers to the people, as on previous occasions they had taken charge during the missionary's furloughs.

On the whole, they enjoyed these visits exceedingly. The peaceful character of the people, their attention to the ordinances of religion and desire for instruction, contrasted so favourably with the warlike and superstitious Tannese. They had the pleasure of seeing their efforts appreciated by a grateful people, and also of seeing some of the Aniwans go out for the first time as teachers to heathen islands. Often did Mrs Watt call Aniwa her "Bethany." It was hallowed by past associations of joy and sorrow shared with her "dearest Mission sister," Mrs Paton. It was a calm retreat for a season from the turmoils and fightings of obstinate "terrible Tanna."

But with all that, it was a very considerable drain on her vital force. There were frequent packings and unpackings, as most of the household stuff had to be carried to and fro; nerve-straining and exhausting boat voyages, and no less wearisome tossings, sometimes for a week at a time, in the "Dayspring." Their connection with Aniwa terminated on the occasion of their visit home in 1889.

In 1886 and 1889 the Mission Synod met at Kwamera. On these occasions Mrs Watt was in her element. She liked to have a crowd of friends around her, and quite enjoyed the bustle of entertaining them.

Towards the end of 1889 they revisited Scotland in order to carry the Tannese New Testament through the press.

The National Bible Society of Scotland had received a legacy which was to be expended in the publication of a translation of the New Testament in one of the South Sea languages. The offer was made to the New

Hebrides Mission, and as there was no other translation nearly ready at the time, Mr Watt, with the sanction of the Mission Synod, accepted it for the south-eastern dialects of Tanna.

"They went home in the "Orizaba," and had an exceptionally fine voyage. The "Jubilee Singers" travelled with them as far as Colombo, and gave much pleasure to all on board by their music. Immediately on their arrival at home, arrangements were made for printing; and for months life seemed to consist in revising and correcting proofs. After the New Testament was finished, Mrs Watt compiled and translated an illustrated Scripture History of 260 pp. 8vo., the lessons being taken from the "Peep of Day" series. The book is an admirable epitome of the Old Testament, and is a great favourite on Tanna and among the people of Aniwa who understand Tannese.

As she had now been twenty years a missionary Mrs Watt was less reluctant to address public meetings.

In a very short time her services in this direction were greatly in request. In Edinburgh, during the sittings of the Assemblies, she addressed several of the annual meetings and breakfasts of Missionary Associations, held at that time. Her mellow voice, and the interesting manner in which she drew on her large store of information concerning the natives and their customs, together with her intense longing for the salvation of the heathen, made her addresses very popular. The interest was much increased by her singing of Tannese hymns. The greatest favourite was an adaptation of "Fade, fade, each earthly joy," which had been translated by a Tannaman named Kaiasi from a hymn he had heard on Epi. Possibly some may be interested in seeing this hymn in the Tannese dialect:

Jesus is mine.

1 Yesu Yerumanu, Yesu asori,
  Yesu Yerumanu, Yesu seiau.
  Ik 'narengi nabien,
  Marengi namisaien,
  Ik 'nane nakwaruarua
    Teini tuke iau.

2 Yesu Yerumanu, Yesu asori,
  Yesu Yerumanu, Yesu seiau,
  Ti arengi nabien
  Fei Yesu tuketaha,
  'Napa sei ya neai,
    Me'ma tuketaha.

3 Yesu Yerumanu, Yesu asori,
  Yesu Yerumanu, Yesu seiau,
  Nangelome ya neai,
  Nermama ya tuprana,
  Tu ani na'ngen aba,
    Yesu ikinan.

4 Yesu Yerumanu, Yesu asori,
  Yesu Yerumanu, Yesu seiau,
  Nehekerien seiau
  Rasori Atua,
  Yesu namuruvien
    Saketaha pam.

5 Yesu Yerumanu, Yesu asori,
  Yesu Yerumanu, Yesu seiau,
  Yesu amasan,
  Yesu Yerumanu,
  Yesu tik abi iau,
    Muvche yesa.

They returned to the New Hebrides by the San Francisco route; and so arranged their journey over America that they were able to spend some time in Nova Scotia and Canada, where they received much kindness from the ministers and people of the Presbyterian Church. It was no ordinary pleasure to Mrs Watt to visit the church which had sent out Dr Geddie, the first missionary to the New Hebrides. In New Zealand they made a tour round most of the congregations, and the hearty reception they received banished their fears that the church had lost sympathy with them and their work. During their absence great changes had been taking place in the islands. The "Dayspring," no longer able to overtake the work of the Mission, was laid up, and latterly sold. An arrangement was entered into with the A.U.S.N. Co. by which their steamers from Sydney to Fiji would connect with the "Truganini," a small steamer which was to run round the group monthly. After running for rather more than a year, the "Truganini" was wrecked at Aneityum during a hurricane, but in less than two months the Company had replaced her by the "Croydon," which was considerably larger.

None of us in the islands considered the steam service perfect; but the frequency of communication was very much prized. Fresh from the magnificent ocean-liners, perhaps Mrs Watt expected too much from the little "Croydon," which was unable to land at their station on two successive trips owing to rough weather. At any rate her first impressions of the steam-service were decidedly unfavourable; but she soon saw cause to think better of it.

The principal event after her return to Tanna was the placing of the New Testament in the hands of the people, and Mr and Mrs Watt were very much gratified at the eagerness of the people to have copies; because books, and especially foreign-printed ones, had always been regarded by the superstitious Tannese as a certain cause of sickness and death. After that came the building of the new church at Port Resolution, for which she chose the name of "The Workers' Memorial," to commemorate all who had taken part in the evangelisation of Tanna—a long roll of missionaries and native teachers, beginning with John Williams and the Samoans, whom he placed at Port Resolution on the 19th November, 1839.

After settling down, Mr and Mrs Watt devoted themselves to a much greater extent than formerly to itinerating among the villages, a work which, while exposing Mrs Watt to much fatigue and discomfort, was rightly regarded by her as of the highest importance. The instruction imparted by native teachers is not of a very profound nature at the best, and when left too much alone it still further deteriorates.

Early in 1893 she had a severe illness which left her very weak. To add to her discomfort the steam-service was discontinued owing to the New South Wales Government having withdrawn their subsidy. A sailing vessel called the "Lark" was sent down by the Australasian New Hebrides Company; but, whilst a more frequent service was provided than had been done by the "Dayspring," to say that this vessel failed to overtake the work is putting it very mildly indeed. In the end of the year, while the "Lark" was lying at

Port Resolution, just about to sail for Sydney, and the "long dark tunnel" of the hot season, which she so much dreaded, was opening up before her, Mrs Watt was gladdened by the return of the "Croydon." During the hurricane season, although she was far from strong, and a tumour on her foot made walking painful, she spent much time in visiting the out-stations; residing alternately at Kwamera and Port Resolution.

Before the steamer was taken off Mr and Mrs Watt had made arrangements to entertain the Synod of 1893 at Aneityum, as a celebration of their silver wedding. The withdrawal of the steamer prevented the Synod from meeting that year, causing Mrs Watt great disappointment. The ladies of the Mission showed their esteem for her by a valuable present of silver plate.

They had planned to go up to New Zealand for a short holiday at the end of that year, but the pleasurable anticipation of the trip was much overcast by a foreboding that if she once left the islands, she would never be able to return. Ever since her father had unexpectedly entered into his rest, she had a strong presentiment that she would be called away in like manner. Sudden death,—so dreadful to most,—had, through long contemplation, lost its terror for her. Although she was devotedly attached to her husband and to her work, yet we cannot wonder that sickness, weariness, and hope deferred created in her at times a longing to depart and be with Christ.

In the beginning of April they came round from Kwamera to Port Resolution to prepare for going to the Synod at Aneityum.

Two days before her death there were very few out at morning school and worship, and Mrs Watt went round the nearer villages in search of them. She found them engrossed in preparations for some heathen rites, but civil and ready to listen to her. On Wednesday, Sani, her Aneityumese cook, being occupied with other duties, she had a long forenoon in the hot kitchen.

> *1894 April*
>
> *Saturday 21st: Had a lot to do + yet saw little for all my time spans –*
>
> *Sabbath 22nd: Good morning meeting – fewer in afternoon. We went to Navotya + had worship with the Martins –*
>
> *Monday 23rd: The "Nupevat" finished this forenoon – W + I 'redd' up the store – we set the old cat at liberty –*
>
> *Tuesday 24th: Missed some in church. So went to Yahumatahi + learned of the new ... being made –*
>
> *Wednesday 25th: Sani at "Yanaius" So I had to be in the kitchen roasting the turkey for the Martins – Lay up all afternoon + am writing now in evening – Mala here to day. –*
>
> *Thursday 26th*

Quite exhausted, she had to lie down with a sick headache, which lasted the whole afternoon. Towards evening she revived somewhat. After tea and worship she spent several hours writing letters and filling up her diary, and, as she occasionally did, entered in it the date for the next day. Just before retiring she read aloud a little leaflet-poem she had found in her desk, on an old man crooning his grandchild to sleep with the psalm tunes he had learned long ago. It concludes :—

" Goodness and mercy all my life
Shall surely follow me :
And in God's house for evermore
My dwelling-place shall be."

" Eighty-seven
His mile-stone,
A home in heaven
Soon his own.
He is only waiting now
For a crown upon his brow."

Next morning she rose about six o'clock, bright and cheerful, to resume her daily duties. Before reaching the bathroom which opened off her room, she complained of giddiness and sat down on the sofa. Mr Watt was at her side in a moment, and found she had fainted. He applied restoratives under which she revived, and said, " How did you know that I was ill? I have no recollection of anything." When he repeated what she had said, she replied, " My dear William, I am thankful you awoke me, I don't think I would ever have come out of it. I never was so near death before." He assisted her back to bed where she lay down, but in a short time became much distressed by sickness. Some little relief was obtained, but in a very short time her feet and hands began to grow cold. By this time she felt she was dying, and said to her husband, " I am going to leave you now, dearie." Struggling against admitting what was becoming only too evident, he replied, "Oh no, Agnes, you have many times been as ill before." Very soon, however, sickness and fainting returned, from which she never recovered; and in less than an hour from the time she awoke from sleep, Agnes Watt had entered into the sunshine of the "perfect day." She passed from the out-post duty of the Foreign Field into blessed and glorious service in the presence of the King.

During one brief interval of the final struggle she said, "How true it is, that in life we are in death," and again, "A dying bed is no place to prepare for eternity."

No sooner did the news of her death spread, than crowds of her dark-skinned brothers and sisters gathered round and poured out their unrestrained grief. All day long they filed through the room to see her for the last time; while some sat on the floor and looked on her from morn till night.

Mrs Martin, the wife of a trader, came over to assist the faithful servants, Ripa and Yecrimu, to lay her out for burial, while Mr Martin hastily prepared a coffin. Meanwhile messengers had started off to tell the teachers all the way along to Kwamera, and in the opposite direction to bring Mr Gray, a brother missionary, from Weasisi. Mr Gray arrived about five p.m., and, shortly afterwards, Mr Forlong, a missionary trader from Kwamera, along with the teachers from that district. As it was too late to hold a service in the church, the coffin was brought out to the verandah, where the natives crowded round to take their last look at the still face of her who had loved them so well. In the deepening gloaming they bore her to her grave, at the place where she had often said she wished to be

CHURCH, WITH MEMORIAL WINDOW.

buried, beneath a breadfruit tree beside the Workers' Memorial Church. A hymn she had herself translated, "There's a land that is fairer than day," was sung, and prayer offered by Pavenga, an Aniwan teacher; and slowly, amid the sobs and tears of the people, all that was mortal of their loved one was laid to rest. There at the very place where she first set foot on Tanna, twenty-five years before, she lies, until the glory of the Resurrection morn shall dawn. What resting-place more fit? Among the people for whom she agonised and prayed, and close beside the beautiful church her pleadings had gained for them.

It is hardly necessary for me to say more. We do not claim for Mrs Watt either genius or very brilliant accomplishments. Her letters reveal her as a woman whose soul was filled with love to Christ and pity for the heathen. Those gifts with which she was endowed she freely and fully consecrated to the Master's service. She gave herself for Tanna. Over and over again in her letters she pours out the yearnings of her soul for their salvation. "I live for Tanna," she said, "and if need be, will die for it"; and her daily life among its people evidenced the sincerity of her words. It was in no conventional style of religious talk that she spoke of the women as her sisters; for with such hearty sympathy did she enter into their lives, their joys and sorrows, their temptations and sufferings, that we cannot wonder that she gained their fullest confidence and affection. A most unexpected testimony as to her relations with the people is given by a journalist, Julian Thomas (The

MRS WATT'S GRAVE.

Vagabond), in his book on "Cannibals and Converts." Speaking of his visit to Kwamera in 1884 to collect the signatures of the chiefs to a petition for annexation by Britain, he says, "We go to say good-bye to Mrs Watt who is standing in the shade of the boat-house talking to the girls and women of the village . . . The women crowd round Mrs Watt with affection. My feelings receive a momentary shock when I see an old hag, so hideous, clad only in a grass petticoat, embrace and caress the lady with fervour. Not only a fashionable woman of the world but any working girl would shrink from such a contact with disgust. Mrs Watt does not like it, I am sure, but she disengages herself without any sign of repugnance. And then I understand the true missionary spirit. I see here the outcome of the vision which the apostle saw at Joppa, when the gospel of humanity and love to all, preached by Him of Nazareth, was first understood as being held out to all mankind, and not only to the parish of Judea. 'Nothing is common or unclean.' Love and charity and the example of good lives; these the missionary and his wife can evidence here—of more value, perchance, than prayers and sermons. In time the seed may bear fruit, but the harvest is long, very long in coming; as yet there is scarcely a germ." So much from one whom none would accuse of being biassed in favour of missionaries. Not only was she sympathetic and loving in her manner towards the people; but she possessed a wonderfully accurate knowledge of native customs and language. This she turned to good account by collecting, at first hand, many of the games, legends and folk-lore of Tanna. In the interests of science it is to be regretted that her busy life and multifarious duties prevented her from doing more in this department. Work such as hers in that line is much more reliable than the hasty generalisations of a passing visitor who is only able to communicate with the people in "pigeon-English."

This same knowledge was also utilized in hymn translation. The Tannese are a musical people, and their desire for new hymns was almost insatiable. Even in heathenism the spirits were invoked annually for fresh music for the season's dances. On no island was the service of song more developed than on Tanna, and the spirited manner in which they sang was the admiration of all who heard them. At present the hymnal contains ninety-five hymns, psalms, and chants. They were also in the habit of chanting the Lord's Prayer and Ten Commandments at the Sabbath service. In the translation of these Mrs Watt took a very large share of the work. To translate an English hymn into a native language is by no means so easy a task as it looks. It is a difficult matter to render ideas which, in most cases, are entirely new to the people intelligibly, and while preserving the idiom, to retain some relation to poetry and music. In all these respects Mrs Watt succeeded to a marked degree. She had a happy faculty of seizing the leading ideas of an English hymn or psalm and turning them into idiomatic and melodious Tannese.

But I daresay that one, if not *the one*, great characteristic of Mrs Watt was her patient continuance in well-doing. The Rev. J. Copeland, who was on Futuna at the time of her arrival in the islands, predicted that she would "wear well." That, perhaps, more aptly describes her than any other phrase. Her humour, her sanctified common-sense, her irrepressible hopefulness and unwavering faith, enabled her to struggle on where many others would have given up in despair. She spared herself no toil, left no means untried whereby she might win her people to Christ. Truly, she gave herself for Tanna. Her death was but a fitting close, was but the seal and consummation of a life freely consecrated to the eternal welfare of its sons

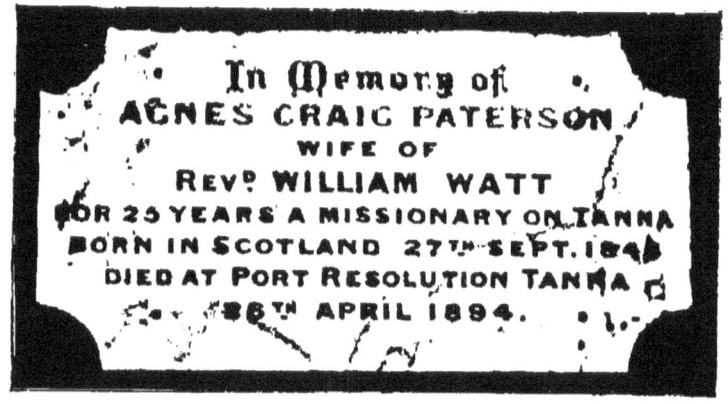

TABLET IN CHURCH.

and daughters. Nor shall her offering, and the offerings of those sainted ones who before her poured out the libations of their lives for that dark land, be fruitless. God's time to favour Tanna is coming; and they who have sown the precious seed in tears and weariness, shall rejoice together with those who reap.

"Except a grain of wheat fall into the earth and die, it abideth by itself alone; but if it die, it bringeth forth much fruit."

On the day after the funeral Mr Gray and Mr Forlong put a border of stones round the grave, and covered it with white coral gravel. Afterwards a

MEMORIAL WINDOW.

railing was put up and a simple tablet of wood placed at the head, bearing her name with the dates of her birth and death and the Tannese words:

"In rabi nakur Ipare."
(She loved the people of Tanna.)

A more durable monument of granite will probably be erected there.

Since then Mr Watt has placed a memorial window in the church. The design embraces a medallion portrait of Mrs Watt over a Scriptural scene. The artist has very skilfully represented Mrs Watt, in earlier years, as Dorcas giving out garments to needy natives. On either side of the medallion rises a Scotch fir and a cocoa-nut palm, while her favourite flower, the white rose, with the Scotch thistle and a Tannese hibiscus are displayed at the base, and the text from Proverbs xxxi. 29, "Many daughters have done virtuously, but thou excellest them all."

TANNA AND ITS MISSIONARIES.

IN 1605 Quiros, a Spanish navigator, sailed from the port of Callao, South America, to search for the great southern continent of Australia. Passing through several groups of islands, on the 30th April, 1606, he sighted land to the south-east, which seemed so large that he felt certain that his long-desired goal had been attained. In pious gratitude he named it "The Great Southern land of the Holy Ghost." Australia, however, was yet beyond his horizon, and all that was loaded with his sonorous appellation was but the largest and most northern island of the New Hebrides group. Into a wide bay opening to the north he and his consort, Torres, sailed. Anchoring near the mouth of a river, which he called the Jordan, he drew up a plan and appointed municipal officers for a city to be built there, and named it New Jerusalem. As one would expect from his manner of dealing with them, he was not very kindly received by the natives. In a short time, skirmishes, fruitless foraging expeditions inland, and the violent illness of many of his people from eating poisonous fish, wore off the glamour of the new discovery, and compelled them to leave. Nothing more was heard of the islands for about a century and a half, when in 1768 Bouganville circumnavigated Santo and discovered several of the northern islands, which he named the Grand Cyclades. In 1774 Captain Cook entered the group from the north and cast anchor in a harbour on Malekula, which he named after the Earl of Sandwich, then First ·Lord of the Admiralty. He sailed as far south as Tanna, which he describes at length in his interesting journals, and north again to the scene of Quiros' discovery. He surveyed the islands so thoroughly, that he considered himself entitled to re-name the whole group as the New Hebrides.

On his voyage southward from Erromanga he was attracted to Tanna by the bright glare of Yasoor, the volcano, then, as now, a pillar of cloud by day and of fire by night. He named the harbour in which he anchored, "Port Resolution," after his vessel. His experience of the Tannese was much the same as that of all who have had dealings with them since. He found them insolent and daring thieves. They picked up whatever was neither too hot nor too heavy to carry off; and were even attempting to tear the ensign from its staff. They laid hold of the anchor buoys, and, when fired at, retreated for a moment, but returned so soon as they found themselves unhurt. He managed to establish friendly relations with a few of them, and learned the names of the surrounding islands, viz.: Erromanga, Immer (Aniwa), Erronan (Futuna), and Annatom (Aneityum). Curiously enough, through a very natural mistake, he put down the native word for "earth" (tana), which in some form is common throughout the Pacific, as the name of the island. The name is likely to remain now, despite all explanations and efforts to change it. It is called "Ipare" by some, but that means simply "inland." The natives themselves speak of the island as "Tana sorè" (the great land), to distinguish it from the smaller islands of Aniwa and Futuna. Now the natives are familiar with the designations of the islands as known to us, but it may be doubted if originally there were names for entire islands of any size, in use by the people themselves. In most cases, the earlier navigators only learned the name of the district on which they landed. Captain Cook also discovered that the Tannese were cannibals, which was a matter of surprise to him, as food seemed abundant. He noted also the curious manner in which the men dressed their hair, which has led some ethnologists to find affinities between them and the ancient Assyrians.

The first attempt at evangelising Tanna was made in 1839, when John Williams visited Port Resolution in the "Camden." Although his reception was somewhat rough, he deemed it sufficiently favourable to justify him in settling three Samoan teachers there. Next day (20th November) he and Mr Harris were martyred on Erromanga. With noble Christian spirit the London Missionary Society determined to win for Christ the savage inhabitants of those lovely isles already taken possession of as it were by the blood of their heroic missionaries.

In 1842 Messrs Turner and Nisbet were sent out to the New Hebrides and landed at Port Resolution, but were only able to remain for seven months owing to the hostility of the natives. Time and again, thereafter, teachers from Samoa and Raratonga were stationed, only to be driven off or killed. In 1858 the Rev. J. G. Paton and his wife with the Rev. Joseph Copeland were settled at Port Resolution, and the Rev. J. W. and Mrs Mathieson at the south-east end of the island now called Kwamera. Shortly thereafter, the Rev. Samuel F. and Mrs Johnston came from Nova Scotia intending to settle on the West Coast, a project which in the providence of God was not permitted. Within four years, however, the gospel light was to all appearance again quenched on Tanna amid war and persecution. Mr Copeland was removed to Aneityum, Mrs Paton with her infant son and Mr Johnston were sleeping in their graves close by the glassy waters of the bay; and Mr Paton with Mr and Mrs Mathieson also felt constrained to leave. After a brief interval Aneityumese teachers resumed the work and held the fort until 1867, when the Rev. Thomas Neilson, accompanied by his wife—a daughter of the Rev. Dr Geddie of Aneityum—was appointed. The fickle Tannese had been understood to wish for a missionary; but when Mr Neilson presented himself, they vigorously opposed his landing, and threw the timber for his house back into the sea as quickly as it was put ashore.

They gave as a reason, that they were angry because H.M.S. "Curaçoa" had bombarded them. The following year they had so far relented as to allow Mr Neilson to settle amongst them. He laboured faithfully until 1882, when he felt constrained to leave on account of his own impaired health, the education of his family, and the long continued unwillingness of the people to give up heathenism. In 1869 the Rev. William and Mrs Watt were settled at Kwamera under very favourable auspices, and when Mr Neilson left they took charge of Port Resolution in addition. In 1882 a new station six miles north of Port Resolution, called Weasisi, was opened by the Rev. W. and Mrs Gray from South Australia. They laboured devotedly for twelve years amid many vicissitudes, and often in no

GRAVES OF MRS PATON AND MR JOHNSTON.

small danger. Quite recently a young missionary, the Rev. A. Macmillan, M.A., from Aberdeen, Scotland, has been appointed to the work demitted by Mr Gray. New ground has been taken up on the West Coast by the third son of the venerable Dr Paton—the Rev. Frank H. L. Paton, B.D.

"Mission work on Tanna," writes the Rev. W. Watt in 1887, "has had a chequered history. Time and again has it been taken up in hope, only to be given up in almost despair. How much is involved in such words as 'giving up,' 'abandoning,' 'being compelled to leave!' We may be sure that none of the European missionaries deserted their posts as long as they considered the ground tenable, and those who know the Samoan and Raratongan teachers would say the same for them; some of them, be it remembered, were faithful even unto death. The story of the evangelisation of Tanna tells of bright hopes fondly cherished, until rudely crushed; days of hard, unremitting toil, of anxious watching and waiting, of trial and reverses. Those of us who are at present at our posts have had much the same experiences as our predecessors, although in the good Providence of God we have been enabled to hold on, and have met with some measure of success."

Letters.

I.

MELBOURNE AND NEW ZEALAND.

TO HER FATHER.

My Dearest Father,—I will write this letter to you as the first of a course in which I intend to give you always a full account of my peregrinations. I will give you all information up to a certain time, and in my next begin at the very spot I left. In this way all my letters put together will form a journal.

Monday, August 1st, 1868. In Rev. J. Clark's, Williamstown. After breakfast, went down to the "White Star" accompanied by Mr and Mrs Clark and little Maggie. Such friendly people! How my heart clung to them seeing I was a stranger in a strange land; and I felt they were kindred spirits. Before we got down to the pier we met the Rev. D. Macdonald of Emerald Hill (a stout Highlander). He had come down to meet us, thinking we would not yet have left the ship; and neither we would, had not Mr Clark got a special permit. We all went on board and had dinner, and having seen after our luggage, we again stepped into the small boat and were pulled to land. As Mr Macdonald was going from home, he wished us to go up to Emerald Hill with him; but I was very tired, and all my things were in Williamstown, so I remained at Mrs Clark's, while William went with Mr Macdonald. I did nothing that day but rested. Williamstown quite fulfils my idea of a place in the colonies. The greater number of the houses are made of wood, and have verandahs. Some of the smaller ones are like match-boxes, but the white painted houses are really beautiful. The town is being laid out in streets, but to the eye of a stranger it looks as if every one just pitched his tent wherever he pleased. Mr Clark gave us encouraging news of the Mission; all the missionaries seem to be prospering and in good spirits.

After dinner on Tuesday, William and I went down to the vessel and got whatever things I wanted, and took a train from the Pier to Melbourne. The distance altogether is about fourteen miles. It was dark, and I did not see the country round about, but I afterwards saw it, and cannot say I was struck with its beauty. . . . The Yarra is a low-lying muddy river. I am told that when they have heavy rain it overflows its banks and floods the streets. . . . You will perhaps like to hear what I thought of Melbourne. Well, it is most wonderful for the time it has been in existence; the streets are wide, and there are some nice shops. Indeed, the buildings and shops are splendid, most of them having shades before the doors, and in them you can get everything " from a needle to an anchor," as the saying is. In the course of a few more years Melbourne will cover as much ground as London. Even now it is a very large town.... There are plenty of theatres and low public houses, dozens of signs,—"All drinks threepence."... St. Kilda is about four miles from Emerald Hill. We took the train there one day with Miss Middleton (Mr Macdonald's sister-in-law), went round the beach, through the town, and then walked home. Really it is the most beautiful town I have ever seen, and were I going to live near Melbourne it is there I would settle. I only wish you could see it! The one drawback for me is, that out here no one can bathe in the sea for fear of sharks. There are, however, public baths in the sea fenced with rails so close that the sharks cannot get through....

I mentioned in my journal that we were going to New Zealand. Rev. J. and Mrs Inglis are to be there, and we are to go and meet them. There would be no use of setting off to Aneityum, while Mr Inglis was not there. We will be able to excite interest in the Mission, see the people who are to support us, and sail from thence in the "Dayspring."

... Monday, 7th August. The Rev. D. Macdonald introduced us to a young man named Daniel Macdonald, who to-day came and took us to the Public Library and Museum. The Library is free; any one can go in and take down a book and read for any length of time without charge. The collection is large and finely bound. In the same building is a picture gallery, and I think the paintings extremely good. There is also a Statuary room. We also went to the Botanical Gardens, where there is much to interest. Most of the plants are foreign to me. Things that only grow in hothouses at home grow in the open air here; such as grapes and peaches . . . I understand this is a very changeable climate; in the morning it will be bitterly cold, then in the middle of the day a hot wind will spring up, and at night a cold damp chill set in. They are much annoyed with dust storms : I have only seen one. The dust comes in such clouds that I am told business is often stopped. Now I must tell you about Daniel Macdonald. He is a young man nearly seven feet high, strong and muscular looking. He is studying with the view of joining our Mission in the course of two years or so. I like him very much, and I think he will make a splendid missionary. If appearance has any effect upon the natives he will have an advantage, for he is head and shoulders above everybody . . .

Manuwatu, New Zealand,
Oct. 22, 1868.

Though to many the jottings I take of my journeyings in a strange land may seem dry and uninteresting, yet I know you will be glad to read anything sent from me; so I will give you a short account of a trip from Wellington to Manawatu. We rose this morning at four o'clock, and, after a little repast, set out on our day's journey. We had twenty minutes' walk to Cobb & Co.'s "Telegraph Line of Mail Coaches" Office, where we took out tickets, got our luggage put in the coach, and set ourselves beside it. We drove past the Post Office where the mails were lifted, along Lambton Quay and out the road by the Hutt. The morning was fine, and I enjoyed the run to Ngahauranga, where we turned into a valley or gorge winding for six or eight miles up. The appearance of the sides was very grand;

they rose about two hundred feet high, and were covered with rich foliage of a deep green and beautified here and there with clumps of whins. After reaching the end of the valley we came to a small village or township named Johnsonville, and just then a thick Scotch mist intercepted our view. New Zealand climate and scenery are very like those of Scotland; one feels almost as if at the coast for the summer months; but there are some things that remind one that we are in the colonies. Some of the houses are such miserable huts, not much bigger than a large hat box, and literally buried in mud. The weather has been wet for some time here, and the roads in many places are a foot deep. When at home in Scotland I could not understand how the missionaries lived in such lonely places; but my knowledge has become greatly extended since then, both with respect to position and quality of houses. Some are miles and miles from their nearest neighbours, surrounded by blacks, and their mansions not so good by a long way as some of our farm appendages at home. You have no idea of the life that some live here to make money. If a story were to get up that there was gold, there would be thousands ready to banish themselves for filthy lucre's sake. It is a disgrace that people are more willing to sacrifice all for that which shall perish in the using, than for the riches that shall stand the wreck of "falling worlds." However, you must not think that all the houses in the country are so poor. No; there are some which make us look one to another and say, "civilization is here."

. . . We were taking notes as we trudged along. We saw fences put up neatly without nails, just tied with "supple-jack," large trees doing duty as bridges having a fence on one side; others trees were hollowed out like canoes and served for drains and gutters. But to return to my journey. After having passed through the last mentioned village we ran along Porirua valley, about two miles long; and having reached the other end of it we stopped at Horokiwi Hotel, where we had breakfast. I can tell you I was ready for mine; for although I had had something to eat, after the shaking and jolting I was beginning to feel sufficiently hungry, as it was now ten o'clock. We had a change of horses and set out once more on our journey through Horokiwi valley, which was about five miles long. The first half, which was over rising ground, reminded me somewhat of the scenery going up to the Falls of Clyde, only far surpassing it in grandeur. You know the insatiable appetite I have for scenery, and you will believe me when I tell you I would not have liked to have missed the feast I had in passing through this and the Paikakariki valley. Horokiwi valley was splendid, having trees of a great height with leaves twelve feet long. The sides rose to an immense height; in some places, I believe, to more than eight hundred feet. The road was often not a foot broader than was necessary for the coach to pass. But the most gorgeous part was yet to come, and by far the most dangerous. In descending, there was an awful abyss below us, and the road was cut along the windings of the hill. At the top we were eight hundred and fifty feet above sea level, and looking down the almost perpendicular rock, sheep on the level seemed like so many kittens; while our path was, if anything, narrower than on the ascent. Had we swerved half-a-foot, or had the horses become restive, we would have been dashed to pieces. It was glorious, and at the same time awful. The driver and horses have gone over this road for three years. We started from Wellington with five horses, but at Horokiwi changed them for two only, which have been trained for these terrific places; and having carried us safely over and left us on the sea level, their work for the day was done. We then got five others and broad wheels, for now we had to run along forty miles of beach. How I wish I could paint our route and describe the view we had! On the right hand sandbanks covered with green and yellow grass so tall that you could see nothing beyond it. If you were transported here you would almost think you had come where human foot had never trod, so lovely yet barren like is the shore. On the left was the ocean, stretching away into the far distance. I could see an island (Kapiti) resembling Cumbrae, only that it was much larger. It called up fond recollections of past friends and associations when I thought of the happy picnics and merry sails we had on and round the little island on the Clyde. The tide was out and we had fine roads. The shells along the beach were truly pretty; some were white as the driven snow, others red and green to relieve the dazzling brightness; we also saw some lovely birds . . . After a few miles of sandy beach we came to Waikanae, where we got a man on horseback to ford us across the river, where the water was up to the axles of the wheels. Having got across, we resumed the beach, the monotony of which was often varied by having little streams to cross. We again turned off along a dirty swamp, all overgrown with flax, which has the appearance of huge bunches of leeks. Fording another river, deeper than the last, we stopped at Otaki and had dinner. Here we saw a great number of Maoris, and looked through the native church. The missionary here preaches twice on Sabbaths to natives and once to settlers. The church is mostly of native workmanship, and is lined with native matting. Some of the Maoris were well dressed, some clad in an old blanket, and others in "puris naturalibus." We saw some noble looking men, but I think the women are far uglier than the other sex, and all smoke!

. . . After leaving Otaki we had some little way to go ere we came to the beach, but once there we had smooth roads. We met some Maoris who said we should not be able to cross the Ohau river, which was discouraging; however, we ran on until we reached its bank, and certainly there was a "fresh" on the river. The parcels were all taken and piled on the seats. I sat on the one side with head pressing on the roof, while William and our fellow-traveller were similarly situated on the other. Thus we sailed through the Ohau river in a coach and five with the water above the axles. You get no such treats in Auld Scotland. Having reached the other side and resumed our old places, we betook ourselves to the beach journey again. After this there was nothing worthy of note until we turned up through sand hills and drew up alongside the Manawatu river, where we bade adieu to the coach and got a boat to take us over. . . . One man told us that the Rev. Mr Duncan was waiting on the other side for us. He was on horseback, but had brought a man with a trap to drive us to his house, which was four or five miles distant. Here we got jolting of no ordinary nature; however, we at length arrived safely. After a drive of seventy miles, occupying fourteen hours, but which I enjoyed immensely, I was glad to sit down at last to tea in a comfortable house. . . .

I am still,
Your daughter,
AGNES.

II.
FIRST SIGHT OF THE ISLANDS.

GENERAL LETTER.

LEAVING AUCKLAND IN THE DISTANCE,
March 31st, 1869.

I now begin to fulfil my promise of jotting down whatever I think may interest you. We came on board the "Dayspring" yesterday morning, and after getting our cabin in order I sat down and wrote to a few friends. In the evening we went to tea in the Rev. Mr Bruce's, and returned about half-past nine, when we found all in a great bustle getting ready for sailing . . . We turned in for the night and had a good sleep, feeling quite secure from cockroaches with our nice mosquito netting. This morning we rose about seven, and after the usual routine of worship, breakfast, &c., a large number of Auckland friends came off to hold a valedictory meeting ; at which Captain Fraser's child was to be baptised. It was a refreshing gathering and a very touching one. There was Mr Inglis, the veteran missionary, who had spent the best of his strength in the New Hebrides, returning to resume his duties ; Mr Morrison also, who had been obliged to rest awhile, returning to the place on which his heart was set; and there were we, young and full of hope, entering on a field totally new to us, only girding on the armour, but ever saying, "If Thy presence go not with us, carry us not up hence." We had the pleasure of meeting the Rev. Mr and Mrs Macdonald, who had laboured fifteen years in Samoa, and I felt much encouraged by their parental counsels and sympathy. They sat and held me by the hand as if I had been their daughter. They had been in my position themselves. All afternoon we were chatting and bidding good-bye until about five o'clock, when we lifted anchor and bade adieu to the shores of New Zealand. One or two friends accompanied us out to the Heads, and went back in the pilot boat, while we were left to pursue our voyage. What a world of meetings and partings! The sick delights to think of heaven as a place where the inhabitant "shall no more say, I am sick." Those racked with pain rejoice to say, "neither shall there be any more pain." We who have our hearts torn with parting, look forward with joy to that time when we "shall meet to part no more." My sorest parting was with my own parents and brothers and sisters; in the light of that, all other partings seem trivial! . . .

On board we have as passengers Rev. J. and Mrs Inglis, Rev. Mr Morrison with his wife, child, and servant; Mrs Logan and her niece (Aggie M'Donald), and Miss Clark, who are going on a visit; Mrs Fraser (the captain's wife), with three children and native servant, in addition to ourselves; seventeen in all in the cabin. Now I will stop writing for a night. Mr Watt is up on deck enjoying the beautiful clear moonlight. I will take a peep upstairs and then retire to rest. How nicely we are going!

April 1st. Little to report to-day. I have been busy attending the sea-sick, for most feel uncomfortable, and as I escape that disagreeable malady, the filling out of tea and a number of other duties devolve on me.

Monday, April 5th. Shipboard life is much alike every day except Sabbath. At eleven a.m. yesterday we had a native service, which Mr Inglis requested us to attend. I wish you could have seen the earnest looks; and though I knew not the language, I felt that these people believed in that God they were professing to worship. At three, and again at seven, we had service in English, at which all the crew attended.

Thursday, April 8th. Yesterday we passed Hunter's Island, and this morning we sighted the lovely island of Aneityum, beautiful in its moral as well as its physical aspect. I soon jumped on deck to see the island, and it did look pretty rising up out of the boundless ocean with its richly wooded hills and luxuriant foliage. The triangular coral reef, forming one side of the harbour, attracted my attention. The wave rising over this is first of rich green, and rolling along, it gets lighter and lighter until it breaks into spray. Once inside the reef we were in smooth water, and soon were lying at anchor. In a few minutes Dr Geddie was on board, and we were gladdened to hear that things were progressing favourably on Aneityum. He brought with him some splendid oranges, which were very large and luscious. After dinner we went on shore. I had to be carried from the boat by two young men who made a seat with their hands, on which I sat with my arms round their necks. I think I see how you will look when you picture me in such a position, for you must remember that they were black men. Once safely landed, what a gathering there was! About twenty-four young women, all dressed in clean clothes, consisting of a native skirt, made of a sort of grass, and a blouse or jacket, each face cleaner than the other. They had brown, velvety-looking skins and beautiful black eyes; they would have gained the affection of any one. As they had come down to welcome us, we had to go round them all and shake hands. This ceremony over we went into Mrs Geddie's picturesque house. Little Ella Geddie and I were soon friends, and she took me away all through the church, a very nice plastered stone building, enclosed by a reed fence. Then we had a walk through the garden to see the orange and banana trees.

Friday 9th. To-day I had my first meal of taro and bananas, and enjoyed them much. The natives are very fond of children, and to-day when Captain Fraser's wife brought her baby on shore, what a crowd rushed to see the little man! They could do nothing but utter shouts of astonishment over him. Coming off to the "Dayspring" in the evening, we had natives pulling the boat. As they were not pulling well, we managed to tell them to sing, thinking that might help; but oh, such music! they shouted so loud that when we wished to tell them to slow, not a word could be heard. When we got to the vessel, those who had been helping the crew and those who came off with us were invited to take tea. I need not say they required no second invitation, as "kai-kai" is a thing that never comes amiss to a native. When satisfied, they went on shore singing as before.

Monday 12th. Yesterday we went ashore to the native service. The church bell rings for five minutes, and the people assemble at nine o'clock. They have two services without an interval. Dr Geddie took the first and Mr Inglis the second. After service a number of the people came round and shook hands with us. In the afternoon we had two services in English, at which all the crew of the "Dayspring" were present, who, by their good conduct, are a credit to the vessel, and set a good example to the natives. The church is plastered, has glass windows, the pulpit and the minister's pew being covered with turkey red, and the floor all laid with mats. It looks very well, and would hold from eight to nine hundred of a congregation. . . . About nine o'clock this morning Mrs Inglis came on board and said to me, "The sea is calm and we are going home, just get your things and come along with us to Aname, and the 'Dayspring' will pick you up on Wednesday." This we most gladly did, and after a beautiful sail of four hours, during which we enjoyed lovely scenery, passing exquisite valleys and sailing over beds of coral of every hue, we were landed at our destination, amidst a large concourse of happy faces, all glad to see "Missi" back, and each more eager than another to carry something. Although Mrs Inglis had been away for four months, she had a house in splendid order to go to; everything was in its own place, which I think says much for her training. Seeing the day was calm, the girls were expecting us, and had roast fowl and taro ready for dinner, so in an hour after our arrival we sat down to a plentiful and well prepared meal. The Mission Station here is quite a model, nothing trifling or flimsy like, and all very clean.. There is a Church, a Training Institution, and a dwelling house with many appendages, such as carpenter's shop, smith's shop, store-room, &c. The situation is not so good as might be wished; but to remedy this Mr Inglis has built a small cottage up the hill where they can live during the hot season. As they pay strict attention to the laws of health they get on well. The Mission ground is well stocked with orange and other fruit trees, and towering above all is the cocoa-nut palm, from which, on the hottest day, one can get a nice cool drink of cocoa-nut milk.

Tuesday 13th. In the morning we were awakened by the church bell ringing the people to school, which all attend from six to seven, before going to their plantations. The Bible is the sole book. It is a real national Scriptural education the natives here receive. There are schools all over the island, within ten minutes' walk of each home, and these are presided over by native teachers. These teachers are of great value, and, I may say, give their labour free, for they only receive £1 per annum for their services. The natives are well behaved; in each house family worship is held morning and evening.

Thursday 15th. Yesterday was the Prayer Meeting day. It is held every Wednesday afternoon, and I was much struck by the attendance. All day the natives came in from every quarter to welcome " Missi," so that when the hour for worship arrived some three hundred people had assembled. . . .

Monday 19th. Yesterday, although the morning was wet, a large congregation assembled. It moves me to see them so much in earnest; they put to shame many in highly favoured Scotland; and when one thinks that a few years ago they were cannibals and most abominable heathen, one cannot help exclaiming, " It is of the Lord." It also incites us to labour, and we hope yet to see the poor degraded Tannese, who have hitherto been proverbial for their wickedness, become, through grace, gentle as lambs. During service several of the men engaged in prayer. They are very original, and pray with great fluency. Mr Inglis takes all the native help he can get, and lets some of the women lead the singing in church. This is a great honour, for in heathenism they are the drudges of the men. In the afternoon I went to the Sabbath School. They chant the Ten Commandments, and have a large portion of Scripture committed to memory. . . . This morning the natives brought the wood for the roof of our house. Some of it was carried ten miles—and that is no joke in a tropical climate. They came in a band, each carrying a load on his shoulders, singing and shouting, and one blowing on a shell. They then laid down the wood as a contribution to the Mission. We feel very grateful to these Aneityumese; for had we to provide what we are doing, it would cost a large sum of money. Our hearts were rejoiced on Saturday by a letter from Mr Neilson to Dr Geddie, by a trading vessel, which informed us of the pleasing prospects on Tanna. He is getting on well, and was round at Umairareker (Kwamera), where we hope to go. All looks well there. The Tannese have burned a large kiln of lime wherewith to plaster our house; they have wattling ready, and there is plenty of material to make a roof, and an

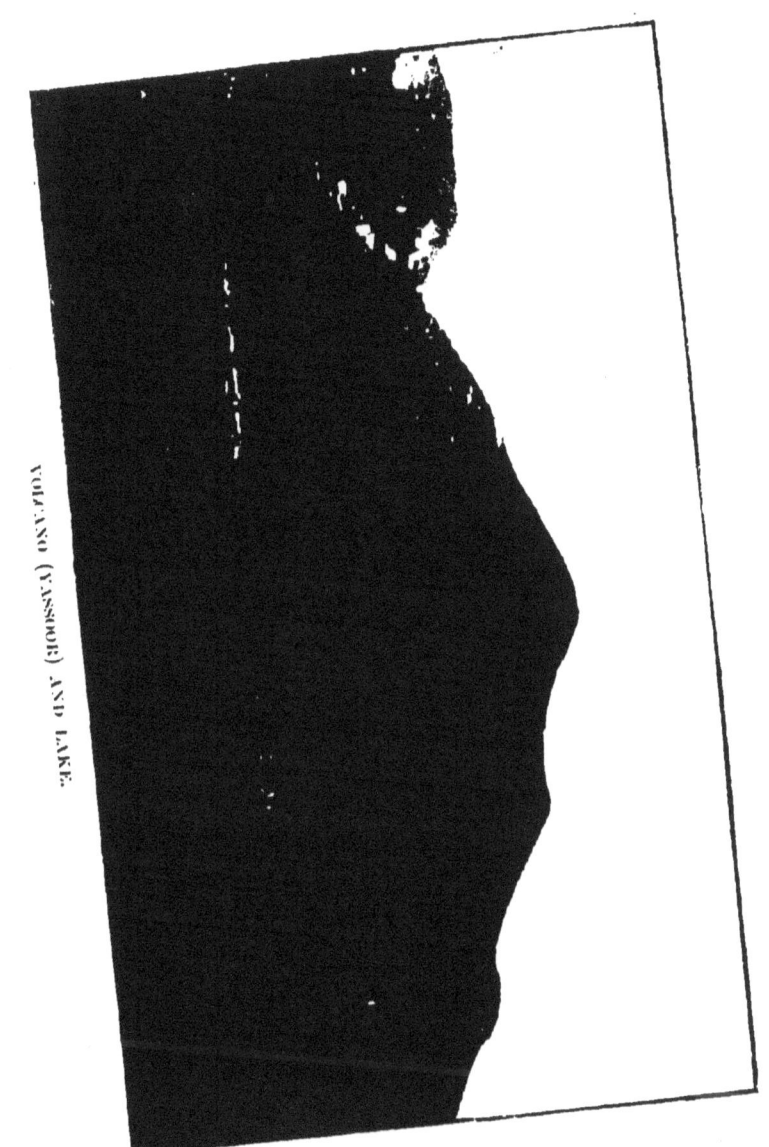

VOLCANO (YASSOUR) AND LAKE.

excellent supply of spring water. This last is most useful, as many of the missionaries are ill supplied with water. There are two teachers and their wives there already, but I have got an additional couple to go with us . . .

Thursday 22nd. We bade adieu to Aneityum for a time, and after a good tossing reached Futuna in the morning. As there is no harbour the vessel had to lie off and on; so we only waited to land Mr Copeland's goods. We found them enjoying good health, and the gospel gaining ground. . . . Here I got my first sight of heathen, and I can assure you I felt the advantage of my stay in New Zealand, where I saw the Maories in every state, else I would have been shocked with the sight that met us here. . . . The island is small, but rises boldly out of the ocean. . . . The population is about nine hundred. We left Futuna at twelve noon, and reached Tanna at six p.m. Futuna is forty-five miles to the eastward of Tanna. We had hoped to get in to Port Resolution with daylight, but the wind being light, the sun went down ere we entered the harbour. However, we were fortunate in having full moon, and the captain thought he would venture in. He is very cautious and does not like to make the land in the dark; but we got in safely with comfort. The one thing that struck me on entering was the volcano, which is very active, and every few minutes sends forth a great blaze. It is a splendid sight, and I hope to see it better some night when there is no moonlight. We had scarcely dropped anchor when Mr Neilson came off, as happy looking as if he were in the midst of his friends. He conducted worship, and chose that most appropriate psalm, the ninety-first, " He that dwelleth in the secret place of the most High shall abide under the shadow of the Almighty." A psalm literally true in the case of a foreign missionary. Mr Watt and I went on shore with him, and were glad to find himself and wife so comfortable among heathen. They have had an addition of a son to their household, to the no small joy of the natives, who think him a wonderful child, because he is a *man* and belongs to Tanna.

Friday 23rd. This morning we rose about half-past six, and by that time a large number of natives had gathered round the Mission premises to see all that could be seen. I shook hands with a number of them, and Mr Neilson told them that we were the missionaries for Umairareker. They said it was "very good," and the people there would build us a house. You may be sure I looked with interest on the people among whom I hope to labour, though at a different part of the island. My impression of them, after having seen them, is better than I anticipated. I long for the day when I shall be able to tell them of the love of Jesus, and teach the poor girls to make garments for themselves. Just now they wear nothing but a grass skirt like the Aneityumese. I liked the women very much. Many a good look they took at me. They touched my brooch and showed me their trinkets, which consisted of shells or pieces of bone. Alas for the poor sons of Adam, they wear next to nothing at all! . . .

As yet you may say that no mission work is done. It is thought better for a missionary to look first after his own comfort and to make all speed with the language, and not to interfere with the natives until they gain confidence, and he can speak to them. . . . Mr Neilson has chosen a healthy site, and has a comfortable house of two rooms. It is pleasant to think that he has been there for eight months and hasn't had the slightest molestation, but all kindness, so far as heathen can show kindness. At eleven a.m. we left Tanna and made Aniwa, which is fourteen miles distant, in two hours. Aniwa is a small island, low and flat, while Tanna is high and mountainous. As there is no harbour there we had to "lie off and on" until the goods were landed. Mr Paton has done much in getting his premises to such a state of comfort. He has a nice church and dwelling-house with a large garden in cultivation. A little daughter was born since the last time the "Dayspring" called. We were happy to find all well, and after staying a couple of hours we left for Erromanga.

Saturday 24th. This morning we landed at Dillon's Bay, a place memorable because of the deeds of darkness there perpetrated; a place holy because of the blood there shed. I felt sad on landing, for so many painful thoughts rushed into my mind. The very hills seemed dark and frowning. The natives of this island, to my mind, are the most disgusting, forbidding creatures I have seen even among savages; but, perhaps, I am alone in that idea. They paint themselves mostly black, and dress their persons in a way too horrible to describe. They have a sullen countenance, and seem very cowardly and treacherous and half-starved. They are good swimmers, and came off in twos and threes to the "Dayspring." The island is large, but not so fertile as Tanna; indeed, they often suffer for want of food. We found Mr and Mrs Macnair well and the Mission work prospering. About forty attend worship, and the prospects are encouraging. . . .

Pango, Monday 26th. We left Erromanga on the evening of the 24th and anchored in Fila Harbour on Sabbath. It is seventy miles from Erromanga, and we hoped to have reached here early yesterday morning, but the wind was light and it was five p.m. when we got in. We found Mr and Mrs Cosh well, and had the pleasure of welcoming the second little Cosh, a fine boy of a fortnight old. They enjoy much better health now than when they were obliged to live in a miserable mud hut. There is much to encourage here, as the gospel is gaining ground. The island is the largest of the six occupied, and is equal, if not superior, to any of the others in scenery. . . .

Erakor, 28th. Mr Morrison lives on a little island separated from the mainland by a lagoon. The lagoon is the finest sight I have seen, and the surrounding scenery is enchanting. The rich foliage down to the water's edge, the bright green sea water covering a rich bed of many-hued corals, and above all a cloudless sky of brightest blue. It is like dreamland or fairyland! The natives of Efate are quite different from the other islanders. The men are tall, and even in their heathen state wear a covering. The women are ugly, have large noses and wear a dress consisting of two aprons. Men and women alike wear bracelets, some of which are beautiful. They adorn their hair by hanging two or three dozen boars' tusks to the ends of it, all round their heads. Their language seems somewhat like Maori. They make beautiful mats with unbleached calico, seventy fathoms of which I bought for my house. So far we have had a pleasant voyage, and have found all the missionaries well. We will have to beat back, as the south-east trade wind is dead against us.

On Wednesday, 28th April, we sailed from Efate, and after a very favourable passage anchored in Port Resolution, Tanna, on the 6th of May. On Monday the 11th, we started with a fair wind for the place of our future labour. We wished to visit the people and ascertain the state of feeling among them in regard to our settling there. At one o'clock we were "lying off," and as there is no harbour and no anchorage, the vessel tacked about while Messrs Paton, Macnair, Neilson, and ourselves went ashore. Long ere we reached the shore we could see that the beach was lined with natives, and we felt very glad to see so many. On landing we were met by one of the Aneityumese teachers (and I can assure you it is a treat to see such, on a heathen island, clean and decently clad), who led us to the little church which they have built. There sat the two Aneityumese women, and what a reception we got from them! We are supposed to have a choice as to the field in which we wish to labour, but in regard to us, the teachers were told of our coming, and the heathen had burned a kiln of lime to plaster our house. Although we had a dozen places to choose from, this would have the preference. We had a meeting in the church with a number of the natives and four chiefs. Mr Paton addressed them and told them of the object of our visit, and asked them if they were willing to receive us as their missionaries. To this the chiefs replied, one after the other, that they were willing, that their words

GRASS CHURCH, KWAMERA.

were all *one*, and that they would be strong for the worship. Before, they said, their words were many, some were for, and some were not for the worship, but now their words were one. After the meeting I went and saw a little room the teachers had made for us to eat in until our house is finished. They seem to be energetic teachers; their wives, too, had sewed up all the roofing for our house and had it all ready in the church. We then went and saw two sites suitable for building on; the one new and the other the site of the former missionary's house. The natives said that they would come to either place. We were accompanied by a number of natives and a chief. The little boys were quite free and came and took my hands. But we had to hurry off as it was beginning to darken, and we wished to reach the ship in daylight. The natives thought we might have brought our house and stayed that day. We really ought to be thankful, it is truly " of the Lord." And though it may be mere selfish motives that prompt them to receive us—perhaps only for the sake of bartering—yet it is pleasant to get such a settlement, and we trust the Lord will open their blind eyes and enlighten their dark minds. Some of the missionaries were hardly permitted to land. The heathen are fickle and have many strange ideas, and it may be that two years hence they would wish to undo all that they are now doing. We have nothing to do with that; the cry has reached us, " Come over and help us," and our duty is to try and lead them to the Deliverer, and leave the future in His unerring hand.

I am, yours very truly,

A. C. P. WATT.

III.
BEGINNING WORK ON TANNA.

1. TO HER FATHER.

June 1st, 1869.

DEAR FATHER,—I have sat down to write a few lines, but ere I put pen to paper I was surrounded by half a dozen natives all wishing to know what I was doing. I told them I was going to write about Kwamera, and they said it was "ramasan" (good).

We arrived here accompanied by Messrs Inglis and Neilson on the 27th of May; and now I will tell you a little about our settlement. On coming ashore we found all in much the same state as when we visited them three weeks before. They were all down on the beach to see the goods belonging to "Missi," and as I stepped from the boat many voices shouted "Missi bran" (the woman missionary). The landing of goods here is no small task, as the "Dayspring" has to lie off and on. In this way it took all day to land our provisions, and then she stood out for the night. The weather since then has been such that we have not been able to get the frame of our house landed. But I have begun at the wrong end of my story. Mr Inglis has brought sixty Aneityumese to assist in building, and they have put up a cook house. I have two of them acting as cook and steward, and I will not be saying too much if I say they do the work well. I wish you could look in on us here. The little church I have divided with a mat; the one end is Mr Inglis and Mr Neilson's bedroom, the other is ours and is also store-room, while the little room the teachers made for us is dining-room, parlour, and reception-room, and we think it very comfortable, all things considered. Saturday was wet, and therefore we saw few people but on Sabbath the weather improved, and we had two services in the open air, at which a goodly number of natives were present. The services were partly in Aneityumese and partly in Tannese. The whole day was spent in peace and quietness, and were I not here I would not believe we could be so comfortable in body and mind on an island of naked painted savages. It is wonderful how soon the eye gets accustomed to such sights as appear here on every hand. All day long we are attended by naked heathen painted with red and black in all the designs they can invent. . . . A man came from inland to see us, and Kapuka, one of our chiefs, brought him into the house. The clock amuses them much. I pointed out to them the hours at which we rose, took breakfast, dinner and tea, when we went to bed, and how long we stayed there; at this the inland man marvelled greatly. Shaking hands is unknown in heathendom, but soon follows the missionary; this the old man knew nothing about, and when Kapuka told him to shake hands with me, I wish you could have seen him, he was so nervous. Kapuka and Kaipapa shake hands with me every morning and say "fakecari." The natives have long consultations over me, and sometimes the chief explains what they say. Some say "very good, you live here," and one said, "I am just wondering at her goodness." So you see I am in high repute just now. The little boys and girls have begun to come with cocoa-nuts, and I barter with them in return. The other day I went to a spring of water, about a quarter of a mile along the shore, and I soon found I had made friends. About a dozen women followed me and did all they could to express their love; they carried the jug of water for me, and gave me the present of a cocoa-nut. Poor things! they are very degraded; some look the very picture of misery, but others are plump and open-faced, and if they were decently clad they would compare very favourably with many at home.

June 10th. Another week has passed over our heads, and I can hardly believe it. How time flies here! Things are progressing favourably and our house is rising with all speed. I hope by next week to write to you from my "ain fireside." We continue to get every encouragement from the natives. They come daily with things to sell, and in this way there is a very friendly feeling between us. We are busy acquiring their language, and each day strive to get some new words. I hope soon to be able to make myself understood. . . .

July 4th. The "Dayspring" came in on the 28th June, and Mr Paton came ashore. He informed us of a successful visit to Santo and Mr Gordon's settlement there. . . . One boat after another filled and went off to the vessel until the last, in which our dear and venerable friend Mr Inglis was to take his departure.

His advice to me was to do nothing I could avoid, and to take care of my health.

But the bustle of that day was too much for me, and I was seized with a very severe headache and had to go to bed. It turned out to be a bilious fever. I lay more or less for four days, but I am very happy to say I am fast gaining strength again. . . .

Your own daughter,
AGNES.

2. TO THE FAMILY.

July 19th, 1869.
KWANAPUKA KWAMERA, TANNA.

MY DEAR FATHER, MOTHER, BROTHERS, AND SISTERS,—To-day one of Mr Neilson's teachers brought a mail overland, that had come by a schooner *via* Fiji. Mr Neilson has been obliged to go to Erromanga, so the mail came to us, being addressed to the "Resident Protestant Missionary." A trader living at Port Resolution has sent round a message stating that his vessel is going to Sydney, so I will write you a letter, and if to-morrow be fine we shall go round to Port Resolution in our own boat. Perhaps this may reach home before the mail by the "Dayspring," which left a week ago.

We are busy getting up some outhouses, and our six teachers have, so far, proved all that we could wish. The men have wrought very hard at the building, so I lighten their work with a little tea at each meal; it does not need to be strong, if it is only sweet enough. The women are none behind them, clearing away the rubbish and making great bonfires. As I have a washing every week, they are kept in a constant move. Warai, the woman who came with me, is my house servant and does everything except bake bread, which I do three times a week, and at which I am becoming quite accomplished. She makes the beds, sets the table, and dresses all the clothes. Except what I work on the machine, my teachers do all the sewing. You will, perhaps, fancy I have nothing to do, but it is far otherwise. Last week I made two pairs of trousers, trimmed three hats for my three women, and to-day, as William was not very well, I have painted all my bedroom; and every day, from half-past seven till four or five in the afternoon, I am kept busy entertaining visitors. In some places the natives have the full liberty of the mission house. When I saw this, I determined, if possible, to have one place where they should not open doors, march in, sit on my chairs, smoke, and gape at me while at food. Two months' experience has now shewn me that if you make a reasonable law and tell them of it kindly, it is at once agreed to. My bedroom is *i-tapu*,—private or sacred; they only see it once, and when I please. In this way I have one place to myself, and if a lot come wishing to see through the house, and I tell them I am going to eat, they are quite pleased, and wait till I have finished. If a man comes in smoking and I tell him not to smoke in my house, in an instant his pipe is withdrawn, and he says, "ramasan, missi" (it is good, missi). Of course you know, all go armed, but no club or weapon of war ever enters my house; all such must be left at the door. But really you can have little idea of our life here. One man came to me to-day and said, "Ik ramasan" (You are good). "Nari saik ramasan" (Your things are good). "Nimwa saik ramasan" (Your house is good). I knew there was something behind all this, so out came "Ik aveipehe miau shoo shap" (You give me a Jew's harp). The harmonium is a great attraction, and many times a day am I told by some twenty at a time, "Ik mo bokis mungkiari" (You make the box speak), or "Ani nupu, missi" (Sing a hymn, missi). This night, as far as we can see, we are on the best of terms with all the natives. Last week there was a great feast, and many from inland came to see us. Some were afraid and would not come in, then one of the shore people, who had more intercourse with us, would march in very boldly to show to his ignorant brother how far advanced he was. Some of these bushmen when they saw themselves in the glass started back, as if terrified out of their wits, to the no small amusement of their advanced friends; others thought it was another room they were seeing. In some such style as this all our days pass; when the sun begins to set, all go home and we see no more of our black brothers and sisters until next day. Of this we are glad, for we can have such nice evenings after six o'clock. Sometimes I work on the sewing machine, sometimes practice sacred music on the harmonium, and at other times get in our teachers and teach them singing. Thus happily pass our evenings, and of our nights what shall I say? I am invariably so tired in body and mind that generally I know nothing from nine p.m. till six next morning, when I rise and have breakfast.

But it is past ten o'clock to-night. As it is very

injurious to health to sit up late here, you will excuse me cutting my letter short. You know that we have to carry it for twenty miles. . . .

I remain your daughter,

AGNES.

3. TO THE FAMILY.

KWANAPUKA, KWAMERA, TANNA.
Commenced July 28th, 1869.

MY DEAREST FATHER, MOTHER, BROTHERS, AND SISTERS,—I promised to give you a description of our house in this letter, so with that I will begin. At present we have two rooms. The parlour is 19 × 14 ft., and has two windows; the bedroom is 15 × 14 ft., also with two windows. We have no ceiling; the room is open up to the rigging, which makes it nice and airy. Now, suppose you were landing here, you would see a nice house enclosed by a pretty reed fence. Coming inside that, you walk up a nice gravel walk to five snow-white steps. Ascend these and you come on to our verandah with its white painted floor and a low reed railing painted green. The outside of the house is pure white, and the doors and windows are painted bright green. Having studied the verandah, will you look around at the scenery? North-east you can see along the beach for a great way, and direct east rises Futuna, reminding you of Ailsa Craig. But you are nearly deafened by the roar of the surf on the reef, and your eyes are dazzled by the bright glare of a tropical sun on the pearly white foam and the pebbly shore. Ah! but the air is delightful, and you feel you could not endure the smoke of a city. But now having got you to the door, I must invite you in. The door opens against the middle wall; and on this wall I have our largest mirror for the use of the natives, and also some coloured pictures which amuse them much. To the left is the harmonium, which also interests them greatly; and a chest, which serves as an ottoman, is under the window. Against the gable wall stands the iron sofa bed, and over it hangs the barometer. Against the back wall stands a meat-safe, another ottoman is set under the window and a home-made chiffonier; above these hangs the clock, and on it I have some books and two kerosene lamps. In the middle of the floor stand two tables put together, which make one nice large one; and when a well cooked dinner, of chicken soup, yam and native cabbage, with a nice plumpudding, plenty of bananas, and a cup of tea with rich goat's milk, is laid out on a pure white table cloth, we are not to be pitied. I have no carpet, as so many natives come in, and I think a clean floor fresher. My bedroom is laid with mats, the walls whitewashed, and the doors and windows painted light green. We have in it a wardrobe, military secretaire, and an arm-chair. On the walls are photographs of our loved ones and the R.P. students. Our bed is made of banana leaves with feather pillows. As there is no ceiling, I have put up four posts on the bedstead to hold up a calico roof and mosquito netting. Now, don't you think the room is a very pretty one? We have about four acres of land, past which a lovely stream flows, yielding an abundant supply of pure water. Besides our dwelling-house, we have a store-room, duck-house, and a house for poultry that are

KWAMERA FROM THE SEA.

bought for food. Soon we hope to get up a goat-house and a carpenter's shop. William is framing a spare bedroom, which we are trying to get up during the cool weather, so that we will have no building to do in the hot weather.

Now, in order to give you an idea of how we live and spend our time, I will keep a journal for this week.

Yesterday,—Sabbath. We rose about half-past six, had breakfast and family worship, and then dressed for church. We dress for church just as if we were at home; William in linen shirt, black clothes and clean boots, and I with a clean muslin or print dress. Before the service commences, one of the teachers beats a thing like a small boat, which is the Sabbath bell. At nine o'clock we went over to the church, which is about two hundred yards distant, and sat down, as it is the custom here to let the minister in first, and the people follow. The service began by William reading the Lord's Prayer, which he has translated through the teachers; then we sang a hymn, one of half a dozen prepared by Mr Paton while residing on Tanna; Kaipapa, the chief of Anuikaraka, prayed, after which William read a chapter from the gospel of Mark, translated in the same way. Another hymn, "There is a happy land," and one of the teachers addressed them. A hymn followed, "Here we suffer grief and pain," another native prayed, then the closing hymn, "Lord, a little band and lowly," and the benediction. After this, the intimations were given out. Paul says that a woman is not allowed to speak in the church; and I wonder what some people would say if they knew that there was only one seat in the church, serving as pulpit and minister's pew, and that, till yesterday, I have always given out the intimations! During the building of the house I had, and still have, most of the intercourse with the natives, and in this way I have picked up a few words sooner than William. The attendance was good, thirteen men and seventeen women; counting the Aneityumese and ourselves there were thirty-seven of a congregation. After the Tannese service there was another among the teachers, to which William stayed, while I went and taught the women to sing. Fifteen followed me and sang most heartily, accompanied by the harmonium. After the music I gave a lesson on the alphabet by means of a box of letters which came in Miss Glen's box, and lastly a lesson in figures on the slate. Sabbath is the only day I can get them to listen to any instruction. While I was busy with the women, William had four or five men. After this we had dinner, and read for two hours, when William and one of the teachers went and had service at Anuikaraka. They came home at five, had tea, and an English service at seven, at which Mr Underwood, the trader who is here, was present. The day was delightful, and our hearts were cheered by so many having come to worship. But I must describe Kaipapa's appearance. He had on a blue flannel shirt, which was a good deal too short; his long hair was tied on the top of his head with a piece of bright printed handkerchief; his cheeks were painted black, a stripe of scarlet half an inch broad began at the right temple, crossed the eyelid, came down the side of the nose and round half of the mouth. A stripe of yellow adorned the other side in the same manner; while a red stripe came down the bridge of the nose! Now, don't you admire him? Well, that is the man who led in the first prayer, and, although he is a heathen and has three wives, still he has manifested a great deal of kindness to us, and was among the foremost in urging the people here to get a missionary. He has brought us several presents which I always took care to pay for, as I do not wish to be in debt to any one. He is not much of a chief, but is a clever, officious fellow. Yesterday week we heard that a man had stolen a woman, that the offended party had declared war, and that all our people would join, as the offended people were many, and it would take all the force they could muster to meet them. Though we were not at all involved, we felt very sad, for our people would be so taken up that our efforts would be stopped for a time, and the pursuers were wild heathen—the worst we know of here. But God, who sets bounds to the wrath of man, had otherwise appointed. Kaipapa sent two pigs and two sticks of tobacco as a present, which was accepted, and thus ended the quarrel. We were rejoiced. Kaipapa is tired of war. He says, now that a missionary has come, his people will not fight. Time will tell.

Monday. We rose shortly after six a.m. Nothing of interest occurred, few natives having come this way, knowing that my beads were all away. William was busy at the frame of our new room, and I at sewing.

Tuesday. This morning we had scarcely got breakfast over, when a number of natives came to "asipau" or look at my house, and from that time till far on in the day I never closed the door, and had to bake in the midst of it all! They were not very troublesome, only I had to sit down with my hands all flour and "make the bokis speak." The trader here came over in great distress, and said that the natives had threatened to make him sick. Those who have any interest advise him to leave no rubbish about, for they believe that if he were to smoke one half of a fig of tobacco, and a native got the other half and burned it, he would become sick; if the native continued to burn it until it was all consumed, he would die. He has got into disrepute somehow with the people. He does not pay so well as we do! . . . They have strange ways of doing things. I engage a boy to bring water; three go, and I have to pay each the same. Now, Mr Underwood agrees to pay two men a fig of tobacco each for scraping a tubful of cocoa-nut. Four helped to scrape it, and all wanted the pay. This he could not, and would not give, so he broke the tobacco in two. It turns out that there is nothing so good as tobacco for making people sick. Therefore they are anxious to get it whole, for if some one burns the other half they think they will die. . . .

Wednesday. To-day, Kaipapa came by seven o'clock,. according to appointment. The natives of a village on the way to Port Resolution had gathered coral for lime for our new room, and Mr Watt with Kaipapa and the teachers had arranged to go for it to-day. William came home in time for dinner, and the afternoon was spent in the prayer meeting. . . .

Thursday. Nothing of importance occurred to-day. In the afternoon William went out to fish and caught some, which we had for tea. In the evening he and the teachers were translating, while I was working at the sewing machine.

Friday. It has been blowing quite a gale to-day. A number of natives came to clear and dig our ground. They came entirely unasked and wrought away till two o'clock. Yesterday morning, long before breakfast, an old woman was digging and fencing and burning, and all the payment was a biscuit! It makes me sad to look at them, especially when they come and put their arms around me and say so lovingly, "Pi-nak" (my sister). Yes, they are; for God "hath made of one blood all nations of men for to dwell on all the face of the earth." . . .

Saturday. This has been a busy day. First I had to bake, then followed cooking, painting, scrubbing, carrying water, killing fowls, re-boiling jam, and an innumerable lot of other duties; besides feeding and paying a number who came to work. Each day by two o'clock I feel as wearied as if I had done everything myself, while very often I have only overseen.

August 9th. Yesterday the attendance was about the same, and much attention shown; although not a single soul has a proper idea of what we live among them for. Their hearts are dark, and, though attending worship, they live in all the abominations of heathenism. For instance, Kiri, one of our chiefs, and a regular worshipper, took an axe and struck a heavy blow at his wife, cutting her arms and forehead, for a very trivial offence. We have heard not a few women screaming, under the blows of their husbands. Oh, if you were just here and saw heathenism, with the wild savage look of the miserable dirty creatures,—in all cases, perfectly nude. Yet they are immortal, they have souls to be saved ; they are degraded, it is true, but Jesus can save unto the uttermost. . . .

August 10th. To-day we went to see the place where Mr Mathieson lived. It is on a hill called Imoa. We intended to have got our house built there, but the natives thought we should be better where we are. I would have liked the view, but I have no doubt that when it is blowing a hurricane we will be glad we are scarcely so high up. The ruins of the old house are still standing, or rather lying ; for after eight years in a climate where hurricanes are common, it is no wonder that it is level with the ground. I saw many pieces of broken dishes, and could trace the garden walks, while I plucked lemons from trees which the Mathiesons had planted. This place tells a sad tale. Many nights of sickness and weariness were here spent ; many tears shed and earnest prayers offered, which shall not be unanswered, although the answer is as yet withheld. The name of Mathieson is almost forgotten. Many have died during those eight years, and those upon whom their highest hopes were set have as yet manifested no desire for instruction. I feel sad when I think how long they laboured, and yet so little sign of permanent success. Perhaps we may have to do the same. . . . We searched in vain for the grave of their infant daughter, whom they were called to lay in the dust a fortnight before they left the island. They buried her near their house and put a fence round the grave, but already it is unknown. Poor little thing ! she had but a short look on this world ; two months, and then fell asleep! Here she lies ; her mother lies on Aneityum and her father on Mare, one of the Loyalty islands. "Their graves are severed far and wide," although there was but six months between the death of the first and the last of the three! . . .

The people are pleasant to us, yet we get much to try both strength and patience. To-day some twenty natives came to "asipau" the house. As they were from a distance, and most expert thieves, I told them they would get in by and by, while I hurried and got all loose articles out of the way. This was about eight in the morning, and from that till four in the afternoon the place was in a constant buzz. I had to go out and in looking after my baking; taking care that some one was left to watch, although the Aneityumese have no power over them. While I was at the cook-house one of the chiefs opened the table drawer and was "asipauing" all in it, which, with some, means practically to look what they can get to steal. The teacher had told him to desist, but he heard her not. However, when I came in I told him that he was not to do that, at the same time shutting the drawer, so he immediately stopped. I often wonder how sturdy warriors feel when I clear twenty or thirty of them out of the house with a word—or a smile—seeing a woman here is a mere nothing; but it is evident that "Missi bran" is more than a Tanna woman. . . . I daresay you may often be uneasy about things which never move us in the least. On Saturday last a native was walking off with our American saw, which, of course, was quite out of the question. We at once told him he could not have it. He said it was to cut wood, and that he would return it; but we knew that if he got it outside of the fence we might bid adieu to it. The command was given to put it down, which he did, in a passion, as might be expected. He scolded and better than scolded, and said he would not enter our premises again for four moons. We, of course, maintained our cause, and said it was very good for him to come and see us, but if he did not wish to come it would still be good. He then said to me, "Ik amucci iau?" (Do you hate me?) I said I did not, that I loved him still. This seemed to cut him worse than if I had seemed either angry or grieved, so away he went. He returned again to-day, came into the house and again laid claim to the use of the saw, which was refused. On leaving the house, he lifted a little hammer and said he would take it. I was between him and the door, and just took it out of his hand, saying that he could not have it. At this he was very angry, but I began tatting and never minded him. Very soon he was all praise, thinking that I was a very wonderful woman. . . .

September 27th. This is my twenty-third birthday, and no doubt you will be thinking about me. William and I feel very unsettled at present, as the " Dayspring " has not yet arrived. She may come in half an hour, or may not come for a week. It is very annoying; for, expecting a visit from Mr and Mrs Milne, we had made some preparations in the way of cakes and shortbread ; but owing to the delay all have disappeared ! Were it not that we are expecting some of our friends in the Mission to come ashore, we would not mind when the boat came.

. . . On the 28th September the " Dayspring " came back from New Zealand. Like " Royal Charlie," she was long in coming, but, when she did, there was no small stir. I was delighted to see Mr Paton, Mr Neilson, and Mr and Mrs Milne. They had a narrow escape from drowning. A heavy sea was running, and just after the boat left the ship the rudder broke. Before they got things righted she took in a large quantity of water, and Mr Milne had to keep baling all the way in, to keep afloat, as she was loaded up to the gunwale. I was happy to see them all, especially Mrs Milne. She seems a lovable person. I think she and I will get on well. We are new to the field, and can sympathise with each other. . . . As Messrs Paton and Neilson were going to visit round Tanna, we thought it our duty to accompany them. . . . The first place we called at was Anamahi, and at Sangalee the missionaries met with a noted trader named Lewin. The missionaries were anxious to get the natives to receive a teacher, and, when pressing them, Lewin said, ".You fools, why don't you take a missionary? a missionary is a good thing." To his no small mortification one spoke out in broken English, "What for you say before, 'Missionary he no good'? now you say he 'very good!'" We had to leave without gaining a footing. A little north of Sangalee the trader seemed a different kind of man. The natives were willing to receive a teacher, and he offered to give the land and every assistance in his power. At Black Beach we met another trader, and there we got the cold shoulder from the natives, who have no teacher; for they liked Charley, and we were to ask him. Here the wind rose and prevented our further progress ; and while we were lying at anchor for two days we saw a vessel that had been taking away natives. She passed quite close, and two young lads from our station, on board the "Dayspring," called out to them on board the "slaver," asking them where they were going. They said, "to Fiji." They were then asked if they were stolen or if they wanted to go. At this there was a long pause, and then one shouted, "The captain says, if we say we are stolen, he will shoot us." Of course, the whole conversation was in Tannese; so the captain could not tell what was being said. . . . We reached Port Resolution on Sabbath, October 2nd. As previously arranged, some of our teachers and Tannese brought round our boat for us. They also brought news of the murder of a trader, whose crime seems to have been that he sold the musket and bullets with which Kasikasi was shot. We do not know his name, but we have heard that he was eaten. A piece of his flesh was sent to one of our chiefs, who refused to take it, saying he had a missionary now, and it would not do for him to have it. Poor man, he has come to a sad end ! . . . We were much gratified and reassured by the reception we got from our own people. They crowded in from every quarter to see us, and tell us how they had cried because we were not here, and how they were now rejoicing because we had returned. . . .

November 9th. The feeling toward us here is friendly, yet it seems cold compared with the reception we got from a tribe four miles from us. The name of the village is Umaiahav. They are very numerous, and they have also been very bouncing. In previous letters I have told you of their thefts and impudence. Indeed, so impudent were they, that when I knew of their coming I either hid all of worth and got William to sit in the house, or else put on my hat and went for a walk to escape them, while the cook locked the kitchen door and sat outside ; thus they could get nothing to steal. They wanted a teacher to go and live among them, but all were afraid of them. However, since we got the lime burned by them their conduct has been better. One of the new teachers is for them, and for the last three weeks they and the teachers have been building his house. . . . Hearing such good reports of their helping, we resolved to go and spend a few days with them, make the door for Manman's house, and give a few small presents. We took bedding and blankets, with a few dishes, and went along in our boat. In a short time we landed, and had a cheering reception. We then had a meeting, at which all the leading chiefs were present. The teachers laid out our gifts, in real native fashion, on a mat spread on the ground. Two of our people spoke, and what occurred that day was the means of stopping the war between them and our people. After receiving the presents, they made a return present of eight large pigs, two of which fell to our share, and one killed for our present needs, besides an immense quantity of yams. The whole ended in good spirits and kindly feeling. That night we had fifteen in to worship in our hut. All Saturday we spent talking to the people and buying food. After breakfast, on Sabbath, William set out for Kwamera, which he reached before seven a.m., and had worship with the people. Forty were present. While he was there I had a meeting with twelve women and ten children, singing hymns and telling them about

Jesus. Though I was but a woman, upwards of half a dozen men came and listened. At eleven, we had service, and though we had built the teacher's house large, so as to serve as a church as well, not one of the women could get in. In the afternoon they asked us to go to the public square, which we did; and no fewer than one hundred and twenty came to worship there. I wish you could have seen us. William in his clean white suit, surrounded by seventy men all naked and painted, sitting under the shade of the banyan trees, and I surrounded by about fifty women, all watching me; if I put my hand to my face, all doing the same, thinking that was a part of the worship. We were a picturesque group. . . . In the evening we had about twenty in to prayers. On Monday morning we bade them adieu; much pleased with their conduct, and loaded with yams.

. . . On December 2nd, we went round to Port Resolution to see the "Dayspring" off. She left us on the 17th, and I stood on a bank and waved my handkerchief till she was out of sight. God knows what may happen ere she again touches our shores. While at Port Resolution we visited the hot springs and other interesting sights; but the most interesting visit of all was the one paid to the spot where Christ's banner had first been unfurled, and where, for the Gospel's sake, God's faithful messengers had suffered. "In perils by the heathen. . . . In weariness and painfulness, in watchings often." I cannot describe my feelings as I saw the foundation of the church, and thought of the bright gleams of promise that cheered the lonely labourers; as I saw the graves and thought of the nights of agony and pain through which the quiet sleepers had passed, the tribulation through which they entered into the kingdom of heaven. . . .

On December 17th, we returned to our own home. I was much delighted with half a dozen little boys who waded up to the waist in water to shake hands with me, saying, " Oh, missi, missi, we are glad to have you come back."

Yesterday,—Sabbath. While William was itinerating I went with Kwatahin to see her husband, Kapuka. He is one of our most influential chiefs, and in Mr Mathieson's day identified himself much with Christianity. He has been absent from church for some time, and no one can give any reason for it. He takes no part in any native proceedings, only sits alone in his house. Having taken such an active part in the last missionary's time, we felt a little disappointed at his manner to us. He is naturally a bashful man, and that may account for it partly; but while he is civil he has at the same time kept away from active efforts on our side, and goes naked like the rest. He was sitting outside of his house, and, though there was a good breeze, he was perspiring profusely. . . . I enquired, Why are you so dull? He replied that his heart was weak, and his body as well. I proposed to bring medicine and cordials, but he didn't want them, as it was his heart and not his body that was sick. I asked what was making his heart weak, and he said it was the talk of the people here, that he wished them to stop fighting, and also to cease speaking of war. . . .

Thursday 23rd. Last night, just before retiring to rest, we had occasion to go out to the teachers' house, and were shocked to hear that Kapuka had committed suicide. At first I could not believe it, but alas! it is too true. Two of our teachers had gone up to dress his corpse and hear the talk, as they were afraid of war on his account. This morning we got the particulars. It was just at sundown, and all the men were gone to drink their kava; he was sitting outside with his wife and children and another native. His wife was laying out their evening meal. He refused to eat any, saying he was not hungry, and rose to go inside his house. His wife, on seeing this, requested him to give her a stick of sugar-cane for the children. He went in, but instead of giving it to her as he was wont, he simply threw it on the ground near her. She wondered at his conduct, but in an instant the report of a musket was heard. Naswai, the man he had left two minutes before, rushed in, and there lay Kapuka, a dying man. The bullet entered his right side and passed out behind. He lingered on till about eleven, and then his spirit took its flight. While he was conscious several asked him as to the cause of his conduct, but to all of them he gave the same answer as to me two days before. Sometime ago he told his wife to lift her child and flee, as he hated them; he hated all men, and his heart hated himself. About two months ago he attempted to flee to a distant village, but did not succeed. One thing he asked me on Sabbath day I shall remember. "When is the 'Dayspring' coming?" and I shall never forget his look of despair when I told him that she had left for the colonies. Since then I have been informed that he intended to have left in her and gone to Aneityum. I verily believe that had she called he would have gone with her and so escaped his untimely end. But we knew not his desire. A probable cause may be, that some time ago a man handed him a musket to shoot a lad who had been misbehaving, or his father. Kapuka was heard to say: "Why did Narin give me that musket? is it really to shoot one of these two, or does he mean me to shoot myself?" Up to that day Kapuka was at church, and, strange to say, he shot himself with that man's musket. Alas, alas! my heart is grieved for Kapuka. He was not far from the kingdom of God, but "many shall seek to enter in and not be able." . . . To-day, Mr Watt went up and saw his corpse. Two of the teachers dug his grave and had him decently buried. A row of stones marks his body, and the head is marked by two long feather ornaments worn by chiefs at feasts and used for this purpose.

The chief Toko, on whose land we are living, had not come down to welcome us. I enquired of his wife the reason, and told her I was wearying to see him. He came to explain his absence, and brought me a nice present of bananas and rose-apples; for, said he, "the two had been wearying to see me, and why should I go empty-handed?" . . . Toko is a genuine heathen, but has all the savage virtues and is free from civilized vices.

Monday 27th. Yesterday, after church, we went to see Kapuka's widow. As we came near we heard the wailing—a sad and dismal sound. If the sound was dismal, what was the spectacle? Inside a miserable hut, full of smoke and filth, sat a few women weeping with the bereaved. All her body was besmeared with powdered charcoal (black is the sign of mourning) and her hair cut as short as possible. The women made way for me, and as I sat down beside her she grasped me by the hand and said, "Missi." For a few minutes there was nothing but loud wailing, but when it was over I laid my hand on her shoulder and began to tell her of Jesus and the family of Bethany. As I dared not speak of the dead, I appealed to the living, and told them that as they knew not the day of their death, they should turn to the Lord, and that Jesus was waiting for them. They listened very attentively. . . . To-day I have had one of Mrs Mathieson's scholars. She comes to talk, and so I practice speaking the language. She is such a nice woman, so gentle and amiable. If she were only a Christian I could love her as a sister. Although eight years had elapsed from Mrs Mathieson's leaving until we came, she remembered nearly all the alphabet, and read very well. We can say this of none but herself. Her name is Yemeitahak.

Thursday 30th. The last four days I have had a few little boys come for a lesson. I wish they would continue. This is one peculiarity of our Mission, we can get no children to worship, or to learn to read. They say their parents would beat them if they came, because they love them and are afraid they will turn sick and die if they become worshippers.

Friday 31st. On Wednesday evening, or yesterday morning rather, a party of Aneityumese who had come to see the trader, and whose conduct during their stay here bespoke the teaching they had got at the trading station, left in a boat, and took away a Tanna woman. While they were here we got complaints on all hands of their evil deeds; for, said they, "You bring Aneityumese who tell us to give up this and that evil practice, and here are their brethren doing worse."

Last night two of our Aneityumese teachers and another man came and pled with us to get our boat to go to Aneityum and bring the woman back; else the village to which she belonged would shoot one of them in revenge. We felt much to give our sanction to sending our boat over forty miles on the open sea; but what could we do? This morning all preparations were made, and after a good deal of ado (seeing we wanted no Tannese to go in the boat, and having turned out three), she started. It happened to be low tide, and as the boat went through the break in the reef, a man ran out and jumped in. In an instant, shouting and wailing by fifty natives began, saying, "Don't take Kasien away! let him out! let him out!" We waved and called to our teachers, and they put him on the reef again. No sooner was he landed than the cry was raised by another party, "You have not let him go, his heart is sore for Kapuka; if he went it would mend his heart, but now he has been stopped he will just shoot himself." I saw there was evidently going to be a quarrel by some if he went, and by others if he did not. The boat was on her way, there was not a moment to be lost. I rushed on to the reef and ran on to the edge where Mr Watt was standing, and told him that they must come back. He gave orders that the boat was to be put in the house, feeling that it was better to be in one quarrel than trying to remedy one leading to two or three. It was a sad affair. One party saying, "You have spoiled his heart by not letting him go"; and the other, "He has spoiled our sailing." We felt quite puzzled what to do; lives had been threatened through the stealing of the woman, and now matters were no better. All day long reports were coming in from every quarter. The one side saying, "It was Aneityumese who stole the woman, and if you don't bring her back we will kill an Aneityumese for her." Others sent to say, "Do not bring her, if you do we will kill one of that village which is requesting you to go." While a third party said, "If you bring her back, we will kill her, and give her as food to the sharks, so you had better go." Nevertheless, in the evening four of our teachers and a Tannaman came and pled for the boat. Was it not baffling? However, we could not give it, for go or stay the threat was, that life was to be taken. We concluded we were better to stay altogether, as if they did fight, the teachers had the boat as a way of escape. We told them that rather than give the boat and leave ourselves helpless we would abandon the station. No more was said that night, and we retired to rest. About nine p.m. flashes of lightning were seen, and at last a severe thunderstorm came on. Thus, amid the turmoil of savages and the raging of the elements, we saw the last hours of the old year pass away, and the New Year begin its course. . . .

With much love to you all,
I remain,
Your daughter and sister,

AGNES.

IV.

MAN TANNA.*

February, 1870.

—— I must tell you something about the people of Tanna in this letter.

As to population. When Dr Turner lived here he considered it could not be less than twelve thousand, but if you consider the numbers that have been taken to other lands to labour, and those carried off by foreign epidemics, such as measles, you will find their numbers much less. The district we live in may be said to be deserted. Eight years ago the Rev. J. W. Mathieson was surrounded by a numerous population. As the natives express it, "they were as thick as the stones on the beach." Now, for miles around, we have not one large village. There is great dissimilarity in the colour of their skins—some are black, others copper like, and some whiter still. Their features, as a rule, are pleasing, and, were it not for the paint, they would compare favourably with other and higher races. They paint in red, yellow, blue, and black. Red is the

---

*For the sake of clearness, I have collected under this heading most of the references to the Tannese and their customs, found in the earlier letters. The body of the chapter is Mrs Watt's journal letter for 1870.

favourite colour, while black is the sign of mourning.
Some show great taste, and paint designs on the brow
or cheeks, while others lay it on as a plaster; some,
again, make their skins glisten as if done with black lead.
One generally paints another, which they do by oiling
the skin and daubing the dry paint on with the thumb.
They seem very fond of it. They think they do honour
to the worship on Sabbaths by putting on an extra coat.
They pierce the lobe of the ear and hang in seven or
eight large tortoiseshell rings, from half an inch to an
inch wide, and three or four inches in circumference.
Nor are they satisfied with that, for they often link one
into the other, until the weight is so great that it
enlarges the aperture and often breaks it through.
Tortoise, or rather turtle, shell is greatly valued by
them, and was worn by chiefs and their wives only,
until traders came and brought it within the reach of
common people. They will give a large pig for a small
piece. Male and female, old and young alike, wear
those earrings. They also pierce the septum of the
nose; yet I have rarely seen any who wore nose
ornaments. A few insert a small piece of wood or a
leaf. They say that should any one die not having his
nose pierced, his spirit will not rest, but fly about in
mid-air. They do not tattoo; but cut or burn some
design on the arm or upper part of the body. They do
up their hair in a very peculiar way. While it is yet
short they divide it into a great many locks, and round
each twine the bark of a tree, leaving two inches at the
end. As it grows, they follow up the dressing till it
hangs down the back; so that one would think they
wore wigs of small cords with curls at the tips. The

labour they spend on these is incredible. For days and days a man will sit, while another twists his hair. After it is done it is drawn back and tied with a strip of red calico. For this there is great demand, especially in the dancing season. The women wear their hair short, and pay little or no attention to it. As to ornaments, there is no end to them. The men wear a number of large white shells round the arm, from which they suspend bunches of leaves and other things. Round the neck they hang whales' teeth and pieces of greenstone (the latter they would not part with for anything). They have also bracelets, anklets and garters of netting or any bits of bright cloth. They are fond of little bits of bright wool, which they stick into their beards. The chief passion with the women is for beads, which they wear in great quantities. They have cords, too, from which they suspend the hair of deceased relatives. Their bracelets and armlets are made of cocoa-nut shells. Married women, as a rule, are decently covered with their native skirts of leaves, but I cannot say that of the others. Full grown women will have on a short apron before and behind, half grown girls a leaf or two, and girls nothing at all. The clothing of the men is so minute that I forbear to describe it. Yet they strut about in their disgusting costume and criticise the Erromangans as if their own style of dress was of the highest order. Their houses are the most wretched one can well imagine. Outside they look like hay-stacks. A cocoa-nut leaf laid on the bare ground serves as a bed, and a few native bags and skirts constitute all their household stuff. They have only a hole which serves as door and window. A few

TANNA MEN—MODE OF DRESSING THEIR HAIR.

of these huts set down in the most irregular way under some trees, with no fence around, is called a village. There the women cook their food or sit and chat; while the men sit in the Imarom or public square. Each village has such a square, and it is generally under the shade of a large banyan tree. There the men hold their parliaments and discuss Tannese politics, hold feasts and dances, and in the evenings drink their kava. In each square is a kava house. The kava (the root of the Piper Methysticum) is prepared and drunk only by men. Beardless boys are prohibited, and women dare not touch it. It is a most disgusting preparation; being chewed and spat out into a basin, mixed with water, and drank. I have only seen two cases of intoxication through it, although many are "glazy" looking after partaking of it. In the evening the call to kava can be heard as regularly as in some lands the Moslem calls to prayer. Before drinking it, the chief prays to the spirits of the departed for every blessing, such as plenty of kava and other things. They have sacred men, sacred trees, and sacred stones. Among the spirits, one presides over the sea, another over the wind, and a third over the crops. If a man goes a fishing and catches nothing, it is because the god of the fish has been angry. To these gods they offer the first fruits of all, but at times not the first in quality. They make this very much to suit themselves. For instance, if only one fruit is ripe they will not eat certain things lest the god be angry; but as soon as another is in the market they eat all and sundry, thereby saying, "We have got plenty without you, you can be angry if you like." When the wind blows some one is making it, and so when it rains. But of all superstitions, disease making is the worst. These disease makers are the gods of Tanna. Here no one can be sick from natural causes. Some one is burning his *nahak* (nahak is any kind of rubbish, such as the skin of food, bits of garments, &c.). Should a disease maker get hold of this and burn it, it is believed that the person to whom it belongs will turn sick, and if burned until it is consumed he will die. Hence, when a person turns sick, enquiry is made, and presents are sent; and you may be sure some rogue is always ready to accept them. I have seen the natives carrying present after present until the person recovered. Should he die, war is the result. Just before we arrived here, a great chief died, and the neighbouring village was charged with burning his "nahak"; war ensued, and they were driven far inland, their houses burned and their plantations destroyed. Thus everything in the shape of rubbish is carefully buried or thrown into the sea. I have seen a man beat a boy, and ask him if he wanted to die, because he attempted to throw away a banana skin. The disease makers themselves are strong in the belief, and if sick, think that some one is burning theirs.

The chief spirit is called Karapanamun. They believe he lives on the top of the highest hill, Mount Mirran, which can be seen from all parts of the island. He is in figure like a man, has a red skin thickly covered with hair, his nails are like birds' claws, only much longer, and with them he tears off the flesh of those who are so unfortunate as to come within his reach.

When they die, they say their bodies moulder in the dust, but their spirits go to another world called Ipai, which simply means " very far off." There they live as on earth, dig and plant, give and are given in marriage. After remaining there for an indefinite time they transmigrate into owls and other animals, and afterwards into sacred stones. As far as I can ascertain, these were their original beliefs, but since missionaries have told them of the " lake that burneth," they have taken up the idea that their spirits are cast into the volcano. With such beliefs, what use is there in refraining from this or that sin ? all go to one place, whatever be their lives. Truly, " darkness covers the earth and gross darkness the people."

Chieftainship may be said to consist only in name. In a village of eight or nine men, six will claim to be chiefs. It is an old saying, that " a man's house is his castle," but really in Tanna a man's *kingdom* is his house and his wives; although they talk plenty about their " great land " and its great rulers.

The men always carry a loaded musket, club or kawas to protect themselves. They are great boasters, and as great cowards. If a man wishes to shoot another he will lurk in the dark, or act the part of a traitor. Hence the constant dread. There is no superior law; might is right.

For four months they are busy with their plantations ; the other eight are spent in idleness and wantonness. The heavy part of the work falls on the women. They are the cooks, and beasts of burden, and should they decline to fulfil the wish of their " lords " they receive a demonstrative proof of affection in the shape of a beating with a stick, or have a knife thrown at them. From this there is no redress; for if she runs away it is only to be brought back and get further punishment.

During a great part of the year they are busy feasting, singing and dancing. Each new season has its new music. In this, you see, they are in no way behind more civilized countries. One of their song-compilers retires into the bush and meets the gods of song, from whom he receives the new dance music for the forthcoming performance. Having acquired it, he returns and teaches it to those of his own village, and so on, until a great many know it. On the appointed day they have a "great sing." Many pigs are killed, and heaps on heaps of native food consumed. Preparatory to the "Taaka," as they call it, the men live away from their villages and fast by themselves, so as to be neat and slender. When the day of feasting arrives they all assemble in the public square; but before anything is done, the song-maker takes a gift of food and retires by himself to a hut, where he presents it to the gods. This done, he returns, and the feasting and dancing commence.

Polygamy is prevalent. I know of no case of five wives; but some have four, three, or two. One is a rare exception. Such crimes as adultery are only kept down by club law; nevertheless, they are very frequent. The natives are passionately fond of children, especially boys, and tenderly nurse the sick.

When a man dies, he and all his personal effects, such as earrings, gunpowder, and shot, are buried in one grave. The strangling of widows is practised, but not commonly; and is said to have been introduced from

Aneityum. A woman who does not manifest a strong desire to accompany her husband at his death is reproached for months afterwards with unfaithfulness. I saw a widow beaten by another woman with a fish spear, because she had not begged to be strangled. A woman, who herself would have been strangled but for certain circumstances, bears testimony that the desire so vehemently expressed is in most cases assumed. They know if they are not to be strangled they will thereby escape the reproach; and if they are to be strangled there is no escape. This woman (Kapuka's widow), although dreading it, did not know that it had been their intention until after it was fallen from. She said, "If it had been finally determined to strangle me, the men who came to do it would have been the first to tell me; and how could I have escaped? If I had made the attempt I would have been shot. But the truth is, 'Missi,' when a woman hears she is to be strangled, her heart rises in her throat; she is astounded and powerless."

Suicide by hanging is very common. At a death, all the friends of the deceased meet and wail. This wailing is the most dismal sound I have heard.

It has been alleged by some that cannibalism is a thing of the past; but during our short residence three cases have come under our notice. One of these was a European, whose body was cut into pieces and sent round the tribes as a delicacy. They said it was just like turtle, which is so highly prized as only to be eaten by chiefs.

They set no value on human life nor on time. Day after day is spent in idleness. They are expert in bartering, and try to deceive you before your eyes. They are expert thieves, ever on the alert to appropriate anything that suits their fancy; and, although naked, manage to hide their spoil. I could go on, page after page, in this manner, but from what I have said you will have some idea of the people who live in this part of Tanna. It is one thing to read about, and another to be brought into daily contact with absolute heathenism. I see no picture that at all seems to describe them save that given by Paul in the first chapter of the Epistle to the Romans.

V.

SETTLING NEW MISSIONARIES.

TO THE FAMILY.

ON BOARD THE "DAYSPRING,"
DILLON'S BAY, ERROMANGA, 4th July, 1870.

—— On May 30th, one of Mr Neilson's teachers brought round our home mail, and, of course, informed us of the safe arrival of our little vessel in Port Resolution. Our hearts were gladdened to receive good news from a far country after such a long silence. We had received no letters for upwards of five months. None can imagine our feelings on reading letters that bear so early a date save those who are like circumstanced. I almost dreaded to break the seal lest they should contain news that would rend my heart. At such times, I almost think I would be happier had I no relative or friend on earth; then I would not tremble to think of what might be happening on the other side of the mighty ocean; but would be able to pursue my course without a care. However, such thoughts are but for a moment; and when I read page after page of encouragement, my heart rejoices that I have so many who are interested in our welfare, and who daily remember us to Him who is a God at hand.

The "Dayspring" was five weeks on her voyage from Melbourne, having experienced head winds and calms. She brought back Mr and Mrs Ella of the L.M.S.; and Rev. Mr Goodwill and his wife, new missionaries from Nova Scotia. After lying at Aneityum for a week, she proceeded to the Loyalty Islands and landed Mr and Mrs Ella, ran to Fate, thence to Erromanga and Aniwa, and arrived at Tanna on the 28th May. She lay there for seven days, first on account of a gale, and afterwards the wind chopping round to the north shut her in the harbour. To expedite matters, the captain chartered a small vessel and sent round our goods.

On Monday, 6th June, we left Kwamera in the "Dayspring's" boat. The wind and sea were dead ahead, but after five hours' hard pulling, four of which I sat up to the ankles in water, we arrived in Port Resolution, and met the "Dayspring" on Wednesday; the wind came round, and we started for Aneityum, where we anchored on Friday. On Monday we went round to Aname, and the Annual Meeting commenced next morning. The only absentee was Mr Copeland, who could not see his way to leave, owing to the unsettled state of his island. The sittings were closed on Saturday, and the next day, Sabbath, we all sat down to the Lord's Supper in Mr Inglis' parlour. The circumstances brought vividly to my mind the company who sat down in a large upper room in Jerusalem.

After being detained by adverse winds for several days, we at last, with a nice light wind, started from Aname with a straight course for Kwamera, which we reached just at dark. As we were anxious to get on shore, Captain Fraser gave us a boat, and accompanied by Mr and Mrs Cosh and two children, and Mr and Mrs Milne, we made for land. On our arrival, we found two large fires and lots of torches lit to guide us through the reef. We were glad to find all well. Mr Watt having been appointed to assist in the settlement of Messrs Milne and Goodwill, next day we made our arrangements, and again bade adieu to Kwamera. Mrs Cosh's two little boys were the novelty of the day. They were carried about in all directions, and much admired by a wondering crowd, who thought Mrs Cosh must be a sterling woman, seeing she was the mother of two such fine boys.

After a pleasant sail all night, we arrived next morning at Erromanga. While the "Dayspring" was taking Mr Milne's goods on board, the missionaries were busy erecting a small cottage for Mr Macnair on a more healthy site. His present house is situated at the bottom of a gully, where they suffer very much from fever and ague. Poor Macnair was very weak during the meetings, he was never clear of fever. He is to have a change this year. We went ashore to the native service. The attendance of Erromangans was good, and the earnestness and fervour with which they sang impressed me much. The address was given by a young man. Oh, how delightful the sight! to see those who once gloried in human flesh, yea, on whose shores the blood of God's martyrs was poured, sitting clothed and in their right minds, singing the praises of the Lord. . . .

Saturday, July 9th. We left Dillon's Bay last Monday for Potinia Bay, the station of Mr Gordon. The wind was light, and it was Tuesday ere we reached the place. Some of us went ashore and spent the night with Mr Gordon. He has a pretty little place, but there is one great want, and that is, he has no wife. No missionary should come out unmarried; his wife can do as much as he can, especially among the women. Mrs Milne and I were the first white women the natives had seen, and you would have laughed at the astonished looks of some of our black sisters. A few collected round the verandah, and Mrs Milne proposed that we should go and shake hands with them. I agreed, but no sooner had we risen from our seats and began to walk towards them, than terror seemed to take hold on them; for they made off, clinging to each other as if pursued by witches. Once outside the fence, they turned to have another look at their supposed pursuers. After leaving Portinia Bay we called at Cook's Bay. The gentlemen went ashore and met with a few natives who seemed friendly, but all agreed that it was not a place for Mr Milne to settle in. . . .

As Mr Milne wished to visit Ifua, Erromanga, we called there next, but on landing found only *twenty* people living there, while the neighbouring tribes were at war. Of course that was not a field for a missionary, and so many hundreds on other islands willing to receive the gospel. Erromanga is now very thinly peopled. This is partly through disease, but chiefly from wars and the quasi-slave trade now so briskly carried on in these islands. . . .

August 3rd. Since last I wrote we have effected Mr Milne's settlement at Nguna, a little island to the north of Efate, under the most encouraging circumstances. His desire was for Erromanga, but none of the places there seemed suitable. . . . The chief of the village received us with pleasure, and said he would give any piece of land the missionary liked to choose. Accordingly a large piece was bought, and operations commenced. Capt. Fraser kindly sent the "Dayspring" men to assist, and, with speed, a nice little cottage was erected; indeed, the captain himself worked daily. The missionaries went in very early, and Mrs Milne and I took their dinner ashore. Mission life is surrounded with a great deal of romance in the minds of some people at home; but were you to see the everyday life of a New Hebrides missionary, your romantic ideas would take flight. It is a very delightful fancy to picture the new station being opened, and the missionary, in broadcloth, with Bible in hand, making known to wondering crowds, for the first time, the tidings of salvation. Such sights cannot be seen here; for the curse of Babel has fallen so heavily on these people, that every island has a different language, and very often those on one side cannot understand those on the other side of the same island. A missionary has many months of hard study before he can declare to the people in their own tongue the wonderful works of God. Mrs Milne and I often wished some of our friends had been there to see us sitting under a large tree or in a native house, with the brown earth for our table, and the missionaries and captain all squatting around. . . . We were very happy, and all went merry as a marriage bell. The natives of Nguna built a store and cook-house, and, while the "Dayspring" went to Efate with some Christian natives who had come to assist, we remained with Mr and Mrs Milne.

During all the time the conduct of the natives was most gratifying. They were always ready to give a helping hand when asked, and manifested good feeling by bringing yams and other native products for sale. On the "Dayspring" returning from Efate we bade adieu to our friends. I felt for them being left alone on a heathen island for the first time; and though the natives are friendly, one has not the satisfaction as in cases where teachers have preceded the missionary. The people can speak a good deal of broken English, as a good many of them have been to Sydney and elsewhere. They dress very much better than those living south of Efate; indeed, if they were becoming Christians they would require no more covering than they have at present. I wish I could get the Tannese men to wear as much. We have good reason to hope for this becoming a large and prosperous station. Not only is the island important in itself, but it is also near a great many other islands, and has a fine harbour in which the "Dayspring" can anchor.

Leaving Nguna, we proceeded to Santo to settle Mr Goodwill, at his own request, at Cape Lisburn. I would have liked to have visited the numerous little islands which lie between here and Nguna. We saw the large island of Malekula in the distance. The natives are said to be so savage that few vessels go there. The cause of their ferocity is not known, but it is supposed that they have been ill-used by some ungodly traders. We need not wonder that these poor heathen are savage to traders, because the cruelty that some have suffered at their hands is almost incredible. Since coming to Santo, we have heard of a case of man-stealing and woman-stealing, in which the victims were carried on board, bound with ropes, then put into the hold, and the hatch fastened hard down lest they should escape. The natives here know about the "Dayspring," and two came off to ascertain who we were. As soon as they found out that we were the missionary ship, they waved on all the other canoes to come alongside. They told us not to send a boat near the place from which the natives had been taken, as the people were set upon having revenge on the first white man they could lay hold of. We are quite safe, but if the natives did not know us we would stand a poor chance.

Mr Goodwill has got a good reception. For the last two days he and Mr Watt, with the "Dayspring" men, have been busy building. In a few days we will be leaving them. I have no doubt he will feel lonely after we go; he has left his wife at Aneityum, and he is upwards of a hundred and fifty miles from the nearest missionary. We can commit him to the care of the Keeper of Israel, who neither slumbers nor sleeps; and who has promised to be ever with those who go forth to preach His Gospel.

. . . The population seems large. The natives, however, go about in a state of greater nudity than any others I have seen; the *ladies*' dress, however, will not stand description. One day I visited a village. They build better houses than the Tannese, and have their villages fenced in. Everything looks neat and orderly. On arriving at the principal chief's house we were invited in, and his royal highness spread a mat for me to sit on. Our words were very few, and we communicated most of our thoughts to each other by signs. After resting a little, and having given his wife a present of beads, we bade them good-bye, and went to see more of their houses.

We were beset on all sides for beads, and as we had given some to a woman because she was the chief's wife, quite a number began to count up the relationship in which they stood to him, so that they might claim beads. Going through the village, we heard a strange noise, and enquired the cause. They said a woman was sick, and advised us not to go. But as some of our party were anxious to see, we went. The woman was dead, and laid in a sort of trough or canoe. Her face and the upper part of her body was painted red, and the lower part covered with a mat. A large bunch of feathers was stuck in the left side of her head. On one side sat two women, and on the other a man and woman, all making a most dismal wailing. The man, I suppose, was the dead woman's husband. As we came up the cries got louder; but on offering them a present of beads their grief was assuaged, and they took them with a smile. The quiet was, however, of short duration, as the doleful sounds began again, and continued until we lost them in the distance. On Santo, they do not bury their dead, but keep them in their houses until they decay, and then take the best of their bones to make spear heads and arrow points. The rest they gather up and bury. This is a most revolting practice. I wonder if, when they are selling the bones of perhaps their father or mother, they never think that some one will yet make spear heads and arrow points of their bones. Every day they came off to the vessel with yams, bananas, spears, bows and arrows. I could have bought any number if I had had plenty butcher's knives, which were in great demand.

August 10th. We are now one week from Santo, and are lying at Fate waiting for Mr Cosh, who is going to New Zealand. On our way, we called on Mr Milne, and found all well, the natives friendly, and the prospects encouraging. . . .

AGNES C. P. WATT.

VI.
STREAKS OF DAWN.

1. TO THE GLASGOW FOUNDRY BOYS' RELIGIOUS SOCIETY.

October, 1870.

MY DEAR YOUNG FRIENDS,—You will no doubt be thinking it a very long time since I wrote to you; but we have so few opportunities of getting letters sent off that our correspondence cannot be frequent. You will have heard that we took a large number of our natives to Aneityum, so that they might see what the gospel had done for the people of that island. It was a serious undertaking, for if any sickness had broken out among them soon after our return, we would have been blamed for it. I am happy to inform you that our visit was a great success, and the results thereof gratifying. The natives returned "strong for the worship," as they express it, and with high opinions of the Aneityumese and their hospitality. They said, "We thought if we worshipped our food would be scarce, but instead of that, they have so much, and gave so much to us, that we were obliged to leave a great part of it behind. They have plenty of everything."

On the first Sabbath of our return we had an attendance at worship of sixty-six. Since then we have not had so many; still, there is an average of forty-five or fifty, which is very encouraging. Not only on the Sabbaths do we see the good results, but their general behaviour towards us has been much more respectful; while they have also manifested a willingness to assist us in several ways. One young man named Kwanung has been bringing and cutting our firewood for the last month, to get a pair of trousers; and now he wishes a shirt, and says after he has got it he will come and worship. A young chief of about fourteen years of age, from a neighbouring village, has come forward and manfully offered to supply us with fresh water. We feel very proud of him, as, after he grows up, he will have great influence, being a high chief. His name is Saba. He is a very smart boy. I am sorry to say that he has not yet come to church, but we hope that daily intercourse with us will help to break down some of the superstitions that at present hinder him from joining us. There are several others who occasionally give us a helping hand. Indeed, we have only to express a wish and a great many come forward, willing to work on very moderate terms. You may think this of very little importance; but were we not respected by them, they would not work for us even for money.

When I received the box of clothing you so kindly sent, I had little prospect of having many calls for garments. Of late, and especially since their visit to Aneityum, the desire for clothing has greatly increased. Among thirty women who come to church there are only one or two who do not wear an upper garment. These they have either bought for a nominal price with yams or fowls, or have worked for them. We do not approve of giving dresses for nothing ; we rather wish them to be independent and value their clothes. So as to put clothing within the reach of all who worship, we have employed them as much as we could in making plantations and arrowroot, besides doing our ordinary work. Now, I have something to tell you which will interest the girls, and, I trust, the boys also. During the last two months we have had two little girls staying on our premises, and although several attempts have been made to take them away, these have hitherto been unsuccessful. The two cry whenever any hint is given of leaving us, and persistently insist on being allowed to remain. They say they want us to be father and mother to them, as they love us very much. Kaianga, the youngest, is a bright little thing, about ten years old. She can now read by spelling, and name all the short words. I have begun to teach her to sew. She is the first that came to school, and she is still the brightest. Kauea, the elder, is not so bright, but she is a nice girl; she has mastered the alphabet, and is making good progress in sewing. Kaianga got a prize for learning her lessons well some months ago, and that was a dress to come to church in. This she wore faithfully until she and the other came to stay, when I gave each a new suit out of your box. After they had stayed a month I gave them others; the latter are kept carefully, and only worn at church. You may be sure they are a great contrast to the naked painted girls around, with their clean clothes, their faces and hands well washed, nice little scarlet turbans on their heads, and a great many strings of coloured beads round their necks. They are much interested in the boys and girls in Scotland who think of them and make clothes for them. They set our table and do any little thing I may require. We have lately added two new hymns to our "Service of Song" on Tanna. We took the sheets of large print hymns you sent me, and cut them up to form the words. We have them hung up on the walls of our dining-room. They have mastered one, and can sing it nicely. The tune is "Morning Light." I will send you a copy of it. We have worship with them every evening, and it is very impressive to see them close their eyes and repeat the Lord's Prayer. The absence of paint, and the wearing of European clothes, has effected such a change on them that one requires to see in order to believe. This is the day of small things on Tanna, but, with the blessing of God, we expect to prosper. Pray for us, and for the poor benighted Tannese, and especially for our two little girls, that soon we may have the joy of seeing them walking in the truth. If there are any questions you wish to ask, just make them known, and I will be most happy to answer them. I feel very happy, when lonely in this distant land, to think that you are all praying for us. We trust and pray that in blessing others you may be abundantly blessed.

Now I must close, as my little girls are wearying to have worship and get to bed.

>I remain,
>> My dear boys and girls,
>>> Yours most faithfully,
>>>> AGNES C. P. WATT.

2. TO THE TREASURER OF THE GLASGOW FOUNDRY BOYS
RELIGIOUS SOCIETY.

November, 1871.

MY DEAR MR MARTIN,—Since last I wrote you, we have been a voyage round Tanna; but owing to a gale of wind we could only visit a small part of the island. The great obstacle to our visiting Tanna efficiently is the diversity of language. There are evidently several languages in this one island; and how many dialects it would be difficult to surmise. Hence our principal means of communication is in broken English; or as it is better known here as sandal-wood English (being the broken English used by the sandal-wood traders in past years), which is very unsatisfactory. The other means of communication, which is the better of the two, is to have a native, who knows the language of the place, to act as an interpreter.

At the first two places we visited, we were told in answer to our question, "Will you take a teacher and 'mafwaki' or worship?" "At present we are fighting, but perhaps after a time we will receive one." They are putting off.to a more convenient time, which may never come. The people at another boat-harbour were willing to take a teacher, but as none of us knew their language, and they spoke broken English very imperfectly, it is extremely doubtful if they understood what we said. They seemed to want a missionary, but in all probability they knew not what that meant. The truth is, it is traders, not missionaries, that the Tannese want. The people here at Kwamera, doubtless, wanted the missionary chiefly for the worldly goods that would come to them, and not for the sake of the gospel; as we have found in our experience. They hate the gospel and its messengers. But can it be otherwise, for the Scripture saith, "The carnal mind is *enmity* against God: for it is not subject to the law of God, neither indeed *can be*"? At the last place we visited, we found a man named Johnny Pata, who could speak very fair English. He told us that he had been stolen away from Tanna by a whaler about fifteen years ago. After he was some time on board, the vessel called at Tongatabu, where he escaped and hid on shore. He was picked up by King George, who took him to look after his plantations. There he received great kindness, and was taught to fear God and shun evil. King George also taught him to read in the Tongatabu language. About two months previous to our visit he had returned home. He has built a little church in which on the Sabbaths he assembles all who will listen; while he, to the best of his ability, tries to tell them of Jesus. Through his influence, the people are anxious to get a missionary. Alas! that there should be an open door, and no one ready to enter; but, sad though it be, such is the case. We have no supply of teachers to spare. Our principal dependence is on Aneityum, and you know the population there is very small. Besides, she has already given out a goodly band of pioneers; of whom, many have died, and even at this present time there are twenty men and their wives stationed on heathen islands. It is only on certain islands or in certain districts that they have any influence. Again, it is well to follow up a teacher's settlement by placing a missionary soon after. These men have but lately emerged from heathenism themselves, and unless supported by a missionary it is doubtful whether they will do much good. I am afraid the name teacher conveys a wrong idea to your mind; the proper word is "pioneer." We are expecting three or four new missionaries next year, perhaps some one of them may be willing to occupy this station. I hope and pray that such may be the case. Poor Johnny Pata will have much to suffer if he remains consistent to his profession. Even his good example in wearing a fathom of calico will be a subject of ridicule. We did all we could to strengthen his hands, and we pray that the Lord, who has the hearts of all men in His hands, may incline some one to enter this wide door, and may it prove "effectual." . . .

Shall we ever welcome to the shores of Tanna one of those boys who bade us adieu in Eglinton Hall? and shall he come supported by that very Society under whose training he was taught that his first duty was to give himself to the Lord, and, having tasted that the Lord is gracious, to make known to his fellow-men the love of Jesus ? . . .

At present we have four teachers and their wives. Two are at out-stations and two live on our premises. Kauaneli accompanies Mr Watt to the different out-stations on Sabbaths, can manage a boat, and is a very useful man in assisting at translating. Yawila, who has lost his eyesight, can do little active work, but his becoming walk and conversation is powerful for good, and his wife is a very active woman; she is extremely useful to me. She has charge of the Tannese girls who live with us. She and Kauaneli's wife assist me in household duties, and teach in the Sabbath School.

Our newest out-station is about two miles from here, and is called Irumien. There Kaka and his wife are labouring, but it is very uphill work. Previous to our coming here the people of that district had been driven inland by a neighbouring tribe, who blamed them for burning *nahak*, and thereby causing the death of one of their principal men. On that account, they seldom came down to their old village, and when they did so it was stealthily. However, about two months ago, peace was made up, and a number have returned and live near the teacher; all have liberty to do the same. Although they wished the Aneityumese teacher to remain, very few attend church, and still fewer can be constrained to try to learn to read. Let me give an instance of how much they dread the gospel and books, and how disheartening it is. I lately accompanied Mr Watt on the Sabbath, and was much disappointed to find only a few old women labouring away at the alphabet. No little girls were allowed to go, and, as we heard one day, they were all hidden as we were approaching, lest we should invite them to worship and they should comply; in which case, they say, they would turn sick and die. . . .

The next out-station, and by far the most important, is Umeiyahau. There Manman and his wife have laboured for two years, and not without success. The district is densely peopled, a good many attend service, and a few are learning to read. . . . We are anxious to do all we can for this important station. During our two years' residence here, besides visiting them on

Sabbaths, we have occasionally gone and spent a week at a time with them, so as to become better acquainted, and make the teacher a little more important among them. We have not been able to stay there for some time, as the only accommodation we have is the teacher's house, which is made of grass, and has only holes for doors and windows. We are thus exposed to the night air, and we have been advised by our more experienced brethren not to expose ourselves to the malaria. We cannot work this station unless we go and live among the people; so on that account we purpose erecting there a small lime house in which we can live for a week at a time, and thus benefit both the people of Umeiyahau and the tribes beyond. We are looking anxiously for the two shipments of boxes from you. We cannot get on without the temporals. As soon as we have the materials we shall have the house built. At Umeiyahau the teacher and Tannese put up a very nice church, for which they received no pay, it being pure mission work; but we do not wish to make the gospel at all burdensome to them. Hence, when they do anything for us we pay them. I fear many of them follow us for the loaves and fishes; but God makes use of the most common things for the furtherance of His own glory. . . .

    Yours most truly,

      AGNES C. P. WATT.

VII.
HOW WE SPENT THE HOT SEASON OF 1870.

ANIWA, October, 1871.

MY DEAR FATHER, MOTHER, BROTHERS, AND SISTERS,
—As all the letters you get during the cool season of the year are only hurried notes sent by passing vessels, I have thought that perhaps you might be interested by hearing what has been transpiring since this time last year. After the departure of the "Dayspring" we had a schoolhouse put up, as I found it very inconvenient to keep school in our own house. I then commenced my girls' reading and sewing class. We read every day, and sewed or wrote on slates two days in the week. During the first weeks we went on very encouragingly. The numbers were small, but they came with great regularity, and manifested a desire to receive instruction. Just then, however, I was laid up with a sore ankle, which compelled me to keep to the sofa. As my scholars were all of my own sex, they would not come when I was unable to attend to them. From that time till this, one thing after another has interrupted our meetings. By the time I was able to resume my duties, all our people were laid down with influenza. Scarcely one escaped, old and young alike suffered, and no sooner did they begin to rally than

they were attacked anew, and that continued until the "Dayspring" returned. Mr Watt dispensed a great deal of medicine, while I was kept busy making up tea. Sometimes a little boy would be sent to get tea and carry it to those who were unable to come for it. I sent it along in old fruit tins, which they could set on the hot embers to warm. There were no deaths, although in some cases the attacks were very severe. Some came along asking for medicine when they were hardly able to stand on their feet, but staggered like drunken men; others were quite delirious for a day or two. No human being, unless his heart was adamant, could look at these poor brothers and sisters of ours in affliction without stretching out a helping hand.

Seeing these natives in health, and during fine weather having plenty of food with very little toil, one is apt to think, "Well, after all, they are pretty comfortable"; but visit them in trouble, see them lying in a wretched hut, like Job, literally lying in ashes, having no bed but the leaf of a cocoa-nut tree, no kind friend to minister to their wants. Although there may be many sitting by, in all probability they will be busy chiding either the sick or their relatives for having neglected to guard against "nahak." In several cases there was severe vomiting of blood; for these, Mr Watt used laudanum, and in each case it was efficacious. The three most valuable medicines to us have been quinine, laudanum, and English paregoric elixir. The last wrought most wonderful cures, and along with a few drops of sal-volatile was the means, with the blessing of God, of raising up some that were very low. At Port Resolution, Mr Neilson's station, they suffered from something of the same kind, but seemingly much more virulent, and the deaths were not a few. . . . During these times of sickness we missionaries on Tanna have an anxious time of it, for a Tannaman believes that few, if any, die natural deaths; they must have been brought about by witchcraft, and the missionary is as likely to be blamed as any other. Hence we have to act with great caution, and never give medicine unasked. One instance will suffice to show the wisdom of being slow to offer medicine. There is a trader, a black man, a native of America, living near us. He has given himself out as a Doctor of Medicine, and professes to cure all. Only you must "pay the piper." He will not prescribe unless you lay down the "guinea" or its equivalent, a large porker. That secured, he "will see what he can do for you." There was one case in which he received either four or five very large pigs. It was a little child who was all covered with sores. He cleared away all the sores, it is true, by means of mercury, I think, but he left the poor little sufferer without eyebrows or eyelashes, and scarcely a hair on its head. In this state, they brought the child to us. We saw at once that it was dying, and told the mother we could do nothing for him. Her maternal feeling made her slow to believe that she was going to lose her little darling, and she pled with us that we would at least try. With great reluctance we gave a little medicine, and two or three days after we administered a second dose, at the mother's urgent request. We trembled to think of the result, as we knew that the infant was likely to die soon. You can imagine what our feelings were when we heard the announcement of his death next morning. We were afraid they might trace his death to us, but instead of that we had to defend the trader from being blamed, as no one can tell what savages will do when irritated. Some time afterwards we went to visit the sorrowing mother, and she told us that she had suffered much from the heathen around, who reproached her with having caused the death of her child through our medicine; and that the trader had told them so. Whether the people were telling the truth or not, we cannot tell. We gave the trader the benefit of the doubt; but it taught us the lesson still more effectively, to act warily in dealing out medicine among a heathen people. Many of them have a superstitious dread of us, believing that we have the power of life and death; that being quite in accord with their notions. May God, in His mercy, open their eyes to see that it is in His hands all our ways are.

Our church attendance is much the same, and our two classes on Sabbath are regularly attended, chiefly by women. The first is like a reading school, and is held immediately after worship. The second is held in the schoolroom in the afternoon, and partakes largely of the character of a Sabbath School and conversational meeting. It is opened by praise and prayer, and closed by repeating simultaneously the Lord's Prayer. I admire a plan followed by Mrs Paton in her Sabbath School, on calling on one of the scholars to engage in prayer. It tends to expand the mind and teach them what true prayer is: " The offering up of our desires unto God." The progress our scholars are making in reading is encouraging, although far from what we could wish; but until they can come every day we cannot expect great strides to be made.

... If the sons of Adam on Tanna were half so pliable as his daughters, both Christianity and education would advance; but they seem to think that the worship is only fit for women, inasmuch as it requires them to wear a garment, and that, of course, is not *manly*. Anything mean, weak, or cowardly, is called by them *womanly*. My dear sisters, you know not how much we owe to the gospel, for having elevated us from that state in which heathenism places every woman. Some who are able to judge say, that the women on Tanna are better treated than on other heathen islands. Nevertheless, their case calls for sympathy. Indeed, the best blessing you can bestow on them is the gospel. Many of them, when born, are left in the bush to die. If spared, they are given away in infancy, and at an early age are sent away to their future homes, where they become the slaves of their husbands; and if in any trifle they offend, they will in all probability receive a more demonstrative proof of affection than they relish, in the shape of a thumping with a cudgel, or having a knife thrown at them. Not but that I think there are times when they require a little correction, for some of them are unsparing in the use of the "unruly member." ...

About two months ago a couple came to live with us, at the earnest desire of the wife. Their names are Naurita and Yemeitahak. I have mentioned her before; they are the parents of the child, of whom I wrote, who died. Yemeitahak used to live with Mrs Mathieson when a little girl, and when we first came to

Kwamera she alone came to school. She has told me since that it was at the risk of a beating from her husband. On Wednesday, we were about to hold our Prayer Meeting when Naurita came in. Seeing us prepare for worship, he rose to leave, when both Mr Watt and I (unknown to each other) invited him to remain. He did so, and every Sabbath since has seen Naurita in his place. Now he has come to live on our premises, and that is a great thing for a Tannaman. To go and live with a trader is nothing, but to live with us is a partial renunciation of heathenism.

Lately we had a grand assembly or "Nukwiara" as it is called. It was a soiree, concert, and ball. For weeks the preparations were going on. The gentlemen were fasting, that they might look slender and neat. They got their wigs powdered with paint, also their belts and bodies coated to their heart's content. At the same time, the belles were getting fine new skirts. Indeed, they seemed to do nothing but bathe and paint. To-day they would have one design, and to-morrow another, until they thought they were perfect. For two or three days previous to the "nukwiari," they all sat up, night and day, lest they should spoil the paint on their faces. When all preparations were completed, they sent invitations to every tribe for miles around. From the west they came a distance of fifty miles, and as it was a time of enjoyment, they were all in holiday dress. While waiting for the feast, each one took his friends to see the novelties of the place, chief of which were the "lions" at Kwamera. The assembly lasted three days, and during these and the two preceding ones we were obliged to hold a levee. They came in bands of from twenty to thirty. We showed them the house and gave them a tune on the harmonium, after which Mr Watt generally gave them a biscuit. They were delighted, and full of wonder. They had to examine our outhouses, hens, ducks, turkeys, and cows. When done, they said "their hearts were weak," and didn't our people feel proud to say, "All these things belong to our Missi." As we wished to see the "Nukwiari" we went up on the last day. All the people were assembled in the public square. In the centre of the square, under the shade of a banyan tree, the women were dancing. Most of them had on white skirts trailing on the ground, and over these were worn short skirts and panniers in light green, yellow, and sometimes bright scarlet. These, with beads, greenstone, paint and feathers, constituted the full dress of a Tanna lady. One chief's daughter had five long feather ornaments in her hair, with her maid to hold them up while she danced. Their songs and dances are dramatical. There was no promiscuous dancing. While the women were dancing, the men and all their visitors were sitting on the adjoining logs, admiring. So far as we saw, the dance was as modest, if not more so, than our own country dances. The part that shocked me most was at the end, when they brought in a lot of pigs, killed in a sickening manner. They were brought in one by one, bound to poles which were carried shoulder high, with a man riding on each pig's back, and holding a number of long feather ornaments in his hand. We have seen some of these feathers twelve feet long. They are made up of a number of small feathers hung on to reeds. Although there was nothing indecent connected with these dances, they ought to be stopped, as they cause sickness, and, in several cases since we came here, consumption.

Pulmonary consumption seems to be very prevalent in these islands; and as none recover who take it, the natives argue the truth of their "nahak." This disease, they say, is caused by it; and as medicine seldom does any good in such cases, they think that a convincing proof; for if it were otherwise, "medicine would be strong to cure." Well may the belief in disease-making be called the backbone of the devil's kingdom here. Break it, and the whole fabric will be ready to fall. They hold tenaciously to it, they drink it in with their mother's milk.

A high chief died lately, and previous to his death, we heard, that should he die, three women were to be strangled—his aged mother and his two wives. We determined to do our utmost to prevent this, but, he being a high chief, we had little hope of success. However, we went inland to see him, and to request the young men of the village to promise they would not do such a thing. On arriving, we found the sick man unable to speak, but told the others the object of our visit, and they promised that we should be obeyed. As soon as the sick man was able to speak, we conversed with him. We spoke of our sinful hearts by nature, and of Jesus the Saviour, of the perishing nature of all earthly things, and of that bright home on high for all who trust in Jesus. As we spoke, he lifted up his eyes to heaven, and when we came to that last sentence, "for all who trust in Jesus," he looked earnestly at me and said, with great pathos, "Yesu."

Poor man, he was unable to speak more; he grasped my hand as I sat on the ground beside him, and I prayed that the Lord would have mercy on him, even at the eleventh hour. A week afterwards he died. On hearing of his death, we hastened to the funeral, as we had our suspicions regarding the sincerity of those who promised that our words should be obeyed. From what we afterwards learned, the dying man had the same, for he could not rest, day or night, for urging them to "hear the words of Missi." At times he was unable to speak, but as he came near death he gave charges as to his burial, and mentioned particularly that they were to do our "word." Lest his wives should neglect to make his wishes known, he requested that witnesses should be brought, which was done. He told them they were to bury him as a Christian; they were to put no muskets nor kava nor gods into his grave, but simply to bury him in a garment; and, above all, to take no lives. When we reached the village we found all the women from the neighbouring villages gathered together to weep with the bereaved. The body was laid out on the ground on mats, and a mat over it for a covering; only the shoulders and head visible. Round this a great number of women sat, while the rest sat at a distance. The approach of each new comer was the signal to set up a fresh howling. Some of them came along laughing and talking till within sight of the corpse, and then commenced to wail. I had some difficulty in keeping myself from smiling. The grief may be real. In some cases I know it is; but in a great many cases it is doubtful. Each village that goes to mourn receives a pig, and each individual, two or three yams, "to make their hearts good," as the Tannese say.

We remained until after the burial. The grave was dug at the side of the house. After digging down a sufficient depth, they cut in under the house, so that the body was literally laid "in the sides of the pit." Even after the corpse was laid in the grave an old chief remarked in a sad tone, that it was a pity such a great man was allowed to die alone. We were informed afterwards that the women, when they saw that we were come to see the funeral, said to each other: "What do these two mean coming here to prevent us carrying out our intentions? Why did not they stay at home, and leave us alone?"

Pray for us and our deluded people. Oh! when shall heathen Tanna stretch forth her hands unto God?

I have been staying here these last three weeks, under the hospitable roof of our dear brother and sister Mr and Mrs Paton, while Mr Watt has been away at Santo and the other northern islands; and dispensing the Communion at Fate, in the absence of Mr Cosh, who is at present in New Zealand. . . .

With much love,
I am,
Your daughter and sister,

AGNES.

VIII.
FIRST EXPERIENCE OF A HURRICANE.

TO THE FAMILY.

January 11th, 1873.

MY DEAR ONES AT HOME,—This is Saturday night, and I am very tired, but I cannot allow this eventful week to close without telling you about our trials and troubles. It is a week past on Thursday since we landed from Aniwa. As the sea was rough no one but ourselves came ashore. . . . The weather continued rough until Sabbath, and although it was dirty and blowing, still we had no idea of what was going to happen. Every year we get wood laid on the top of our roof over the sugar-cane leaf to keep it down in case of a hurricane. We generally get it put on in the first week of this month; for, according to some who ought to know, a hurricane has never occurred before the twelfth of January. Believing that, and partly owing to our being away on Aniwa, we had not put on our storm rigging; and thus were ill prepared for what followed.

On Sabbath, as it was very wet, we had short service so as to let the natives away home quickly. The day was very dull, and as we were newly home we felt a little dull ourselves. After our English and native worship we went to bed about nine o'clock. There was a good blow of wind then, but as it was only the fourth of the month, I did not think much about it, although the aneroid was very low. I went to sleep, but whatever was the cause of it, William could not sleep. About twelve o'clock he wakened me, and said he thought he would go into the dining-room and look at the aneroid. . . . By this time the wind was coming down in great gusts; accordingly we both rose and went to the dining-room, and found that the glass was falling fast. I took the precaution to take down the pictures from the walls, which I put in a chest. All our albums, work-boxes, ornaments, &c., I put in boxes or drawers; I put the lamps and all breakables in the sideboard, and a large tray over my seam basket and sewing machine, so as in every way possible to be prepared for the worst. While this was going on the aneroid was still falling, but as we could do no more I lay down on the dining-room sofa. The house shook at such a rate, and the wind having torn off the roofing up at the ridge pole, the rain soon soaked our beds through and through. Not knowing the moment the roof might fall in, we thought it better to abandon the house to its fate and seek shelter in a native house. At this time my chief anxiety was to save my locket for the sake of your cartes, and also our albums; but William assuring me that there was no danger of the walls falling but only the roof, I left all. We betook ourselves to the yam house. I took out a lot of cushions and, laying them in a row, made a bed for myself. William was groping about in the dark, being too excited to lie down, and at the same time adding to my excitement, as I feared that a tree or something else might fall on his head and kill him. All was dark as pitch, and the wind was roaring like a mighty cataract; we could hardly hear ourselves speak. The wind came down in fearful strength, and caused the house in which I was to shake at such a rate that I felt as if I were on shipboard. Being cold and wet, and fearing the house would fall on me, again I made another "flitting," trying the teacher's house, in which was a good fire. I thought to warm myself, but here all our strength was needed to try and hold up the walls of the house. I once more rushed out into the darkness amidst pelting rain and terrific wind to make my way to Kaipapa's cook-house, which, being made after the native shape, was less likely to be blown down than our European-shaped houses. I was not long there until our teachers, having given up their house to its fate, came in, as also did William, wearied with his watching. There being a good fire, we warmed ourselves. One of the natives gave me his bed, and the wind being a little calmer, I lay down and dozed. About five a.m. the day dawned, and William proposed that we should leave the native house and go into our own and try to get some rest. The wind was now quite moderate, and I rose to go into our own house to have a sleep. On coming out of Kaipapa's house the sight that met my eyes drove all thoughts of sleep far from me. All around was desolation. Yards and yards of new and old fencing lay on the ground; fencing that had cost us pounds and the natives many days' work, all laid level in one night. On we came to our desolate house, with every floor swimming and the roof torn up; not a dry place to sit on. The house looked so dismal that I went out to look about the premises. What a sight! The teacher's house and yam-house were blown off the straight, the mangle-house was a heap of ruins, and so was our washing-house, &c., &c. During the day we heard that the church roof was also injured, the church fence lying flat on the ground, and that the boat-house was a total wreck. Our premises were in a fearful mess with broken fences, fallen trees, &c. We did not know where to begin; and, shall I confess it? I began by a good "greet." This cleared my eyes a little, and I was able to see my way somewhat, although, owing to having had no sleep, I felt unable for much. At first the natives could do nothing but stand and shout in wonder and amazement at the thorough desolation, and instead of trying to put things to rights, only stood and talked. I daresay that was the chief cause of my shedding tears. Soon afterwards, however, a band of Tannese came and, along with our Aneityumese, put our house in repair, so that by twelve o'clock we had a roof over our heads once more. William remarked to me in the morning, "We are homeless wanderers." How much cause for gratitude have we when we think how readily the Tannese came and helped in our extremity. Two days afterwards we had all the fences propped up, and now, January 15th, our new boat-house is finished and the cow-house is to be commenced to-morrow; and all our other houses have again been made water-tight. The severity of the storm and grief at the loss of property unnerved me very much, but fear as to the impression which might be left on the natives' minds troubled me most. They believe many can make wind, and I feared that they might blame us, or each other, and so lead to war. The latter was the case as far as blaming each other went. The shore people had a previous quarrel with the inland people, and the hurricane raised all their latent wrath. War seemed likely to ensue. On Sabbath we heard that they were going to fire on each other, so we determined to see what our intervention might do. Early on Monday we, and Kauea, who comes from that district, went inland and succeeded in getting the people there to promise not to fight. After that we hastened down to tell the shore people and try to get them to do likewise. On our return we found them all gathered together in the public square, and to our delight were informed that they had decided not to fight; because if they fought their plantations of yams would go to ruin. Thus this untoward event was brought to a happy conclusion. It was not fear of war that caused us to interfere, for we are on the best of terms with both parties and had nothing to fear as to personal safety; but when quarrels are abroad the natives are so excited that we can do little among them. Just last Sabbath the people at church seemed so indifferent to what was being said, that I felt sad to think that we were labouring as if in vain. Now this was out of no disrespect to us, but just because their minds were taken up with other things. As I have said, we have got our houses and premises into pretty fair working order; the natives are coming forward readily to help, and we will get over our loss (though native food will be very scarce), but I have my fears as to the safety of our dear little vessel. She would be near Aneityum.

Has she escaped unhurt? or is she lying a wreck on Aneityum?* If she is safe you will have heard of her arrival in Sydney ere this reaches you. When we will know it is hard to conjecture. I am glad we have plenty of stores for ourselves if anything is wrong. We are expecting a mail daily by the vessel that will take this up to the colonies. In all probability she will tell us of the "Dayspring." We are sending this overland to Mr Neilson, to be posted there. We have not heard from him since the hurricane.

Kauea is still with us, but during our absence on Aniwa, Kaianga was married, and owing to the natives quarrelling she has not been down since our return. She is very young, not over twelve years of age, and her husband is about eighteen or nineteen. They have built a nice European-shaped house, and have taken up housekeeping already. All the rest of our establishment remains as it was, excepting Yemeitahak, who had a baby girl on Christmas eve. They carried out our request, and performed none of the heathen ceremonies usually done on children, and I am happy to say she is a fair, bright little baby. The fears of those who thought that some evil would befall the child, because they had departed from the commandments of their fathers, have been disappointed, and we are much gratified, as we hope others may follow their example. When we came home from Aniwa, I made up a little present for them, and named the baby "Nancy," after myself. The natives could not pronounce "Agnes," besides William always calls me

---

* The "Dayspring" was wrecked on Aneityum.

Nancy when alone. I visit Nancy and her mother several times a day, and it is pleasant to see how she is thriving. If spared, she will be my little table-maid by and by. While I am writing this Kauea and Yarere are busy making dresses for themselves, by the light of the lamp. Yarere is quite a little old-fashioned woman of ten years old, and sets the breakfast and tea table daily. How precocious the native children are! They could buy and sell children of the same age at home, so far as knowing things is concerned.

Friday 17th. All is quiet. Yesterday, no fewer than thirty natives came forward and repaired the church, and the fence round the grounds, also cleaning and sweeping the premises, for nothing. We told them that if we asked them to work on our own private premises we would, and always did, pay them, but that this was quite different. The church and its fence were public property, and that if they felt the worship to be a good thing, they would repair it for nothing. Our invitation was responded to by the thirty. I felt very much gratified. I boiled a large pot of beans, and another of rice, besides a piece of salt meat, for their dinner.

September 30th. I fear you will be writing to enquire why I am writing so few letters this year, but it is no fault of mine, I can assure you. I am thinking and speaking of you all every day. The reason for my letters being fewer is the want of time. In past years I wrote long letters in the hot season, but then we could not get the natives to come to school, and had long days to devote to writing. On the contrary, last hot season we had school for five hours a day three days in the week, and that broke up my time very much, besides I was so wearied after it that I could not write. With making up seams for them, over and above my own sewing, I had more than I could overtake. That state of things continued until Mrs Paton and family came here, and after they left I wrote a good long letter for the mail which left here about a month ago by the Mission vessel. What we have been doing since then I will tell you presently; and though it may look small on paper, it has been so big as to put writing out of the question.

When the Mission vessel left, we had just got the pantry finished. The doing of it made a great mess; what with chopping wood and mixing lime, every corner was more or less abused. After the vessel left, we commenced another lean-to at the back. It consists of two apartments—one a bath-room, the other a printing-office. These two are finished, except the doors and windows, which William hopes to finish to-morrow.

You understand that all our roofs are thatched with sugar-cane leaf, which requires to be renewed now and again. Ours have lasted since we came till now, and this year we are putting on new thatch. Now we have no ceiling on our rooms, all is open up to the ridge pole; so you can fancy the mess when the old thatch is stripped off. Our bedroom was done last week; and I can assure you that the day after the new thatch was put on, Yemeitahak and I had a hard job cleaning up. The day after to-morrow we hope to get the dining-room done, and after that the study and the store-room. We have also been getting a new roof for our school-house. To-day, William has been superintending the putting up of a cow-house.

But you will say, what have you to do with all that building? Well, I will tell you. I bought all the thatch, and am still buying it, although I have got upwards of five hundred roots already. Then I have to see that the workers get some food, besides helping William with my sage advice.

The bustle we are in with building, thatching, bartering, &c., has been increased with printing. We have spent two days last week, and the same this week, printing a copy of our hymns. The Society (Glasgow Foundry Boys') only sent out as much of the large type as would print one page; and as the small is so very small, and our natives prefer the large, we thought it better to spend extra time and give it to them. They are not too fond of reading, so we wish to encourage them as much as possible, and humour their likes and dislikes. I have no doubt but, if the Tannese make a good use of this book in large type, the Foundry Boys will send us out as much more as will do at least four pages, and save us all the extra trouble.*

Another thing that is occupying our time, and I do not grudge it, is the evening school. Three weeks ago we commenced it, and seven outsiders came, making a class of eleven, who are learning to read and write. William printed one hymn, a translation of the Hundredth Psalm, and we are teaching them to read without spelling. Mr Inglis seems to think they learn quicker that way, and certainly it is the more interesting way. We have

---

* A large supply of type was received later on.

tea about six, and about seven we beat the bell and the service commences. We have it in the dining-room. The new-comers are mostly boys; five of them are under seventeen. . . .

But I must be done, hoping this will find you all well. May *our* God bless you all both temporally and spiritually,
    Is the daily prayer of
      Your own
         AGNES.

IX.
A GLIMPSE OF CIVILISATION. THE MARTYRDOM OF TAUKA.

1. TO THE FAMILY.

ANEITYUM, 14th July, 1874.

MY DEAR ONES AT HOME,—I will write a family letter now, for though I have a large mail ready for you all, there is still a month's news to write up. My last letter was from Aniwa, where I was enjoying myself immensely in the good company of three worthy ladies, Mrs Paton, Mrs Milne, and Mrs Annand. Aniwa, with the dear friends there, is the dearest spot in these seas to me, and I shall ever look back to the pleasant days spent there. We four "sistern" were three weeks together, and were very sorry to part. On leaving us, the Rev. Dr Steel of Sydney said he supposed we were going to hold a New Hebrides Ladies' Synod, and that he would be much interested in seeing a copy of our minutes. However, we must have thought it more judicious to keep our resolutions to ourselves, as we did not put any of our deliberations on paper. We spent our time writing letters, playing and singing hymns, sewing, reading aloud, and a little painting in water-colour.

On Saturday, June 20th, the Mission vessel returned and brought back our husbands. On Monday we all left, except Dr Steel (who was to spend a few days there), and shaped our course for Tanna. It was evening when we left, and we ladies kept on deck till near ten, admiring the volcano, talking of pleasant memories, and, I fear, building castles in the air. Early next morning we were off Kwamera, where Neptune seems to hold his revels, and very often puts a veto on passengers going ashore. Mr and Mrs Inglis and we two had to land, as those dear people were going to honour us with a visit; and although there was a good deal of sea on, Mrs Milne braved it all, only to be an hour or two on shore.

On landing, we found our people rather shy; the cause of which we afterwards found out. There has been a great deal of sickness, and the devil had been busy. He always is; and on Tanna he has succeeded in breaking up the Mission twice through superstition connected with sickness. The Tannese, as you are already aware, believe that they have the power of causing sickness and death by means of "nahak" or witchcraft, and the missionary being a sacred man, they attribute the same powers to him as to themselves. Now, as there has been much sickness during the whole season, they sent messengers daily among themselves to enquire who was causing it, and met daily to harangue each other in their villages. As they could find no clue, they came to the conclusion that it must be the Aneityumese teachers. From the teachers it passed to the missionaries, and during our absence they came to the conclusion that they had better ask us to leave. But how could they get quit of us, with our teachers, and the gospel? If only we had never come! —but to drive us away would doubtless be followed by sickness and death wholesale. Some took our part, and some were against us. One man volunteered to burn our house, as he thought that would be the most effectual way of getting us to leave; or he would fire on the boat as we were going to land. But they had not said, "If the Lord will." The devil overreached himself; for we landed in safety and found not a single fowl of our stock awanting, nor the slightest damage done. Those who were friendly before have become more attached to us; having suffered shame for His name and for His servants.

Mr Inglis had brought Nokoanpakou, the chief of the one side of Aneityum, from whose district our teachers come. He is quite an authority among our Tannese. I think his was a most providential visit, and did much to restore a right state of affairs. Our "noble" Tannese confessed their faults, said there would be no more of it, and exchanged presents with the Aneityumese.

Now, I fully expect to hear that you are worrying yourselves more about these things than we do who are on the spot. The Tannese talk plenty, and are very brave in words, but there it ends. Not even an Aneityumese teacher has been killed by our people. But I trust in higher strength than theirs. They have no power except it be given them from above, and till the Lord will, no evil can befall us if we trust in Him. When He shall see fit to will it, neither we nor any mortal can avert it. How comforting are those words: "The Lord reigneth," "My times are in Thy hand."

As our cow and bull have been very troublesome in breaking into the natives' plantations, we killed them. We distributed a good deal of the beef among our Tannese friends and enemies. Some could hardly eat it, as they associated the cow's death and their bad talk together. Others took a different view of the matter, and said we had killed it to feed them and "make their hearts good." We had roast-beef every day for a week at Kwamera, and all the way to Aneityum on board. I don't know how others feel, but I could wish myself in Old England for the sake of its roast-beef. We get sick tired of the unchanging round of pork and fowl, fowl and pork, occasionally changing to salt beef, and may be, on some other island, to nothing at all.

On Saturday, the 11th, the good ship "Paragon"[*] came off Kwamera, and oh, what a bustle we had. The "Kurimatau" had to be killed, so as to have a piece to take off; and to help us forward, the natives came selling yams. I was quite worried to get all done, but shortly after dinner we finished, made all necessary arrangements for leaving, and walked down to the beach, where the boat was waiting. What a contrast from the day we landed three weeks before, when the natives were all ashamed! Quite a crowd came down to bid us good-bye, and many asked us if we were really coming back again. Considering their bad talk, and seeing we had killed off our cows, they

---

[*] The vessel chartered to take the place of the "Dayspring," which had been wrecked in January, 1873.

seemed rather doubtful. What a waving of hands as we pushed off from the shore! A few good strokes and we were outside the reef, and exposed to the fury of the waves. It had been calm in the morning, but was now blowing half a gale, and we were close on the wind, as the sailors say. As the water was coming in and drenching us, I took refuge under good Mr Inglis' shoulder and got but little, but William and Mrs Inglis got a good deal. Dr Steel, who saw us from the ship, said we were more like a flying-fish than a boat, as our bows were quite out of the water at times. Soon after getting on board, we became very meek, and were glad to lie down quietly. What a queer thing a ship is; especially a mission ship. At times we have missionaries with their wives and children. white men from the captain to the sailors, black men from the king of one of our islands, or a part of it, to the most degraded of the devil's slaves. We have cows, pigs, goats, and fowls. What a gathering, and all in a small vessel! and yet, not one stands in another's way. Things are all so well ordered and regulated on board ship. The punctual bells, the ready "aye, aye, sir" to the captain's commands, are all very pleasing to one who admires discipline.

But now I had better tell you where we are, and where we are bound for. Well! we are at Dr Geddie's old station, enjoying the company and hospitality of those good people the Murrays, who do so much to make one feel at home. I can assure you that down here, where we have to bake our own bread, superintend the firing of it, not to speak of the thousand and one other duties we have to attend to, it is a great relief to be where you do not require to look after the culinary arrangements.

To-morrow we leave the harbour for Sydney, where, among other things, I will gratify you by getting a photograph taken, a life-like one I hope, of two real live missionaries from Tanna.

With much love,
I am, my dear ones,
Your affectionate sister,
AGNES C. P. WATT.

2. EXTRACTS FROM JOURNAL.

Thursday 16th. After dinner, saw the "Paragon" start full sail for Sydney. We followed after in the boat about six miles, and got on board at dark. I told the captain that surely he thought I had a weakness for the vessel's side at sea.

Monday 20th. Heavy sea, head wind. Saw Mare yesterday. To-day, running more freely. Saw Isle of Pines.

Wednesday 29th. A stormy day and stern sky. The captain, William and I were sitting on the hencoop when up came a sea and ducked the two former. Dr Steel conducted the Prayer Meeting, and spoke on "Be ye followers of God, as dear children." He expressed his satisfaction at seeing so many turn out regularly to worship.

Thursday 30th. The wind fell light during the evening, and during the night we were becalmed. Oh, the rolling and the rumbling of the blocks on deck!

All day we found ourselves alternately becalmed and in a fair wind till about three p.m., when the wind fell light and we began to settle on a lee-shore. For an hour and a half we were drifting in. I saw the captain was beginning to look uneasy, and glad was I to see the telegraph flag go up, and soon a tug steamer in the offing came up. "What will you give us to tug you in?" "What do you want?" "£10." "Oh, that is too much!" "We wont take you for less." "All right, take us in at £10!" So here we are in Sydney harbour. How I did enjoy seeing everything; the lighthouses, and the steamers passing to and fro. I felt what I had not experienced for more than five years, viz., a touch of civilisation. Though it was raining hard I stood on the deck dressed in my waterproof and large plaid. It was only after the tug came alongside, and we were at anchor, that I went below.

3. TO THE FAMILY.

KWAMERA, October 17th, 1874.

MY EVER DEAR ONES,—I purpose making this a family letter for you all at Pollok Road and elsewhere. The natives are very busy with their plantations during the day, and the fact that they prefer to imitate Nicodemus prevents them from coming to day-school. So we, striving to our utmost, in season and out of season, have a night-school about an hour after sunset. We had it last year, and it was well attended, and since our return from Sydney we recommenced it. We have worship first, read half an hour, and write the other half. Our own establishment provides eleven worshippers, eight of whom remain to school; six outsiders come to worship, four of whom remain. Thus at worship, seventeen meet every evening in our dining-room, and twelve remain to read and write. They are all making fair progress. Now this breaks up our evenings completely, so that Saturday is my only clear night. We have some who have come long distances during all the years of our residence here, every Sabbath while in health, and yet they seem as far as ever from the Kingdom of God. Many a time my spirit fails me when I think of the days and years we have spent here, the thousands in Glasgow and elsewhere that are praying for us, and yet, these bones are still very dry. Showers of blessing falling all around, and we like Esau still crying, " Bless us also, O Father." If there is an Achan or a Jonah in our work, O for sight to see it, and grace to cast it out ; and for patience to wait the Lord's time.

Our goats make havoc in the natives' plantations. We are anxious to keep them because they give us milk and mutton. The natives are very much annoyed with them, and proposed selling us a piece of land and putting a fence around it; to this we agreed. During our absence they made the fence; but, alas! for our purse, and alas! alas! for our feelings ; no less than *sixty-two* people had been at it, and really I do not know how much they expected to get. We gave about £10 worth of goods, chiefly in adzes and axes, and yet they were not pleased. One man gave us a fearful tonguing ; but as no one backed him, he felt rather small and left. Public opinion was on our side, and he was held in disrepute.* A week later he brought a pig as a peace-offering, and we gave him several yards of rope. He was delighted, and since then he has been quite friendly with us personally; but he is a very wicked man. His name is Misauarin. He was seven years in Fiji, and judging from his conduct since he came home, I think Tanna might bless the trader who took him away. While in Fiji he was involved in a murder, for which he was nearly hanged, and was kept in gaol for a long time. The natives say that his long confinement in prison is the cause of his ill-nature. I very much doubt it; still he has said that he will never rest until he has killed a trader in revenge. He breaks the seventh commandment on every hand, and for some time back he has dogged the footsteps of a woman who lives with us. Her name is Tauka, and she is a very nice woman. He has tried to seduce her several times, and last Thursday renewed his request. She told him that she had joined the worshipping people and could not do that great wickedness. The villain ran for a club and struck her two severe blows on the forehead, breaking her skull, and ran off leaving her for dead. Some people happened to come to the place soon after, who came and told us and her husband. He brought her home, and she now lies in a precarious state. The villain is under the protection of his father-in-law. Our young chief Nahi-abba is very angry about it, and says he will not rest until he drives the wretch out of the place, although it should be by war. There was a

---

* The fence enclosed three or four acres of land, and would have to be renewed every two years at longest.—T. W. L.

murder here early in the year; the victim was the mother of Houye (one of our boys). The murderers fled and took refuge in a village near. Soon after, in that village, two people died, and all the rest, with only two exceptions, were sick, whilst the instigator of the murder died of a grievous running sore. This has been a lesson, but seemingly not to all. I believe that the Lord often follows up crime by punishment, in a very marked manner, when dealing with heathen. In cases, where no one has remarked it, the person concerned has spontaneously said it was a judgment.

20th October. We were afraid the above-mentioned quarrel might hinder the people from coming to church, but last Sabbath the attendance was about the usual. We have commenced lately holding two services on Sabbath, but they are lazy as regards the second. They have again got reeds and put a new fence round the church, free; and I think a few are more interested in the services than before. These few, and those who come to school at night, with those living on our own premises, are our earthly stay here, and impart a comfort to our hearts, in this dark heathen land. What could I do without the few loving ones who live with us? The least in age, but not the least in love, is Nancy. She calls me "Tattin," a word of her own making. I take her on my knee at night at worship, and she sits quite quietly. She beats time to the hymn with her hands, and when the prayer commences, it would make you laugh to see her pretend to put her hands over her eyes while all the time she is peeping through her fingers. When the rest say "Amen" she gives a long sigh of relief and looks up, quite glad that the service is over. When her mother is cooking their evening meal, and Nancy feels hungry, she puts her hands over her eyes and mutters in imitation of asking a blessing. This she does over and over again until the meal is ready. As her mother, Yemeitahak, says, she seems to think that she has only to ask a blessing and the meal will be cooked.

I said before, that I got much comfort from my home letters. I always prized them, but since the visit of Moody and Sankey, they have been peculiarly dear. Often I find myself saying, "Oh that I had been at home, how I would have enjoyed the hymns." I sing and say,

"Lord, I hear of showers of blessing
Thou art scattering full and free,
Showers the thirsty land refreshing;
Let some droppings fall on me."

I got and copied the words and music of "Jesus of Nazareth passeth by," while in Sydney. I wish I had a copy of the book, well bound, and in large type. Often I play a hymn when I can't be bothered with secular music.

October 24th. Poor Tauka died on Saturday morning. She suffered a great deal. I had hope of her recovery till Friday, when she grew quite listless. I asked her if she were dying, and she said she was. When I said, "Who are you trusting to help you in the hour of death?" she at once said emphatically, "Yesu." We trust she has gone to be with "Yesu" in that happy land where people of every kindred and tongue, who have trusted in Christ, shall be.

November 17th. We had a severe gale on the 11th which lifted the thatch off the roof at the ridge, and drenched all our bed. We didn't get to bed at all. William slept on the top of the dining-room table and I on the sofa. It reminded me of the hurricane in which the "Dayspring" was lost, but it was far less severe. I think I must be getting more hard-hearted now, or else stronger-minded, as I have not bothered my head crying over it as I did last time. It is a sad drawback that we cannot get some kind of roof here which would last, and not be damaged by every strong wind. There is no appearance of the "Dayspring" yet. Since the storm, we have been rather anxious about her safety. I will have letters ready for any chance vessel after she leaves, but really we know of no chance until she comes back again. If you get no mail for months, don't wonder at it. As so much has been said about the "slave trade," few vessels are seen here.

My dearly beloved ones, I know how trying these long waits are to you; but do ever strive to realize that we are on our Father's footstool and under His fatherly care. There is a "need be" for every trial, and we know that all things work together for good to them that love God. . . .

  I am,
   My dear, dear ones,
    Your affectionate sister and daughter,
            AGNES.

X.
"EARTHQUAKES, WARS, AND RUMOURS OF WARS."

TO THE FAMILY.

KWAMERA, TANNA,
July 7th, 1875.

MY DEARLY BELOVED ONES,—I do not know whether you have noticed it or not that I have written a great deal less during the past year. The chief cause of this is the long unsettled state of things. The past twelve months have been the most trying we have had since we left home, and often when I ought to have written I felt loth to do so, because the only news I had was such as would alarm you, and in all probability the cause of alarm would have subsided long ere the letter reached you. I was very dull at the time the vessel left in November; for owing to the state of ferment we had been in at the time of Tauka's murder, and the subsequent quarrels among the natives, I had a strange presentiment of coming evil. That night after the vessel left, Nahi-abba shot one of his wives in the arm. We were awakened by an old woman coming to tell Yemeitahak, to see if she would go and dress the wound. The young woman got better, and soon after got another proof of Nahi's affection, in the form of a burning. Although Nahi-abba is our friend, he is, I think, the most wretchedly cruel husband on the island. He is jealous about his wives' conduct while he was away in Fiji for seven years, and when in the least they offend him he takes a lighted stick and scorches their bodies. When it gets cold he puts it in

KWAMERA NATIVES AND TEACHERS (NAHI-ABBA TO THE RIGHT).

the fire again for a few minutes and then resumes the diabolical process, no one daring to interfere. He was very ill lately, and the application of medicine was blessed by God in a very special manner. He seemed surprised at the speedy cure, and I took the opportunity of refreshing his memory regarding his evil deeds and

God's great mercy to him. I hope his spared life may yet be devoted to Christ and His cause, though, in the meantime, he never comes to church. . . .

On the 30th December the Neilsons came round to spend New Year's Day with us. We invited the natives to come and shoot at a bottle and have games. I am sorry to say it failed, as the non-church-going people came in great numbers, and instead of looking on the games as mutual fun and the prizes as proofs of our generosity, they seemed to think that they were playing for our amusement and the prizes were payment. They sometimes wondered whether the pay were enough for the feats they had performed. We gave them dinner of native food; rice and tea, &c. The rice was in two basins, and, as we had lots of spoons, we told them they could keep them. We knew we would not get them all back, so to prevent them from stealing part we gave all. I felt rather annoyed, however, when I heard they had taken the two basins to the bargain, saying, they would do well to feed their pigs in. You may be sure I sent messengers after the delinquents and got back my two basins. We have made up our minds, if spared till next New-year's-day, to have a soiree in the church, and in that way only church-goers will come. . . .

On the 14th of January we had a hurricane which destroyed our church and school-house, also much of the natives' food. This added fuel to the flame, and about a fortnight after, one poor wretch was shot dead and left in the bush until the morning. Narin, the murdered man, was notorious in more ways than one. He often gave us no small trouble by spearing and stoning our goats. Among his own people he was very officious. He had killed more than one, and was plotting the death of other two when he was treacherously shot by the party into whose hands he was playing. He was nearly killed two days before, but a friend took him away in time. Knowing this, he adorned himself in holiday paint and earrings, so that when he was killed he might be dressed ready for burial. In this attire he sat on the day of his sad end, seemingly waiting for a signal from his friends. A single shot was heard, and, saying to his wife that he must go and see what that shot meant, he left the village in all the style of a Tanna chief and warrior, carrying his loaded musket. It was supposed he went to inveigle two of his own relations into the hands of their enemies, but, as was afterwards seen, it was to meet his own untimely end. On the day that his body was found and buried, war was declared. His friends were strong for revenge, and most extravagant were the threats made, even by those who had been regular church attenders for years. We were amazed to hear some of the most hopeful talking about making an oven of some of their enemies. Of course their blood was up, and they said many things they never performed. There were several skirmishes on both sides; two villages were nearly burned, and the people moved nearer here. There was then a lull for a week or two, and they plotted a morning attack. Both sides seem to have laid the same plot, unknown to each other. They met in the grey dawn, and could not distinguish between enemies and friends. Muskets were fired at random; a man on the one side and a youth on the other were shot, and buried in the same grave; and a few days afterwards a man died from injuries received in the affray. Although this was the last blood shed, yet the alarming threats did not cease for long after. We had our share of them; and our house was to be burned over and over again. I think things were pretty much this way. Our people knew that their enemies were on friendly terms with us, and from that, fancied that they would not come within range of our house, and so, to disabuse their minds, the enemy kept making our house the subject of all their threats. We knew this, and I must confess that I felt rather uneasy, seeing that, as a rule, houses are burned at night. About seven miles from here, our old teacher, Luka, had five shots fired at him. One knocked off his hat and another grazed his side. Since then, Luka stays with us. The wife of a man who had been killed gave a poisonous fish to Milliama, Luka's wife, and she, being in delicate health, died from its effects. In this state of uncertainty we slept but little, never knowing when the rumours might prove realities.

On Sabbath, 20th March, we had not long retired to rest when, at a quarter-past eleven, we were startled by an earthquake. We rose and ran to the door, lest, if it were becoming severe, some of the rafters might give way. It soon subsided, however, and as we have been six years here and have never experienced a severe one, we went again to sleep. Again at half-past three we had another, and repeated our exit. This was severe, and as the house rocked to and fro, I was half way out to the cook-house before it subsided. We again went to bed, but not to sleep. I sat all the time till daybreak, and ere the morning dawned I counted no fewer than *seventeen shocks*.

After breakfast, as Mr Watt was engaged, I was acting the part of architect in the erection of a new grass church; and the girls were in the pantry washing the breakfast dishes. I had just been putting in marks where the windows were to be, when suddenly the ground began to shake and the trees to rock violently. I ran home as best I could and found the girls in a great state of anxiety, as so many dishes had been broken. This was at half-past seven. We had all resumed our duties, and I was over at the church again; the few who were working were getting on well; when, without any notice, a volley of shots were fired toward us. I saw several bullets fall into the sea, but the excitement was so great that I could not make out where they came from. I went up to where Mr Watt and the girls were and we went into the house. Very soon, thereafter, every native in the place was off in the direction from which the bullets came. That was the final volley, and seems to have been levelled at no one, but only fired into the air; and, although no formal peace has been proclaimed, there has been no more war. I cannot say the same about the earthquakes. They occurred at all hours and in all weathers, and gave no warning. Between the 27th of March and the 7th of June I have *twenty-seven* marked in my journal. They came at irregular intervals. On some days there would be three and four, then perhaps none for a week. After a day when we had one or two, I never went to bed, but lay on the dining-room sofa, with the door unlocked, so as to get out quickly; for if you are nervous and shaking with the house rocking, it is a difficult thing to unlock the door. Again, after a few days had intervened, I took courage and went to bed. If there had been none all day, we tried to persuade ourselves that we would have none till morning. Strange to say they often occurred at eight or nine o'clock, and served to put sleep out of my head at least.

Between hurricanes and wars and earthquakes, this has been by far the most trying season we have had. As yet, we have suffered little from the earthquakes compared with those on other islands. On the first night, one of the earthquakes was accompanied by a tidal wave, of which we knew nothing until the next day. At Erromanga, the sea rose and broke away a stone wall four feet thick, washed up close to Mr Robertson's door, and I believe he, with his wife and child, took shelter in a cave till morning. On Aniwa, the tidal wave ran far inland and left a great many fish, among which was a fine turtle. The Patons kept blankets on the verandah, so that when they rushed out they would not be cold. At Mr Inglis' station on Aneityum the tidal wave broke through the front door and went through the house. Mrs Inglis was sick, and happened to be up and dressed. Hearing the natives call that the earthquake had brought up the sea, she escaped in safety. Mr Inglis was behind her in fleeing, and the sea was already up to his waist. It was only by the assistance of the natives that he was saved from being carried off his feet. At the other side of Aneityum there is a small island, on which has been a trading station for twenty years. The sea broke down all the houses on it, and the inhabitants were in great danger. Several houses, and the stone church on Aneityum, were rent. But we have to sing of mercy as well as of judgment. A trader's house, within two hundred yards of us, was smashed to atoms by the January hurricane, while we escaped, having only our thatch damaged. . . .

Notwithstanding war, excitement, and hurricanes, we succeeded in getting our new buildings finished and the ground laid out in good order. While the natives were running off day after day to fight, their missionary was busy correcting and printing the "Parables of our Lord," and the four little girls and I kept up our daily sewing school. Some of our teachers seem to have despaired of the power of the Gospel on the Tannese, and expressed freely their opinion of our foolishness in persisting to finish our premises or print books. They said, "These are times to flee, not to build." Our reply was, "You can flee if you like; as yet, we see no cause to flee." And so here we are, as safe as ever, and in some ways we never had more encouragement in our work. Like the walls of Jerusalem, our building was done in troublous times, in which, owing to the excitement among the natives, we could do no Mission work. I often said, it was fortunate we had it to do, otherwise we would have been idle. If the mind is distracted, it is hard to study, but not so hard to do manual work.

We have had evening school more or less regularly for two years. Our experience here has been that the natives turn out then, when they will not look near during the day. About two years ago a few boys joined, but a boat from Aneityum came and took them away to labour for a trader there. Those who were left came only occasionally. After Tauka's murder they were afraid to come, so only those living on our own premises attended. The excitement was abating, and they were beginning to come back, when Narin's murder led to war and so stopped their learning once more.

However, in the end of March the boys came a great deal about our premises and bothered us much coming into the house and touching everything. As a punishment, we told them that every one who came in must take a lesson on the alphabet, and whenever tired of learning was to go out, as this was our private house and we would not allow stragglers. One boy named Yako took quite a fancy to his punishment and came day after day for his lesson, and hearing that we had evening school came to it also; others followed. In order to induce them to attend more regularly, we keep a roll which is called nightly. I offered a prize for regular attendance, and the thing most valued is a good fishing line. The number on the roll is nineteen, and the average attendance fifteen. We ring the bell at half-past six, have worship, teach a passage of Scripture. I read and they repeat a new verse every week. Those already committed to memory are, "Behold the Lamb of God"; "God so loved the world"; "Seek ye first the kingdom of God," &c. We have now begun to learn the Ten Commandments. After that the roll is called and the reading commences. We teach by syllables, and read until half-past seven, then those who write get their copy-books and write till eight o'clock.

On Saturday night we have only worship and singing of hymns; and on Sabbath, worship and a Bible story. We have also a mid-day school, but the attendance is very irregular, somehow or other they cannot be induced to come in daylight; not Nicodemus-like for fear of the Jews; but just because there are so many other things, such as work and play, to take up their attention during the day. We also give a prize when one masters a given task. Four boys got clasp knives, and five girls necklaces of red and blue beads. A goodly number wait for reading after service on Sabbath, but alas! some have been so learning for over six years now and cannot read yet, and never will at the present rate of progress.

Our out-stations at present are few and unoccupied. As I have already said, old Luka has had to leave his station after being fired at. The natives there were very unkind to him, and he was too far off for us to help him. Meiyahau is also vacant, as Manman has been forced to leave on account of his health. He had a very severe illness in January last; indeed, we almost despaired of his recovery. He has since returned home, whether permanently or for a time we do not yet know. He was our most energetic teacher, and had by far the most missionary spirit. He held service at several places besides the one at which he was located, and was very much liked by the people.

. . . The Aneityumese are somewhat weary of well-doing on Tanna. They have told the people what is right and what is wrong, and, because they have not obeyed their word, they think them unworthy of being taught. They fear the Tannese, who are very rude;

for although their knowledge is very limited, I have even heard a little boy criticise a teacher forty years old.

Some time ago, we went to see a place called Ifefe, where in heavy rain there is a waterfall. The natives profess to jump from the top into the pool below, a height of fifty feet. There was a good depth of water in the pool, yet none were brave enough to show their jumping powers. The water was too shallow, they said, so we had to content ourselves with a sight of the place from which they ought to have jumped. The natives are very much given to exaggeration, and I doubt if ever they did it. . . .

I must not forget to tell you of Kauea, who, although owing to the surrounding darkness is obliged to be one of two wives, has never joined in any heathen dance, and never returned to the custom of wearing heathen ornaments, nor of painting her face. Lately, when all the women in the district were dancing they called on her to join. She gave them an evasive answer; but fearing their entreaties might prevail, she went twice into the house and prayed. She told me that after she prayed the second time she felt strong, and would not have yielded; but the temptation was not repeated. She is now teaching a few to read every morning. She has been a great comfort to us, and makes us feel that our labour has not been in vain.

When sick the natives try all means in their power to escape death; still, although they fear death, they do not fear the after consequences. Hence the frequent attempts at suicide. They generally take care to be seen. The men shoot themselves, and the women

WATERFALL, IFEFE, TANNA.

either climb a cocoa-nut tree and throw themselves down or hang themselves; very often for paltry quarrels.

Perhaps it is the heat of the climate that leads to the custom of every individual man, woman, or child having their separate things, such as house, bed, blanket, or axe. In a house there was but one blanket, which belonged to the wife, who is a regular attender at church; she had got it from us in payment for some work done. Her husband took a fancy to it and took it over to his side of the fire. For this his better half took him to task; but he retorted that he had both the will and the power to strangle her, and so saying, drew a small rope to him and began to trifle with it. All of a sudden she snatched it from him, saying, "I'll save you the trouble, and deprive you of the honour of strangling me." In less time than it takes me to write this, she tied one end to the rafters of the house, made a noose of the other end and put it over her head. Had not her lord and master cut the rope smartly, no doubt she would have died.

If a wife wishes to chop some wood she must either take her own axe if she has one, or else break the sticks over a large stone.

Among the many bad traits of character among the Tannese there are a few good ones. Whatever food one gets he divides among those around him. Even little children are taught to share their things with others. Those who do not are called mean. Meanness is considered one of the cardinal vices, and liberality one of the cardinal virtues. If a native has been out all day, and has cooked, and is just about to eat the only bite of food in the house, he will offer it to a neighbour if he happens to come in, and if it is accepted he will go supperless to bed, rather than be called stingy. You will rarely meet a native woman who has not her bag on her arm, in which she carries whatever cooked food she has. She offers it to those of her friends whom she meets, and if after having given it all away, she meets another, she opens the bag to let her see she is speaking the truth. Hence if they want to keep anything for themselves they have to deny that they are in possession of it. Need I say they do not think lying a sin? With regard to stealing. If one steals and is not found out, he is praised for his cleverness. Alas! if he is found out, he is "a thief."

If I had to study my writing and composition, it is rarely I would write, for endless are the interruptions I have had in the scribbling of this lengthy epistle. I meant to have a nice quiet afternoon to-day; but, as usual, we have had visitors. I have just to look as pleasant as possible to our intruding friends, who walk in without asking leave. While writing the first part of this page two friends came in. They chatted away quite freely, to the extent of putting an end to my writing, and paid no attention to the many hints I gave as to the desirableness of being left alone. I at last took refuge in flight, and paid a visit to the goat-house and saw all our little kids. On my return, I found that the object of my absence had been gained. But as I fancy you will agree with me that I have written enough, I will add no more.

I remain,
Yours affectionately,
AGNES C. P. WATT.

XI.
RAIN-MAKING.

ANIWA, August 24th, 1876.

MY DEAR FATHER, MOTHER, BROTHERS, AND SISTERS,
—. . . After the "Dayspring" took away our mail for Sydney in the end of December, we had very dry weather, and the natives became much concerned about their crops. As they believe in their power of making rain, they set about it. I have not seen them do it; but I know they have sacred stones, which they use somewhat in this manner. When rain is wanted the rain-maker takes a canoe, puts it somewhere in the bush, and fills it with water; fresh water, it must not be salt. He proceeds inland to some known pool, accompanied by several others, who, though ordinary men, want rain, and help him. Each makes a cocoa-nut leaf basket, into which he puts leaves of certain trees and plants (I am not aware that any of them are from fruit trees), such as stone palms, &c., and a small banana plant. When they think they have enough, taking a few leaves, or a branch of kava, they go direct to the aforesaid pool, where the rain-maker commences his incantations. Taking a basket of leaves, he calls on his departed father and friends and asks them to join him and his party in making rain, and then places the

basket in the pool. He does the same with each basket, until he has placed them all in the water. He then rolls a large stone over them to keep them down. This done, he places the twig of kava on a ledge of earth or stone near. He calls on his departed relatives to note the fact of his having brought kava for them to drink, and enjoins them to see that even now the clouds may darken the sky, and that by the time they reach home the first drops may be falling. The whole party then start for home. On the way the rain-maker suddenly breaks from the party, and following a bypath, gathering certain leaves as he proceeds, he carries them to the place where he had previously put the canoe full of water.

On reaching it he puts in the leaves he has gathered and the sacred stones, only reserving one or two. With a prayer to his departed relatives he returns to the village. That day he must not eat anything that has been cooked in an oven; only such things as have been roasted on an open fire; nor may he bathe in or even touch the sea. I knew once of our young chief Nahiabba being under some such vow when a vessel was seen coming. He was very anxious to get on board for some tobacco, and in order to do so, he caused the boat to be pulled up so far on the beach that he could step in without even wetting the soles of his feet. Some of the more scrupulous objected even to that, suggesting that if the boat were leaking he might touch it in that way.

But to return to the sacred man. While he has been thus employed, a little boy or girl has been fishing. What has been caught is cooked, and the rain-maker presents it on an altar, formed of two or three reeds, set up near the enchanted canoe. He again calls the attention of his departed sires to the food he has prepared for them, and invokes their help. The food is generally the poorest possible. Unripe fruits, miserable fish, or the worst parts of a pig are selected for the altars of the gods. Nor are these gods the spirits of long ago; many of them are men who were living in our own day. It would appear that as soon as a man dies he is worshipped. The power of rain-making is hereditary; and, as all a man's brother's children are his children, there is seldom difficulty in finding a successor. In the evening the rain-maker, having drunk his kava, spits, crows in his usual way, and calls on the gods to send rain. Next morning, a while before day, he is up and away to visit his baskets in the pool. He removes the stone, stamps the baskets down a little, replaces the stone, and returns. Although he should see no signs of rain he will go on from day to day, calling on his gods over his kava, putting in new leaves now and again, and replenishing the altar. If it seems likely to rain soon, he puts the remaining stones into the canoe, and when the rain has actually begun to fall he goes to his kava with a glad heart; praises the gods for assisting him, and appeals to his fellow-drinkers, if he is not good to them in causing such a plenteous rain to descend on their crops. To all this they assent most emphatically.

But I think I hear you saying, "If there is no rain, does he not feel put out?" Not a bit. If his rain charm does not succeed, it is because some one is making such doses of sunshine, and perhaps messages to that effect will be sent out in different directions. If no one will own that he is making sunshine or wind to keep away the rain, then they are telling lies, and doing it secretly. I have known cases where the rain did not fall for weeks, and yet their confidence in their power did not slacken in the least. We have tried every argument to persuade them of their impotence, and taunted them with their failure; all to no effect. The furthest that they will go is to say that it is wrong to make it; but as to their power they have no doubt. . . .

On New-year's-day we had a "Soiree." At about ten a.m. the drum was beaten, and we assembled in the church. After singing a hymn, and prayer, several speeches were made by teachers and Tannese. Mr Watt addressed them on several subjects of a temporal and secular character, which he thought hardly fit for Sabbaths. After the speeches, they were served with as much rice, goat-mutton, pine-apples, and rose-apples as they could eat, and as much tea as they could drink. The tea would not hurt their nerves, as it was very weak; but there was plenty of brown sugar in it, which is the principal thing. When I say they got as much as they could eat, I mean they got a sufficiency; for I really do not know the limit of their eating. They can eat an immense quantity of food at a time; and on the other hand they can do with very little. The power of endurance in them is very strong. I have seen even children go for a whole day without a morsel of food. At work, or on a journey, they do not care to stop for food, not even to eat what they may have brought with them. They prefer to go on, and then fill up and go to bed. I often wonder how they can sleep comfortably after such heavy suppers of rich cocoa-nut and banana, or cocoa-nut and yam-puddings, or taro and pork. Of the last, they eat ravenously. I have known one man sit down to a leg of pork, without either yam or taro to eat to it, and consume the greater part of it, go to bed, and next morning resume his tearing at it (for they have neither knives nor forks), and leave little or none.

The past hot season has been a very pleasant one; fine clear weather and few earthquakes, and the absence of war in our immediate neighbourhood. About two miles from us there has been a deal of firing, through which several of our parishioners have been wounded, and two have died of their wounds. It did not affect what we may call "our people," except that every other day they went to assist in the shooting, and came home laden with spoils.

In this late war I saw that should it reach us, I might well say, "Save me from my friends"; for as soon as a district is vacated in time of war, whatever has not been carried off in the flight is a prey to all; and generally to your allies. In passing through the village, they will do more in the way of plundering than the enemy. Fowls, dogs, cats, pigs, yams, &c., are all taken; and yet, after all, though you have had the worst of it, when there is a cessation of hostilities, you have to give them a large pig and other things for fighting for you. Of course, the tables will be turned some day, when you find yourself the ally, helping yourself to whatever comes to hand, and getting a large pig for your valour.

Although the season has been a pleasant one, it has been the hottest since we came to the islands. The perspiration poured off us from day to day, and we felt quite unable for work. We both had wonderful health until the 25th of March, when William took a severe vomiting of blood, which left him very weak. It came on in the evening and continued until nine o'clock, when he got rest. Abel, our cook, stayed with me until he got relief; and neither Yemeitahak nor the girls would go to their own houses till they knew he was out of danger. Next morning, old Luka and Kauaneli came. It was quite affecting to see how they sobbed and cried when they shook hands with him. He had scarcely recovered strength when, on the 1st April, I took ill with fever and ague of a very severe type. My head ached for days; and although William gave me double doses of opium, I could not sleep. This continued until the 17th, when we went round to Port Resolution in our boat, hoping to catch the "Dayspring," and go north with her to Nguna, to see if the change would do me good. The "Dayspring," however, was gone, but a home mail cheered me up, and I grew stronger every day. There was a great deal of sickness among the natives. Nearly every one was laid aside for a time, and some were brought to the very brink of the grave.

You know their notions of "nahak" and "foreign disease," for which the missionary, being a sacred man, often gets blamed. I am happy to say that in this instance they did not blame us, but showed their confidence by coming for medicine, which they afterwards paid for. With regard to children, they have unbounded confidence in my skill. Many a dose of castor-oil have I administered to the little black things, who often manifest a determined opposition to my wish that they should open their mouths for the nauseous dose.

So remarkable were some of the cures that we could only say, "This is of the Lord." One woman who had been ill for some time was taken for dead, and had her grave clothes put on. She was laid out to be wailed for, but as the pulsations of the heart continued, some proposed that they should come to us for medicine, though others pooh-poohed it. Toko, one of the chiefs, came himself. When he told me how she was, and how they had dashed cold water on her face in vain, I said it was no use sending medicine. He was very importunate, so I gave him half a glass of raspberry vinegar, with a little extra acid in it to make it irritate the throat. (She had a cough, and I understood that the phlegm had gathered in her throat.) I told Toko to give her that if possible, and if she opened her eyes and could swallow, he was to come for other medicine, which he did the next day. He said that our medicine had made her live, and soon she would be down to see us. In a week she was able to walk about, and now she is as strong as ever. He showed his gratitude by giving us a pig. . . .

I am,
Your loving daughter and sister,
AGNES.

XII.

THOUGHTS ABOUT HOME-GOING.

TO HER PARENTS.

Kwamera, Tanna,
June 22nd, 1878.

MY DEAR FATHER AND MOTHER,— . . . Truly it never rains but it pours, for from the middle of October until the end of April I never saw a letter, and since then you know what a budget I have received from home, besides thirty from colonial and island friends. All your letters were intensely interesting, and I will answer them individually, though this letter to the heads of the family may be looked upon as *the* letter. When the first lot came in April, after such a long silence, I could not trust myself to read my mail before any one, and so went to my room, where I could laugh and cry as I saw fit, or as my highly-strung nerves might cause me to do. . . .

This letter will convey news to you which will occasion you both joy and sorrow. In your last letter, my dear father, you say you cannot think of my coming home only to leave again. That I cannot altogether understand; for ten years ago you parted with me to go to an unknown region, and that, too, when my husband and I were to be supported by a church which neither knew us nor our mission, at a salary of £120 to cover all our expenses. I can assure you I sometimes felt homeless then. But now we have a comfortable house, a salary of £200 a year from a church which gave us such a welcome two years ago. We have the respect of all the tribes by whom we are surrounded; and many other blessings. I think it ought to be less hard to part with me now. True, our second parting is more likely to be our final one on earth; but why, if we believe in the recognition of friends in our Father's house, nay, more, of our love being perfected towards each other there, why cannot we part and tryst to meet *there*? You are no nearer Home in Glasgow than we are on Tanna. If it be the Lord's will, I hope to lie in a forest grave; for I have no desire, indeed, I dread being buried in a crowded graveyard. Did I think my coming home would pain you because of the parting, I would forego the hope on which my heart has been set all these years; for although it will be like plucking out a right eye or cutting off a right hand to sever myself again from home, still I believe that afterwards I will be only glad that I have again seen your faces in the flesh. Our Great High Priest, who wears our nature and knows our every feeling, who gave us strength to part and live and labour so long separate, will give us parting grace again when the time comes.

I am almost afraid to say we are coming home. It seems too good to be true, and "there's many a slip 'twixt the cup and the lip." I suppose you feel like me, that you wont believe it until you see it. Well, well, so let it be! We have got leave of absence from the

New Hebrides for sixteen months, and if all goes well we will spend next summer with you. We are afraid to come home earlier than April or May, lest the sudden change from the tropics might affect our good health. William especially is very "cauldrife."

I cannot get over the thought of how good God has been to us, seeing we are all spared for these ten long years, and such a large family. Some day there will be changes, but wont it be grand to be all gathered Home safe, never to part? . . .

I am sorry I failed to tell you how well all the things had come out, but in writing one is apt to miss something if it is not noted just at the time. We notice omissions and repetitions in the letters we receive, and I suppose you do the same. But though correspondence is unsatisfactory, what would we do without it! I see the want of it among the natives. When one of their number goes to the colonies he is nearly as good as dead until he returns. It is no uncommon thing for a father to hear of his son's death, which plunges him into sorrow and makes him long to be revenged on the supposed disease-maker. The family goes into mourning, cuts down trees, kills pigs, and gives presents. Soon after another report comes to the contrary, which also is believed, causing quite a revulsion of feeling. Perhaps by this time the man's wife has been given to another, she is taken from him to await her former husband's return; and so on, until either the one report or the other be verified by the young man's return, or his wages being sent on by some one else.

The Neilsons have had a trying time of sickness. The

little twins which were born about Christmas had poor health, and are now for ever free from sorrow. So the Neilsons have now three infants' graves on Tanna. They came round and stayed with us for a few days after Charlie's death. The boys and girls were much delighted with Tommy and Jessie.

After they left I made preparations to receive my dear sisters Mrs Paton and Mrs Milne. Owing to a terrific hurricane which occurred in January, near Fate and Nguna, the "Dayspring" was detained until Mr Macdonald's house was made habitable. While in the colonies he got a letter from Mr Milne informing him that his house was blown over. The first intimation we received of the hurricane was when the "Dayspring" came down from the colonies in April. The two ladies and their children and I enjoyed ourselves immensely for a fortnight. . . .

As to our proposed transference to Aneityum, notwithstanding that the two churches were agreeable, the Synod disapproved. . . . They said that were we to leave Tanna the island would go down; nobody could fill our places there; that Mrs Watt (not Mr Watt, mind you) had the true ring of a Tannese linguist; and to take us off Tanna would be to write Ichabod over it, &c., &c. . . . I would rather go to Aname than see it left without a missionary; but if we long for fame and the praise of the churches, this is the sphere. . . .

I remain now, as ever,
Your loving daughter,

AGNES.

XIII.
BACK TO TANNA.

TO HER FATHER.

KWAMERA, TANNA,
27th August, 1880.

MY DEAR FATHER,— . . . We stayed two nights with Mr Dean in Sydney, and again resumed our watery way, not in a big Orient steamer, but in the wee " Dayspring," which was lumbered up with tanks, wood for houses, new boats for missionaries, mission-boxes, and stores, maybe for starving folks. Hearing of the hurricane made us very anxious regarding our friends in the islands.

On leaving Sydney, we set out upon a heavy sea; and how the little thing did pitch! We all made for our bunks at once, and but for the kindly visit of the captain to see how we were getting on, or to reproach us in sport for being bad sailors thus to give in to Neptune after having come all the way from England, we lay in a state of silence and semi-seasickness for two or three days. Gradually we began to crawl on deck, and although it was rough weather, there was no rain, so we spent a good deal of time there. On the whole, it was a dull voyage. The sea was rough, the vessel was heavily laden, and we made slow progress.

Mr Mackenzie, who had gone up for his health, was very ill, so it was with joy that we saw dear old Aneityum again. We were detained there for a week with adverse winds and a rough sea, so that it was the 4th of May ere we landed at Kwamera. We got a fairish day to land, and were met on the beach by a few people. I was disappointed at our welcome, for they had made such demonstrations of grief at our leaving that I expected a much more hearty reception. But knowing there had been a hurricane, the sight of the gaunt, hungry faces told me why they were sad. Besides, some had died in our absence, and our return reminded their relations of their loss. How wild and desolate the country looked! great trees blown down in every direction, their bleached roots pointing to the sky, and bare branches instead of rich foliage. Our house looked like a weather-beaten ship, "only, not a wreck." It seemed very dreary to me, after the nice well-carpeted rooms I had lately left. The natives had done well; had repaired the thatch, whitewashed the walls, and scrubbed the floors. Outside, they had put up a new goat-house and servants' houses, and had put a new fence all round the premises. As the sea had been washing up inside the fence, they must have had a great deal of work to bring things to the appearance they presented.

. . . Gradually we came to know of all the changes that had taken place during our absence. We were glad to see that, although there had been a high death-rate among our people, they had continued to attend church and school as when we were here. The great cry here just now is, "If we worship, we will die"; and as more

YAM GARDEN.

of the church-goers in proportion than of the heathen have died in our absence, there seems to them some ground for it. He who rules above will do all for the best. I was gladly surprised at being met once more by all my girls. It was more than I expected, for some of them are far bigger than many that are married. However, they all came back and are still with us, and can all read and write fairly. After unpacking, &c., we began to settle accounts. We had left some twenty men and women to fence and look after the premises, so that if a hurricane should come they would the sooner get the place in order. I see from my day-book that twenty-five men and women have worked; each of the men for at least four days. The women had brought from five to twenty-five bundles of reeds each. It was no small business to get all these people paid justly, giving them neither too much nor too little. We gave them from sixpence to a shilling a day in blankets, axes, adzes, knives, print, &c. Axes, adzes, and blankets were in great demand, and one or two saucepans. It was pleasant, however, to see all arranged to the satisfaction of every one. William was kept very busy repairing the damage the natives had not been able to repair. No fewer than twenty-three panes of glass had been broken, and the school-house had been thrown over. With a block and tackle and a band of natives, he got it straight again. We were sorry to see the bairns coming round with hungry faces and having nothing to give them. We needed a great deal of help, and altogether we had nineteen mouths to feed. We gave out bread and tea in the morning, soup and rice at mid-day, and bread and tea again in the evening. In that way we used a cask of flour, a cask of biscuit, and two bags of rice in a month; even then it was only a mere existence. I was glad when the month was over and we got the chance of escaping, for a little, from distress we could not relieve, for we had only two casks of flour and were 1300 miles from the market. We knew that when we were away they would scour the bush for roots and leaves, and so put in an existence; besides, we left sufficient flour and rice to spin out the time till we returned. We had arranged with the captain that if it were calm weather he was to call here before going to Aniwa, so that we might visit our dear friends the Patons. We got a lovely start, but were becalmed, and took five days to do what we have often done in our boat in eight hours. We got our usual hearty welcome there, and oh what a happy ten days we spent together! . . . From Aniwa we went on to the Annual Meeting. We were but one night on Erromanga, where we were delighted to see the change on the people. Such a band of clean, well-dressed natives! We were present at the second opening of the Martyrs' Memorial Church (a wooden building presented to the natives of Erromanga by friends in Sydney in memory of the five missionaries who were murdered on that island). It is a nice building, but the devout appearance of the people assembled in it was still more pleasing. Next morning we were off Erakor, and found Mr Mackenzie a great deal better, although not able to go to the meeting. The next again we entered Nguna Bay, and were ashore in time for mid-day dinner. We were introduced to little Miss Milne, a splendid baby with lovely dark eyes.

Next day the gentlemen and Mrs Robertson went off in the "Dayspring" to Havanah Harbour, where the meeting was to be held, leaving Mrs Lawrie and myself to keep Mrs Milne company. We spent a pleasant time together, and I was delighted to see the change that had taken place on Nguna since we were last there. Then, scarcely one would come to church; now, the same church is filled with earnest, devout people.

After the meeting was over the "Dayspring" came round, and we proceeded north to Tongoa, where we landed Mr Michelsen. Nearly all the mission party accompanied him ashore. The landing is not of the easiest, as there is a heavy surf. The boat lies out in the water while natives wade out and in, carrying passengers and goods. The gentlemen are carried on their backs, while the ladies have a queen's chair, made by two men crossing their hands. One moment the men are up to their knees in water, the next, the wave has receded until they are standing high and dry. On the way to the Mission Station we passed through a native village. The women and children turned out in a body to see us. They expressed little wonder at the gentlemen, gave a look or two at the ladies, but, getting a sight of little Johnnie Lawrie, rushed round him shouting and yelling in great excitement. I suppose they had never seen a white baby before, for they seemed like to devour him. Mr and Mrs Lawrie had considerable difficulty in getting through them. Some of the women were rather good-looking, although covered with yellow paint and grease. If only washed and clothed, they would be quite passable. The mission house is some little distance from the beach, and as it was near sunset, and we have little twilight, we had to make haste. After the same how-d'ye-do getting into the boat through the surf, we got safely on board, leaving poor Mr Michelsen all alone. There is not one white person on the island but himself. He looked so lonely as he stood on the beach waving his hat to us. Next morning we were off to Epi, and the missionaries went on shore to see about Mr Holt's settlement. He is a layman sent from the Church of Victoria, and appointed to Epi in accordance with his own and the Church's desire.

Leaving Epi we came south, calling at all the stations, and at last arrived back here, having got some flour, rice, and beans, which we purchased from our neighbour missionaries, to help to feed the starving. Since our return, things have been going on quietly. While we were away, two of our people took to themselves wives according to heathen custom. We got them to be married after the Christian mode in church. One of the men had two wives; but at our request he gave up one, who has since been married according to Christian fashion. These are our first Christian marriages here, although I hope they will not be the last. It is really painful to see how backward the Tannese are in adopting any of our Christian or civilized customs.

Last Monday, with the help of two of my women, I made seven shortgowns. Some of the women could not sew, and two of them lived ten miles away. They had sent fowls in payment for dresses. They have no teacher in their village, but a Tannaman conducts service with a few women. Poor man, he is very ignorant, for he has had but little teaching, but he endeavours to walk up to the light he has. He was along here lately, and stayed one night. Next morning, as usual, I sent out to Yemeitahak a canful of tea and a piece of bread. He happened to enter her house just after she had eaten all the bread and had only a little tea left. This she offered to him, but before he drank it, he took the covering off his head and thanked God for watching over him during the night, asked Him to give him His Word as a relish or "kitchen" to the tea, and to watch over him in the way he was that day to go. When Yemeitahak told me, I thought what a reproof it was to many of us, who, unless it be a regular meal, never think of asking a blessing. He was talking to the people here, and telling them how many greater advantages they have than either he or his people. They are midway between two mission stations, and have not had a teacher for years, yet they cling to the form of worship.

One of the single men now living with us is a young Tannaman. He has been to the colonies, and, since his return, has attached himself to our party. His name is Kaiasi. He is about twenty-two years of age, and, if spared, he may be a comfort to us. He is learning to read and write; the latter he does well. I felt so cheered by his coming and offering to stay with us to be taught.

Since our return, William has resumed itinerating. We are ill off for teachers, so the work devolves on the missionary. Every morning we rise between five and six. On weekdays we have to do so for the sake of our reading and writing school, and on Sabbaths for his itinerating. On the Sabbath he goes four miles along the coast, has worship, and converses with any he finds on the way. Some days he is encouraged with good gatherings; other days cast down, having only seen a few persons. Some weeks ago, I accompanied him, along with some of our girls; and as their eyes are much sharper than ours, we were often amused, yet vexed, to hear them say, "Missi, there is So-and-so making his or her escape." Once or twice I saw a young man stooping and running under trees to get out of sight. In some cases it was because they did not wish us to catch them naked, and ran to get their girdles; but in others, they wished to avoid the service we were about to hold. You can fancy what a hard day Sabbath is, walking eight miles, either along the beach or inland, in such a climate as this, holding short services at several places, then the usual service here, followed by the Sunday School and a meeting for men, a women's meeting, and in the evening, meetings for teachers and boys and girls. One of these last is conducted by the missionary, and the other by his wife.

The great obstacle to the progress of the gospel, and the chief cause of war and quarrelling, is the belief in "Nahak." Till that is given up, we have little hope of decided success. On Aneityum, the disease-makers gave up the practice of it and broke up their sacred stones. I doubt much if they do not yet believe that they had the power; only they feel it is wicked for Christians to exercise it.

One Sabbath morning, when Mr Watt was away itinerating, a labour vessel came off here and sent in her boats. From my bedroom window I saw one of the white men in charge of the boat hold up turkey-red and muskets to excite the cupidity of the natives, and get them to go as labourers. I saw one or two take down shallots for sale, and then I went off to look after something else. Soon the cries of the people led me to look out, and I saw they had succeeded in getting three to embark. The wife of one of them was crying bitterly to get away with him. On going out, I heard the people on the beach calling on some young men to launch a canoe and take off the man's wife to him, as she was running along the edge of the reef. The boats returned to a ledge of the reef, and soon a crowd was gathered to the spot. Two more of our parishioners embarked, although they had to swim through the surf. The lads in the canoe got up to them, and, one of the white men having spent two months here, while we were away in Scotland, Kaisai knew him, and said, " Dan, if the missionary had been here you would not have come in on a Sabbath morning for nought. Why do you come from the religious land of Britain and teach us to break the Sabbath ? I shall inform the missionary of your conduct."

Having got the five natives they again left without the woman. Meanwhile, William returned and we resumed our duties. The bell was ringing for service and the people were all gathered, when the cry of "the two boats are again coming" was heard. We saw we would have no peace as long as they were there, so William went down and awaited the arrival of the first. He accosted him with, " I am amazed at you, my fellow-countryman, openly profaning the Lord's day."

He replied, "I do not like it myself, but I am under authority and must obey." "Well," said William, "it is very sad to see you, of whom we expect better things, trading in goods and men on Sabbath." He seemed to get angry at this, and said that Sabbath was a lucky day, for he had got five. "Yes," said William, "but I question if you will gain much by your luck; you shall yet have to answer for this day's work." Whether some chord in that man's heart had been touched, or how it was we know not, but he turned himself round in the boat and sat down and never looked up once again. The natives say the tears were streaming down his cheeks. For some reason or other they did not take the woman, but slipped away out to sea where the other boat was lying, never having plucked up courage to come in. . . .

Your loving daughter,

AGNES.

XIV.
FORMATION OF THE CHURCH ON TANNA.

TO THE FAMILY.

Kwamera, Tanna,
25th June, 1881.

My dear Father and Family,— . . . I had written to no one since the "Dayspring" left here in December till the day she returned in April, and, even then, it was but a note. To my grief, I have had no cause to write all these months, for we have been, as it were, buried alive or banished. We have not had the remotest chance of sending off a mail, and, of course, we have received none. Often have I said, that the four hurricane months looked like a tunnel to me. I fear to enter, and I breathe freely when I reach the further end. The longer I am here, I feel it the more. Perhaps never since our settlement have we been so shut up as during the past year. Very few traders have called at Tanna, and still fewer live on Tanna. I am not aware of any white trader being on the island at the present time. One poor fellow died of dropsy during the year. He lived all alone, except for some foreign natives, who, after he died, went in a canoe for Mr Neilson's teachers to bury him. They brought his body to the Mission burying-ground, and laid him in his last resting-place there. I know not all who lie in that little "God's acre," but I know of some. There Mr Johnston rests, having only put his hand to the plough. The club of the savage did not break his skull, but he never recovered from the shock he received when he saw what a narrow escape he had had. There lies also the first Mrs Paton and her infant son. There several native teachers rest, who have been found faithful unto death; and a goodly number of little children. There, too, was buried all that remained of John Underwood, who was blown up with his own gunpowder while in a state of intoxication. So shattered was he, that only one foot and his chin were left to be buried. Near him lies Dana, who, while out shooting on Sabbath, accidentally shot himself, and died of tetanus. Close by, we buried poor Bell, who was killed by a shot from a Tannaman some years ago. What a strange medley, gathered from many parts of the world! Scotland, England, Nova Scotia, Germany, Raratonga, Aneityum. The helpless infant and the sinner old in wickedness; all awaiting the resurrection morning. That is at Port Resolution, and from there to here, a distance of fifteen miles, I only know of one European grave. It contains the precious dust of little Minnie Mathieson, aged but a few months. Her father is buried on Mare, in the Loyalty Islands, and her mother on Aneityum. Their graves are severed far and wide, but their spirits are united before the throne of God.

When the "Dayspring" called here last December I went on board according to appointment, and was put ashore at Aniwa. On arriving, we were almost afraid to ask how Mrs Paton was, she had been so low when the vessel was last there; Mrs Braithwaite, the captain's wife, had kindly remained with her. The captain, Mrs Mackenzie, Mrs Milne, and I, landed in the moonlight, and so came upon them unawares. While Mrs Mackenzie and I stood upon the verandah, fearing to enter lest we might disturb, we heard an infant cry. Soon we found that Mrs Paton was improving, though still very low. She had been ill for six months, during which time she passed through much trouble. I spent Christmas and Newyear's-day there, making toffee for the children to cheer their young hearts. About the beginning of January, Mr Watt came over in his boat to take me to Kwamera; and as Mr Paton had so much to do, we proposed to take Frank and James with us, and this being agreed to, we started on the 10th. We got a lovely day, but so calm that we had to row the whole way, and thus were nearly twelve hours on the sea. We landed in the moonlight and got such a welcome, not only on account of the children but because Mr Watt had left on a rough day, when the natives feared that he and his boat's crew would be drowned. About six weeks after our return we got a letter by canoe from Aniwa telling of Walter Watt Paton's sudden death, only ten days after we had left. What a shock to the lonely parents, as the child was but an hour and a half ill. The father made his coffin, and the next day, he and Robert, with the natives, laid him to rest beside his sister Lena. Jesus only knows what the parents suffered.... As the Synod is now past, we expect the "Dayspring" back here soon, on her way to Melbourne, whither it is to go with the Patons. Mr Paton will reside there at present as agent for the Church of Victoria, whose funds are at present very low. The Holts go too; they came down last year with us, bringing with them a beautiful house. They got a promising station on Epi; and through their own indefatigable efforts and the help of others, in a few weeks they found themselves in possession of a fine house and grounds. But they had put the stove pipe through the thatch of the cook-house without a fender; so on the day that the vessel was to leave them for five or six months, and while Mr Holt was on board with his latest letter, the flames of all he possessed rose to heaven. He rushed on shore to find all reduced to ashes. What a mercy the "Dayspring" was not off. She made a trip to Havanah Harbour and got what she could for them; and the captain having given what he could spare, left them with an anxious mind. After that, Mr Holt set to work to build a house, cutting the wood in the bush, but in a short time was so prostrate with fever and ague, that they were glad to get off by a chance vessel to Mr Macdonald's at Havanah Harbour. . . .

On Aneityum the chief topic is the destruction of "kava." For some years back, the growing and drinking of it has been far too prevalent. Lately a movement has been set on foot to repress the evil. Several have publicly rooted up and burned their stock of kava. The missionaries have also instituted an "Anti-Kava League," and numbers have signed the pledge neither to give, nor take, nor grow it.

The kava question will be a grave one on Tanna,

where every adult male drinks it at sundown. It will be like plucking out a right eye or cutting off a right hand to give it up. But we have still graver sins in our midst to war against, which more than occupy all our energies. The missionaries were pleased to see the marked improvement on our people. The recital of what is going on in other islands is stimulating our backward Tannese. Matthew and Kapere have commenced to conduct morning worship in two villages.

. . . November 17th. I am afraid that the events of the last two days will cause a tinge of sadness to pervade my correspondence. Yesterday and to-day we lost seven of our church-going people by emigration to Queensland. A vessel from Brisbane has been lying off, and sending in her boats to recruit labour for the colonial market, and I am sorry to say she has got many willing labourers from our immediate neighbourhood. One of the recruits was Keianga, our first girl, as you may remember, and of whom we had such hopes; for she *did* promise well. Alas, she fell deep into sin, and many an aching heart we had over her.

Lately, she and her husband came to live in our neighbourhood, and for some time we have been cheered by her earnest desire to follow that which is good. Her husband, who left her and went to the colonies for three years, is the very personification of jealousy and revenge (though truly she gave him cause). Since his return, three years ago, he has beaten her unmercifully; yet, poor thing, she bears it patiently, without a grumble, believing it to be the cross she is called upon to bear on account of her backsliding. She told me the other day that she prayed for grace to be patient, to bear the just rewards of her deeds, and that her trials might be sanctified to her. This morning, she came to ask my advice, as her husband wished her to go. Would it be right for her to go away from us who had taught her to worship God? I said she ought to follow her husband, and that she could worship the Lord wherever she went. She was so pleased to hear me say so, and said, "I'll try to give my heart to Him. If I pray in my heart daily to Him, will He love me although I cannot get to church?" Having got our consent, she went away cheerfully; and though I mourn her absence, still it is so hard for a young woman to live a pure life, when left by her husband, that I think it better she has gone. May the Lord guide her into a Christian home!

Since writing the above, we have had a letter from Mr Neilson, informing us that the "Dayspring" had called there from her northern trip, and landed Kiri, one of our lads who has been acting as boat's crew. On hearing that so many of his companions had emigrated, he would, no doubt, wish to join them. Unfortunately for us, the same ship called there two days after he landed, and he, with some others, sailed in her. I cannot tell you how sorry I am, for he was such a hopeful lad, could read well; and, believing the Scripture, "The entrance of thy word giveth light," we looked forward with pleasure to his approaching manhood. They will go for so much per head in Brisbane. If they fall into good hands, they will be cared for; if not, they will be attended to according to their market value.

The vessel's name is the "Ceara." The man in

charge of the boat is what the traders call a "good shot." He captivated the natives here by lavishing articles of barter on them, throwing bunches of tobacco on shore for them to scramble for, promising £2 10/ a month as boat's crew, and giving gin all around for nothing. How far he succeeded in his mission here, you already know. Those got here would realise at least £70; not a bad return for two days' hunting. Our church is manifestly thinner, and at morning and evening school the blanks are even more noticeable.

Though the love of novelty has a great deal to do with taking our lads away, as well as the desire for property, yet the chief cause is discomfort. In this district, Nahi-abba, the chief, is a constant torment. He is always causing trouble by stealing other people's wives, beating his own, and otherwise leading all connected with him into trouble. The lads here have been saying that they are tired of carrying muskets daily for the protection of one who is so fool-hardy and wicked; and that if they got the chance they would emigrate. This they have done. You say, "Why do they defend him?" I cannot tell you; the only reason they give is, "He is our chief."

While I was in Melbourne, William had a visit from a man-of-war, H.M.S. "Miranda." A trading vessel reported that she was fired at by the natives here, and Her Majesty's ship came down to caution the people. Of course the charge was refuted. A boat had been fired at away to the west of us, by people who are at enmity with ours. After a very pleasant visit, Her Majesty's representative took his departure, and my old man was again alone. I never felt anxious about his comfort, for I knew that with Yamen as cook and Yamen's wife as bedroom maid, these matters would be duly attended to. The other helps are not so efficient ; still, with a little supervision, they get on very well, and I hoped for the best. All went on favourably in my absence; and having a splendid passage both up and down, I arrived before being expected, and gave them a glad surprise. There was a great "hurry-scurry" that morning trying to put things in order before their exacting friend arrived. There was a sort of pride in letting me see how nicely they could get on without me. Nevertheless, it was not difficult to see that I got a hearty welcome from the Kwamera missionary and his parishioners.*

The printing of the Acts of the Apostles had been finished a few days before, and our best readers had been presented with copies. They were pleased to get them, for they had been reading for a long time in Matthew.

The second annual free contribution of arrowroot was made, amounting to about 450 lbs. The people did not enter so heartily into the work as they did last year; but then they had put up a large grass building to worship in, and so well did they turn out, and so heartily did they work, that the whole structure was up in four days. The proceeds of the arrowroot we intend to use in lengthening our school-house and making it do duty for a church as well. At present it is too small for our congregation ; hence the erection

---

* Mrs Watt had been under the necessity of going up to Melbourne for medical advice.

of a temporary grass building which, along with the arrowroot, is the *free* contribution for the year. They also put up a school-house, but that was in payment for medicine.

Almost from the beginning of our Mission we have got the natives to put up their own places of worship, but to give anything for the gospel's sake is a new idea on Tanna. Like many of old, they follow Christ for the loaves and the fishes, and thought they were conferring an honour on us by attending service, expecting to get all their clothes for nothing. These erroneous ideas are being dispelled.

In anticipation of my return, the six girls had learned by heart the fourteenth chapter of Matthew's gospel, and repeated it to me; in many cases without a mistake, in others with only one or two promptings. I gave them each a shoulder handkerchief in acknowledgment of their diligence.

The most important event of the year, nay! of our whole mission life, if not of the history of the missions of Tanna, is the formation of a church here. We have had a communicants' class for over a year. First we waited for Mr Neilson's return, thinking it would be nice for us all to be together; then for the Annual Meeting, and, finally, my absence postponed it till October 6th. After all, Mrs Neilson could not leave her station, but Mr Neilson came. On the Friday evening Mr Neilson preached, and William baptised two men, four women, and three children. On Sabbath, October 6th, eighteen of us sat down at the table of our Lord: three Europeans, nine Aneityumese, and six Tannese. Mr Neilson administered the sacrament.

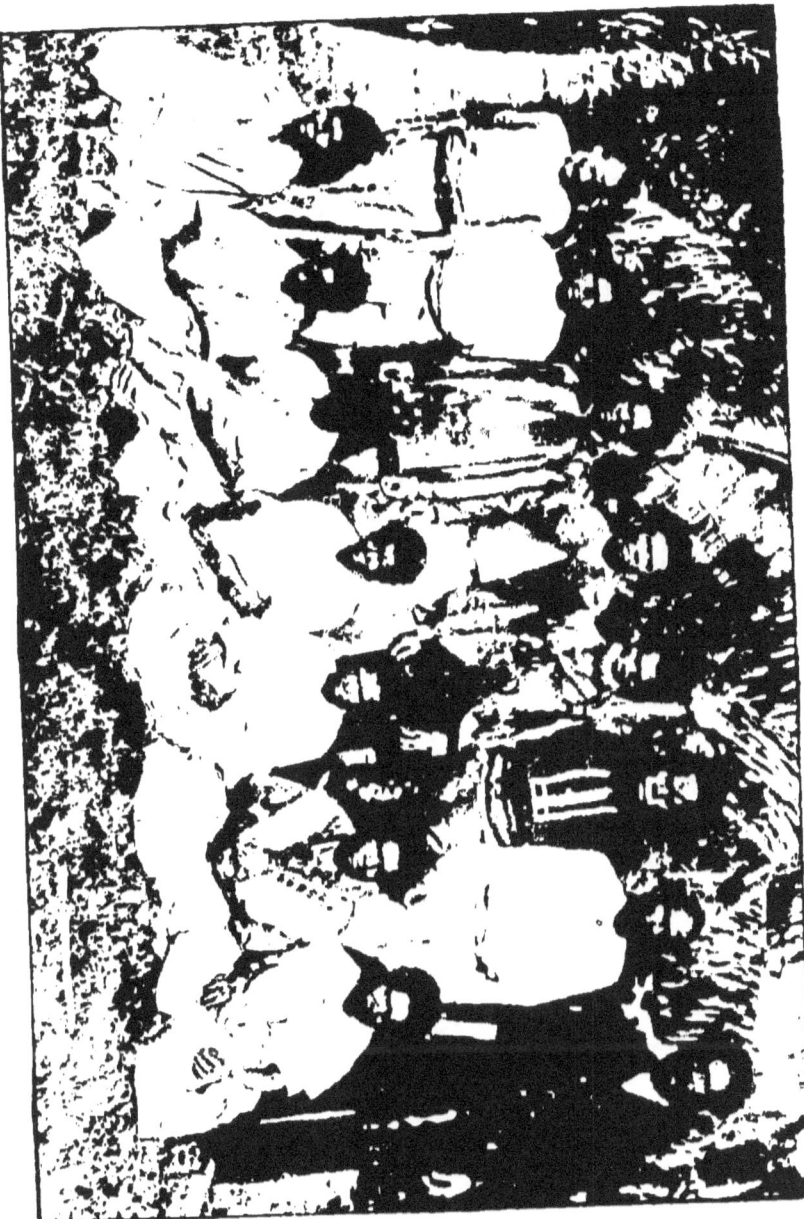

It was a happy, solemn time. In the course of my daily Bible reading I got this promise: "From this day will I bless thee."—Haggai ii. 19. May we indeed realise that precious promise! Mr Neilson expressed himself pleased with the general demeanour and appearance of our people. He took a severe attack of asthma and was detained for several days, thus causing, I have no doubt, much anxiety to Mrs Neilson, who was expecting him back on Monday.

Having made abstinence from daily kava-drinking a term of communion (on account of heathen associations), several were kept back, as they were not prepared to give it up. Like Felix, they put off, saying: "By and by, missi, we will join you." . . .

With heart's love to you all,
Ever yours,

AGNES C. P. WATT.

XV.
INCIDENTS—FOLKLORE.

COMPILED FROM LETTERS IN 1882-83.

... On the 17th of December, 1881, we went to Meiyahau, where Nalvatimi is teacher. We have only a reed church there, and one end is partitioned off for our use. A reed bench and a mattress stuffed with banana leaves form our bed. We hung up our mosquito curtains, which kept off lizards, centipedes, and rats, with which the house is infested. We had taken a number of traps which we got in Scotland from a good Midlothian friend, and every now and again I was awakened by the screams of our unwelcome visitors. On Sabbath I had to talk and sing from six in the morning to nine at night, and, need I say? I was perfectly exhausted. We had good meetings, and, for Tannese, they listened well. Next morning at sunrise we started again for Kwamera, overland; as good as four miles over rocks, up and down, now through bush, now sinking deep in sand, then over rough stones. We must have looked a grotesque company, for many natives followed us carrying our mattress, &c., on poles. Our own good house with its boarded floor looked so cool and inviting after camping out in a grass hut, and our hot walk that morning.

In April we had a sore trial. Wabu, who was born in December, 1869, and was thus far too young to be married, was dragged away and lifted into a canoe like a pig, and sent to a heathen district ten or twelve miles away, to be trained in heathen manners and dress, and at last become the wife of a heathen. Some time previous we heard that this was proposed; then a deputation waited on us. We said we could not agree to it, that they ought to let her stay until she was full-grown, and then the intended husband might come and get properly married; and, as she had long conformed to Christian customs and dress, they ought to have respect to the same. In vain were our expostulations. I felt it so keenly that I neither ate nor slept for three days. But time heals the sorest hearts, though I have still a tender spot for poor Wabu. She was so affectionate, that on my return from anywhere, when she came to meet me, she leapt up and clung to my neck like a big dog. Her cries when being dragged away rang in my ears for weeks. Dark, dark Tanna! She sells the bodies and souls of her children for a piece of pork and a drink of kava. Wabu was a good reader, could sew well, and was exceedingly smart at committing Scripture to memory. May her knowledge be blessed to herself and to those among whom she is sent. I have called her "Joseph"; for, like him, she is sold by her relatives into a heathen land. If only the Lord would bless His own word, so that she might become a light in a dark place! It is hard to see those you have thus watched over, taught, nursed and prayed for, compelled to return to their former life. We have had much to grieve us in this way from time to time. But the work is God's. Oh to be able always to remember that is so! . . .

STREAM AT KWAMERA.

The other day I noticed that the run of water was rather slow in the stream, and said: how dry the brook is! Oh, said Reriapui, the source is going dry. How is that? is it want of rain? I asked. Oh no, there has been plenty of rain lately; but the spring that bubbles up is going dry. Some one has bewitched it. There is nothing in earth or heaven that these people do not profess to be able to do. Even the story of Joshua commanding the sun to stand still would excite no wonder; for they believe they can do that. William saw a reed with its leaves tied together, and asked what it meant. He was told that if one saw the sun was going to set before a certain piece of work was finished, and was anxious such should not be the case, he tied up the leaves of a reed round its stem.

Many of their beliefs they hide from us, because they know that we white people laugh at them. It is only now and again that we find them out. There was an old woman to the west of us who professed to have communication with the unseen world. Many who had lost relatives sought unto her; and she brought beads, turkey-red, tobacco, pipes, and knives, from the departed. One man, a very sensible fellow in many respects, brought a knife he had got from a deceased son-in-law; I forget the maker's name, but it was a Sheffield-made knife. In vain we showed him the maker's name, and told him it was all a hoax, that the old witch was befooling him. He declared that he heard his deceased son-in-law speak to him, and tell him to stretch forth his hand in the direction of the voice and he would receive the knife. He did so, and there was the knife;—now, was not that proof positive?

Day by day new messages came from the dead; some sending for goods and others giving back return presents. As one piece of turkey-red is much the same as another; why, the poor deluded creatures actually believed that that very piece of turkey-red or that pipe which had been buried with their relative, was now sent back from Ipai (Hades)! Of course, we were branded as deceiving the people. We challenged the old witch and her believers to come and take something out of our house. If she did so, with closed doors, as she professed she was able to do, we would reward her liberally. "Oh, she was coming, she was coming; Missi, you will see that you are wrong. She can get things out of a house without opening the door; her deceased husband is the medium." I fancy she was more rogue than fool; she did not come, and, as a reason, she told the people that her husband refused to go to premises where there was so much worship. He could not work where the gospel was. Lately she has given up her trade, and is now a poor decrepit body, unable to walk.

We often purpose gathering together all the folk-lore, &c., of this people that we know; for, doubtless, many of their old beliefs are passing away.

One of their legends is very interesting to me. It seems to speak of a vague belief in immortality, of the depravity of our nature, of our willingness to remain in condemnation, of our rejection of eternal life, and our preference for the things of this world. The legend is this:—An old woman went to the sea along with her grandchild. She set the child down among the pandanus trees that fringe our beach, and went to the sea. There she cast off her old wrinkled skin, as lobsters cast their shells, and she became a young and beautiful woman. She returned to her grandchild and said : "My grandchild, let me take you in my arms." But the child refused, saying, "You are not my grandmother; she is old and wrinkled: and I'll not come to you." In vain the grandmother pled; the grandchild would not go to her. So after many entreaties, she said to the child : "I willed good for you, I offered you good, but you have chosen evil." So saying, she returned to the sea, put on the old skin, returned and called the child, who immediately went to her. Thus it was designed at first that we were not to die, only to be changed.

We have tried in several ways to find out who were the parents of the child, if the grandmother was anyone in particular, and where she was said to have come from; but the people say, "Oh, it is only a legend; we do not know any more about it."

There is a large rock on the other side of the island which is spoken of as "that old woman"; but whether they believe that her spirit dwells in the stone, or that she has turned into stone, I cannot make out.

Not far from us there are a great many stones representing different actions of, or articles belonging to, a being named Yanuavau. He must have been a person of like passions with themselves; for they showed us the impress of his knees where he knelt on a stone, raising himself up over a rock to see and admire the women who lived at the neighbouring point. There is also a cave full of moss-grown stones representing the many pigs he had killed at a great feast which he had made.

XVI.
IN PERILS BY SEA.

GENERAL LETTER, 1884.

—— Isn't it strange to be writing in February for a mail in August? but that is what I am now doing! January is past, and with it many cares; for in that month we have always experienced the worst hurricanes; but our fears were not realised this year, for we have had a pleasant month; only we are sadly ill-off for want of rain. The grass is parched and looks dead, and the natives are crying out at the loss of their crops. The rain-makers are at their wit's end, but remain unconvinced of their powerlessness. The Lord alone can dispel such darkness. . . .

The statistics of our mission do not figure largely on paper. One hundred at the principal service does not sound much, but when we know that many of these have come over long and rugged roads, I tell you that we feel glad to see them, and give them a hearty smile of welcome.

Many are inclined to ask, " Can any good thing come out of Tanna ? " I am grieved to hear people harping on the old story of how Tanna has resisted the gospel, of how long she has had it, and how strenuously she has opposed it. I found lately in a newspaper a statement to the effect that while Messrs Turner and Nisbet were on Tanna, mission work was commenced in earnest. True, but it was only *commenced*. Any one who knows the Tannese language, or indeed any of the New Hebrides languages, will agree with me, that it is but lame mission work one can do during the first twelve months. Besides, the Eastern island teachers never learned to speak Tannese properly. Even after fourteen years' chattering away in this tongue I have difficulty in making out the few sheets of *Samoan-Tannese* which I have seen. Thus I say the Tannese never had a fair offer of the gospel until a much later date, and even then in only one small part of the island. Why condemn the whole, for the backwardness of one or two tribes?

Tanna *is* a hard field. The network of superstition is close; the people cling with a tenacity worthy of a better cause to the traditions received from their fathers; but is *that* any reason why we should give them up, or that we should send men past Tanna, saying—"Wherever you go, don't go to Tanna: Tanna is doomed"? We trust in God that poor doomed Tanna shall yet shake herself from the dust, and arise and shine; and that on the last great day it shall be said of her as of Zion, "This man and that man was born there."

To us who labour down in this deep mine of heathenism, in darkness, loneliness, and longing,— receiving, from time to time, from those who are working in the light and sunshine of social life, messages to the effect that we are wasting our time, spending our strength in vain, and digging where gold can never be found,—it is cheering to realise that to our Master we stand or fall, and that work faithfully done in His name shall not only be rewarded, but rewarded openly. Besides, we never know when, in digging, we may strike the precious ore.

What an amount of discomfort we have endured in twelve months! During that time we have re-thatched and lined our own house, re-thatched the printing-office and store-room, taken down our school-house and put up a new church, and re-thatched Mr Neilson's old house at Port Resolution. Mr Neilson gave in his resignation at the Synod; and we are left in charge of his station; but the general opinion is that it would be well to let the people take charge of themselves, for a time at least. Thus, you see, we have the care of three stations—Mr Neilson's, Mr Paton's, and our own. Formerly the house was thatched with cocoa-nut leaves, which require to be renewed every two years. Now we have succeeded in procuring sugar-cane leaves, which at Kwamera last five years. A great quantity was carried for miles; yet in one day we bought nearly eleven hundred reedsful!

Next day a band of men and youths came to put it on; and just after the whole of one side of the roof was bared, down came a heavy shower. Soon the floor was flooded. We dragged our bedstead to one side and barely saved it. In despair I took off my shoes, and with a long-handled broom switched out a good deal, and so kept down the water on the floor.

Things did look a bit dreary, and led me to exclaim: "Who would be a missionary's wife?" and how many hundreds a year more would it take to induce me to continue such a life? But we have higher motives to live for.

However, the shower, though hearty, was soon over; the sun shone out again, all became dry, and the men were again at work. When one half was done we gave them a lunch of rice and tea; and as both we and our boatmen were anxious to be home again, we urged them to go on with the other half, and by sunset all was finished. Meanwhile, the women had been cooking; and two pigs, one fowl, and a lot of native puddings were brought and laid down at the back door, as a present to the workers. We gave return presents, and paid for the thatch and labour.

We had much to discourage us during February. About the beginning of the month, a promising young man died, and his death threatened to shake his father's reason. The father had begun to come regularly to church, and had cut off his long hair, wore clothes, and was otherwise a hopeful character, but this sudden and unexpected blow was too much for him. On Sabbath 10th, we went inland to visit him, and to hold service at his village. Whether he hid or not, I cannot tell, but he was not there; and as Mr Watt had to preach at other villages, he and a teacher went on, while I and a little lad waited patiently. A long weary wait we had, but, just before sundown, Tero came. He looked wild and restless, but I spoke kindly to him, and tried to impress on him the fact that sickness is in God's hand alone, and even if some one had so hated his son as to do what he believed would cause death, it was not his to avenge, but that God would do so. He listened to all I said, and promised not to

OLD MISSION HOUSE, PORT RESOLUTION.

take revenge, and by and by to resume his church-going. In the gloaming I returned home, not over sanguine of his promise, but hoping for the best. On the Friday following, just at sundown, a poor, miserable wretch was crossing from the water's edge to the "kava-house," carrying a bottle of water to prepare his evening potion, which was being chewed by a little boy, when he discovered Tero peering at him through the surrounding under-scrub. The poor victim said, "Tero, wherefore art thou here?" The reply was a shot that laid him low, followed by a volley from the people who had been hid in the bush, who now rushed out and fired on the lifeless body. This over, they fled and left Kauki to lie till some of our servants—who were the first to recover from the shock of so much musketry fired close to our house—took up the mangled body and buried it. Thus Kauki, well and intent on heathenism at sundown, was laid in his grave ere another day had dawned. He was a noted "nahak-taker," a notorious thief, and an arch deceiver. No actual war followed, but the state of excitement consequent on such a tragic occurrence thinned our previously well-filled church. I indeed feared that we would have no worshippers on the following Sabbath, but upwards of fifty came, and soon after it rose to seventy, and continued so. According to native ideas, revenge must yet be taken; but a better spirit rules many of the aggrieved people, and we trust that peaceful counsels may prevail.

When the "Dayspring" came, Dr and Mrs Gunn came ashore to stay with us while the vessel went north.

William had arranged to go for arrowroot to Port Resolution and thence to Weasisi, and Dr and Mrs Gunn expressed a wish to accompany him.

We intended to go, stay one night at each place, and then return home. So, taking what was needful for a night's encampment, we started. The sun was strong, and there was no wind; but we were sick. We landed at Port Resolution, had a cup of tea, and again resumed our voyage—the voyage that gave us such experiences that we won't seek another for many a day. I call it our famous trip; William says, *infamous*. We reached Weasisi that afternoon, and left next day at 1 p.m. It wasn't looking over bright, but little did we think that we would take from that hour till eight p.m. to reach our destination. As we passed the volcano or Sulphur Bay, darkness fell on us. Though the flame from the volcano seemed lurid and terrible, we were glad to watch its ever-recurring eruptions. The men were worn out pulling, but as the moon was rising, we struggled on for Port Resolution; and, although we had but an empty house without a fire to welcome us, we felt glad to be thus far on our journey. We got a fire lit, and tea made, and having thanked the God of life for preservation, retired to rest. I slept little, as I knew from the howling of the wind that we should be prevented from getting to Kwamera. The note in my daily journal speaks volumes. Here it is—Thursday 8th. Still blowing, and no food, but the "Caledonia" (French ship) came into the harbour in the afternoon, and my spirits rose. Dr Gunn and William boarded the "Caledonia" for supplies, and returned laden with much kindness. The captain would take nothing, but only asked them to give a few francs as a contribution to the "Company." Mrs Gunn and I did our best at housekeeping under the difficulties, and so we lived until Monday, 12th May.

We rested the Seventh day, according to the Commandment, and had two services with those who met for worship. On Monday morning, two of our boat's crew, who had walked to a point of land where the sea is usually roughest, pronounced it practicable. They and William would go round in the boat, while the Gunns and I walked over a neck of land and saved a nasty point. This agreed to, we dismantled our beds, packed up what was to go with us, and divided all our cooked food. The boat started, and we did the same. We had a pleasant walk, and got some cocoa-nuts to drink on the way; so in good spirits we emerged from the bush to see our boat careering along like a racehorse. Our spirits sank; but how could we go back? All our necessaries of life were in the boat, and it could not turn; while once home we would be all right. On William and the natives landing and saying that they had been out in worse days, we put a brave face on it, and stepped into the boat. The men pulled with a will, and soon we had up sail and were away before wind and sea at a tremendous rate. We thought that the worst was past, and hoped that the further on we went, the calmer it would become. But alas! other sad experiences were in store for us. The wind was puffy, and the sea was evidently rising. Now and again a spray broke over us, but the good boat mounted every wave; and the taking in of a spray was only followed by a shake of the head from the recipient and a laugh from the spectators. Already we were in sight of our house. Having risen over so many waves, and having kept ourselves pretty comfortable by constant bailing, we were hopeful. As we thus careered along, cheered by the steersman's "It's all right," and the prospect of soon being on shore, a heavy wave is seen coming behind us. It breaks over my devoted head with a heavy thud, fills the boat, so that we are now wet from above, and our feet and legs in water. Things are floating! Bail, for your life! Away with that paltry meat tin, and get a bucket! Vahai springs over two thwarts, and Dr Gunn renders efficient help; while Mrs Gunn looks after her sleeping infant gasping for breath—having been rudely awakened by a wave dashing on his face and filling his little mouth with salt water. Old Niath looked round him in bewilderment, then recollecting his position, set to and bailed also; only he poured the water on Dr Gunn's legs instead of over the side. To this the Doctor objected, and calling the good man's attention to the fact, he came to his senses. Another wave may come and swamp us; but a few more plunges and we are landed on the beach, like drowned rats, hardly able to crawl with the weight of water in our clothes.

Thus were we baptised in the cloud and in the sea; nay, we had passed through the sea. As we looked out on the still rising sea, after a cup of warm tea and a change of clothing, we felt more than ever what a merciful providence had been vouchsafed to us. I told Mrs Gunn she had indeed experienced the romance of "a missionary's holiday trip."

XVII.
ON ANIWA.

COMPILED.

For a number of years Mr and Mrs Watt were appointed by the Mission Synod, at the request of Mr (now Dr) Paton, to take charge of the work on Aniwa during his absence. Besides visiting that island by boat from Tanna, they usually went over in the "Dayspring" when on her way north, and stayed with the people until the vessel returned. Their visit usually lasted from six to eight weeks at a time. Some of the most interesting references to these visits are presented in this chapter.

1882. Aniwa. We arrived here on the 1st July. We were landed, with all our train, including goats, kids, helps, boxes, &c., and the vessel went away north before seven a.m.

We found much to give encouragement. The people were glad to see us, and clamorous for clothing. In two days I had disposed of one hundred girdles (fathoms of calico) for men; cut, pinned, and saw made, twenty women's dresses. Another day I cut eleven. My fingers were blistered. I got a fowl for a dress; still they came and came till I had torn up all the sheets I could spare, and had even made dresses out of a sofa cover. My inventive powers were severely taxed; every scrap I had was used; even the parings of the dresses were sewn together for a handkerchief. I was indeed sorry I could give them no more; it was so pleasant to see them wish clothing, and be glad to buy it.

On the second day after our arrival, they gave us a present of four pigs and twelve fowls, with a pile of yams. We gave a return present of shirts, calico, axes, and soap. . . . From what I have said, you will see I have not been idle. I have had to write all this to-day, with many interruptions; bartering, giving out medicine, and seeing my new cook, who, by the way, is an Erromangan, and cannot speak Tannese; so we carry on our conversation in broken English, thus: "What for you no cook yam?" "You no speak me before." "You tell woman belong you, he eat this fellow yam." "He no like him," &c., &c. William accuses me for writing "jumpy" letters. If you think this one "jumpy," just remember all I have to do.

After the Communion here we returned to Kwamera.

1883. We arrived here on the 9th July, about five p.m. We got a hearty reception on the shore, and the people carried up our baggage at once, though the Mission house is a good way off. As the sun was down, and all was dark in the empty house, I did feel like entering a dungeon. The rooms had been whitewashed three months before, but no one had been inside since; and cobwebs can be spun in three days. The rats had been trying what sort of a meal they could make out of the straw palliasses, and they did not look inviting after their doings. However, after sweeping up, we got out our napery and stores, and had a fairly comfortable tea, and a good night's rest. On the afternoon of Thursday, 12th, Mr Watt gave out new books in the church, and I never saw such anxiety manifested for the Word. The people seemed quite desperate when they knew the Gospel of John had run done.

The darkest-hearted man (Nesi) in this island has now begun to attend church; so that heathenism can truly be called a thing of the past, as far as open profession is concerned.

I have had a great deal to do in millinery and dressmaking. The week before the Communion we were kept busy from morning till night—so many wanted new dresses, and there was so little time to prepare them.

On Sabbath, August 5th, fifty-nine sat down at the Lord's Table. On the previous Friday, which was our Fast-day, Mr Watt baptised five adults and ten children. The little children specially interested me. In one case two little boys and their sister stood in a group, being admitted on the faith of their mother, who had just been baptised. Their father is still outside the pale of the church, though a regular attender. The little ones looked up so enquiringly into Mr Watt's face as he sprinkled each in the name of the Triune God. I thought of the Saviour's words: "Except ye become as little children."

One of the unusual events that took place while we were here was a *divorce*. A young man and woman were married some few years ago because their parents and guardians had arranged it; but they publicly disowned each other, and were causing great scandal. Lately, the wife, who has all along been a gipsy, eloped with another man. The deserted husband wished divorce, and all the island concurred. On Wednesday, after the prayer-meeting, in presence of the whole congregation, the husband and wife stood side by side in front of the missionary and declared their desire for divorce. The missionary read, in their own language, all the Scripture on the subject; and after a short address declared them put asunder. The divorced husband then left her side and went to his seat; while the claimant came forward, and they were formally married: the bride giving as emphatic a "yes" to the question whether she would marry this man or not, as she had given when she declined the former. I sincerely hope this is the end of the unhappy affair.

1884. On Tuesday, 24th June, we started on our watery way. When we reached Futuna, it was blowing hard, so I did not go on shore, but Mr Watt did, and, through some mistake, we did not get from there that night. Next day, the boat went in and brought off our passengers, and we sailed away for Aniwa, where we landed at daybreak, after a rough night— Messrs Mackenzie, Fraser, Murray, and two children accompanying us. Having only two tea-cups, we had to use tin pannikins, but our friends expressed much relish for the tea and sweet milk (thanks to Mrs Annand, who had given us two milk goats). Three boat loads brought in all our things; our friends left us, and we began our third annual visit to Aniwa. When once our boxes were unpacked, and the necessaries of life conveniently laid out, we began to feel somewhat at home. The people gave us a very hearty welcome, and we found things in fair order. An attempt to steal a girl last year after we left, and of which we heard at the time, had caused some unpleasant feeling, but it went no further; and since we came, the man who wished to steal her has come again to church, and is now attending the candidates' class. He has made considerable progress in reading during the past year, and we earnestly trust the Word may be blessed to him, and that soon he may become a help to us and the good cause here. We are pleased to note the marked advance in reading during the year; it speaks well for the teachers, who only get £10 divided among six of them. Soon after our arrival, we set the people on to their annual contribution of arrowroot; and after the grown up people had made theirs, Mr Watt proposed that the young people should follow the example of the children at Aname and Kwamera, and make some as their special love-token, for they had already assisted the grown up people.

It was very encouraging to see one after another of these bright boys and girls coming along, laden with a basket of the raw material, having scoured the bush in search of it, and now bringing it to be weighed, for we wished to see who had gathered most. Even after all had brought in their offering, and the day had been fixed for grating it, a few rose at daybreak and searched for more, thus supplementing their previous lot. The making day was a great day, and from early morning till late in the evening these young people scraped, grated, and washed at arrowroot. So now we have the pleasure of saying they have made a whole cask.

Yesterday, July 25th, the year's contribution was exhibited in church, and formally dedicated to the Lord, as a free-will offering for the Gospel. We have celebrated here three Christian marriages this year. As has been the custom, the three brides never saw the dresses they were to be married in, till within half an hour of going to church. I then called them in, arraying them in nice print robes and new straw hats, and a silver(-less) ring each. They were quite delighted. In the meantime, the bridegrooms were dressing somewhere else; I had given them a trifling present of clothing. Two of the lads had been in the colonies, and turned out in splendid style, even to boots. (Had they any socks?) I accompanied the brides to church, and each sat down in front of the pulpit, by the side of her respective betrothed, but in a manner that would have made you laugh, as each one was more anxious than the other to keep at a respectable distance. After the prayer meeting (for it was the weekly prayer meeting day), the three couples stood up in the presence of the congregation, and were solemnly married. Then came the benediction, and, headed by the missionary and his wife, the whole congregation shook hands with the happy couples, wishing them much joy. We then all separated, the brides going out at the one door, and the bridegrooms at the other, as if nothing had happened. We were just in the heat of the arrowroot-making, but as I stood a minute to speak to some one at the church door, fancy my surprise when, on entering the house, I found one of the bridegrooms with a big sheet full of arrowroot on his back; he had thrown off his coat, and was thus giving a helping hand at putting past the arrowroot for the night. So you see we have no stealing away of the happy pair, no wedding tour, no honeymoon holiday; but three couples are sensibly married, and seem well matched. Next day there was a big feast, almost like a welcome home, and the minister got his marriage fees, in the shape of two large pigs and five fowls, from two of the couples, and one fowl from the third, with the promise of something better by and by.

It is rather unfortunate that our mail and our visit to Aniwa come together; for while here I have such an amount of cutting and pinning of dresses, repairing of books, &c., while Mr Watt has school examinations, elders' and teachers' meetings, that our time is much occupied. Last week we had an ordination of five deacons—one of them goes as a teacher to Tanna. We are also sending out another teacher and his wife to Futuna. Two years ago we sent out the first teachers from Aniwa, a couple and a single man; and last year a couple left to help at Weasisi. (The first Aniwan teachers on Tanna were Natshia and wife, and Pavenga. The couple who went to Weasisi last year were Litsi sori and her husband Nuperau.)

On Sabbath, 3rd August, we joined with the people in commemorating the death of our common Lord. We numbered from fifty to sixty, and were much encouraged to see the progress in the appearance of this band, compared with a similar company that sat down some years ago ; and we earnestly hope that the outward improvement is an indication of advance in heart.

1885. We have had charge of this island for four years, and this year we were much gratified by seeing the progress that had been made in the art of reading. We utilise the best readers by employing them to read the Scripture for the day, both on Sabbaths and at the Wednesday Prayer Meeting. It is amusing to see each take his turn. It may be an old man with spectacles in the morning and a child of twelve or fifteen in the afternoon. To be deprived of one's turn is regarded as a loss, and to have one's name struck out is considered a disgrace. We baptised seven : five infants, one man, and his son about ten years of age. The man is by birth a Tannaman, but was adopted here in infancy. His name is Nesi, and he has been a notorious character. For years he was the dread of Mrs Paton's life, and a decided opponent of the gospel. Two years ago we spoke earnestly to him and he promised to reform. Last year he began to read, and we commended him for so doing, telling him to ask God to bless the Word to him. He has attended the catechumens' class for a year, and professes to have undergone a change. As all the elders esteem him worthy, we have, at his own earnest request, admitted him to the membership of the church. He is a clever man, and we hope he may yet be a power for good in his own land.

Till we came here, none had left the island on Mission service, as teacher or servant. Three years ago we sent three to Weasisi, and since then others have gone there. Last year we placed one couple at Port Resolution and sent another to Futuna. The man was an elder in the church, and very energetic, though far from strong. Alas, in a few short months, he and his son fell ill and died. . . . Even to write this, though months have passed, wrings my inmost heart. I feel so deeply for the afflicted woman losing first her only child, and then her husband, while she was a stranger in a strange land.

On the 19th of August the "Dayspring" reached Aniwa, and our pleasant visit was at an end. The natives cheered us as we went off, with a thorough British "Hip, hip, hurrah!" We had only eighteen miles between us and our destination, and as the weather was moderating, we thought we were sure to be there next morning. One night of cockroaches wasn't much; and so comforted, we went to our bunks. But alas! next morning, "No landing at Port Resolution." "Well, let's try Weasisi." Away we go, and I feel the squeamishness vanish before the hopes of landing. Though we would be twenty miles from Kwamera at Weasisi, and might undergo great discomfort in the boat voyage, still, the present being disagreeable, we will shut our eyes to the future. Knowing that we are nearing Weasisi, I rush on deck just in time to hear the captain say, "No landing here to-day." To-morrow is Sabbath, we can do nothing till Monday. No landsman, none save those who have been in a wee 150 ton vessel in a stormy sea can tell how miserable one feels in such a position. *Mal de mer*, like toothache, elicits little sympathy, but both try the temper in no small degree. With her head to the sea, under easy sail, the poor tossed "Dayspring" ploughed into the waste of waters. I retired to my little stuffy cabin, where in a small bunk I got fixed or jammed, and, having my head down, felt comparatively comfortable. All that day, and Sabbath, and till three p.m. on Monday, we did penance in our floating, tumbling prison.

On Monday we called at Futuna, and found the Gunns well, then stood away for Tanna, for now wind and sea were really going down. At break of day we stood in for Port Resolution, but the wind headed us off, then it fell calm, and it looked almost as if we wouldn't get landed that day. However, a gentle breeze brought us to Kwamera, and we took it first, though we knew that as soon as possible we should have to go back in our boat to Port Resolution.

1888. Aniwa is a delightful place to land at. Although the sea was high outside, it was wonderful the shelter we got from this little, low-lying island. As we ran close along the shore we heard the glad shouts of the people rejoicing at our approach; and just as the "Dayspring" was wearing round in order to lower her boat, one on shore called out in English: "Ready, bout"!

What a welcome we got on shore! But, as the vessel was in a hurry, we told them to show their joy by quickly getting some pigs, fowls, and oranges for the ship. This was soon done and all put into the boat, ready for a start.

Every day has been well filled with useful work, and a good amount of it.

The forms or pews for which they have paid in arrowroot are expected by the "Dayspring"; so we set them on to put a lime floor in the church, and also to thatch one side of the roof. While some were mixing lime, and plastering, the women and frailer men were making sugar-cane leaf thatch. What the Aniwans do, they do heartily, so in less than a fortnight all was finished. Meantime, I took ill with fever, and vomiting, and was very miserable for eight days. During my enforced retirement, the poor missionary was terribly worried, having so much to attend to. He was medical attendant, general store dealer, and overseer of labour; had to hold session meetings and general consultations; and one day he had a marriage. Ill in bed, I had to direct the dressing of the bride; for we always deck out the young couple, and they, in return, sometimes give us a present as a marriage fee. In this case, as they were people of some importance, we got a splendid porker, some fowls, and a pile of yams. Some one has remarked, that the advantage of receiving a present is, that you can give the donor far more than its value in return, and feel that you are not wronging him.

On the Monday after the Communion we had our Thanksgiving service, at which we laid in front of the pulpit, as is the custom, the annual contribution of arrowroot.

We received the boxes sent by Mrs Mackie, South Yarra, and Mrs Boyd, South Melbourne, and found them very useful. Seventy-three people had weeded and cleared all the Mission ground. We gave them each as much print as would make a lava-lava; besides, we had eighteen regular sweepers of premises. Of three dozen dresses and fifty hats I had brought from Kwamera not one is left. Everything goes here. Why, even old shirt fronts or "dickeys" have been made to serve as garments. Two seamed together formed a little boy's blouse. Last Sabbath, while looking at some young darkies thus arrayed, walking out and in at their pleasure, during service, I thought how much harder a mother's life is at home, where the care of a large "small" family may keep her from church for nearly twenty years. Here no one is left at home. Whenever the mother can come the infant is brought, and the stirring "two or three-year-olds" do not tend to quietness in church. I carry a bag of broken biscuits and hush many an impatient spirit with them, until I am charged by the missionary with giving too much attention to the loaves and fishes. But I dearly love the little brownies, and often picture the time when their parents, having served their own generation and fallen on sleep, the promise will be fulfilled, "Instead of thy fathers shall be thy children."

I have called this place my Bethany; where, after the turmoil of Tanna, we enjoy comparative rest among more like-minded spirits than are in the "great land" (Tana sorè). This year it is a perfect land of Goshen. I never saw food so abundant, large yams and plenty of them, while the orange crop has been so great that, as the natives express it, "They are weak to eat them."

We expect the "Dayspring" any day now to take us to Tanna, and we hope and pray for good weather for our landing there.

I am tired with writing to-day, so 1 crave you to be lenient in your criticisms and continuous in your help. Be not like the man of whom the Rev. R. M. Thornton of London told, who said, "I've given a shilling a year for the last twenty years, and do you mean to tell me that the heathen are not converted yet!"

A. C. P. WATT.

XVIII.
A MONOTONOUS SUMMER.

GENERAL LETTER, 1885.

As the "Dayspring" will soon again be leaving for the colonies, I suppose you will look for a few more jottings from my daybook. So little to interest and encourage has taken place since the last "General" left, that I had almost made up my mind to write none this trip; but the deep interest many express in these, causes me again to pen a few rambling sentences. One word would express all that has occurred in the past half-year, viz., *Monotony*. Nothing striking has occurred. Things go on in the even tenor of their way,—we hope advancing; but daily we feel how suitable the passage of Scripture is to our case, ".Ye have need of patience." Emphatically we have; for the night of toil is proving long. In dark times I try to remember that the darkest hour often precedes the dawn, and thus hope against hope; or else cry out, "Oh that my head were waters, and mine eyes a fountain of tears, that I might weep day and night." Not that crying does them any good, while it gives me a violent headache! It makes me feel desperate at times to see so many going down to death eternal, and we cannot save them. Daily do I remember that hundreds of Foundry Boys and Girls say that they are praying for Tanna, and yet the light is weak. We are a small and feeble flock, while the heathen are numerous, and talk *big*, as in the Second Psalm. Nahi-abba has been raised up from the gates of death—where he longed for and got our daily administrations—only to return again to his heathenism. This is the time of year when feasting and dancing goes on, and so engrossed are the majority in these affairs that they have no ear for anything else.

The past history of Missions on Tanna has been a sad one, and, in our experience, the present is not unlike the past. For instance, since the formation of a church we have lost two of the four who first joined us, and these the two youngest and most promising. Now this tells sadly on our work, as many say, "See how the Christians die! They become Christians, fall into sin, and are cut off; therefore shun the Gospel, and you may live as you like." You and I know how silly such reasoning is, but yet we are altogether unable to uproot this belief. About a month ago, a young woman, who had identified herself with the worship, died, leaving a helpless infant. Her death, too, has been a sore blow, and has taken many away from attending the church. How foolish! you say; so do I, nevertheless it is true. "This people's eyes are closed, lest they see." Like the Church at Pergamos, we dwell where Satan's seat is. I would despair, did I not know that the Gospel is the power of God, and that it is that Gospel we preach.

Had we but an outpouring of the Spirit, what an incoming there would be! So many know the truth theoretically. We are like a ship ready waiting for

wind, every sail set; but what if there is no wind?
"Ye have need of patience." . . .

This has been the finest hot season we have spent. It has been quite unique; and were all the seasons like it, half the misery of our life would be gone. We have neither had a blow, nor a big sea, nor an earthquake. Besides, I have enjoyed exceptionally good health; not for years have I felt so well. This only confirms the medical man's opinion, that my trouble was on the nerves; so, there being nothing to cause them to tingle has permitted me to enjoy perfect health. In the end of March and beginning of April, William had a severe illness, which ended in his vomiting a little blood. He had excruciating pain during the night previous to this occurrence, but after that he soon recovered. These are the times when we long for human sympathy, and would fain have medical advice. True, Dr Gunn is on Futuna, and we can see his rocky Ailsa-Craig-looking-island out of our windows, but fifty miles of ocean divide us, with no conveyance save an open boat. In all likelihood, going there would be impracticable, and so would his coming here, even although we could bottle up our sickness until he arrived. In vain I try to persuade William that we are getting old—having been seventeen years in the Mission field, and that soon we must retire. He, however, shows me how some of our New Hebrides folks were as old as he when they entered the field, and yet laboured for over twenty years. So I have to keep quiet. Rest will be very sweet when it comes; that is, if I *can* rest.

January and February were filled up with the monotony of daily life—cutting and sewing dresses, reading proof sheets, correcting and printing Exodus as far as the end of the Ten Commandments, making and printing a number of new hymns, which brings our collection up to *sixty-nine*. The chief favourite among the new ones is "The Great Physician." I must send home a copy to the Glasgow Foundry Boys' Society, from whose Press they were printed. . . .

The event of March was the opening of the new church at Ituko, where Yamen was settled in the end of last year, and where we have had more to encourage us than at any previous station. Almost without exception, every man, woman, and child lent a willing, helping hand in its erection, and that without any hope of fee or reward. On the 26th of March the place was formally opened, by our going up and holding a service in it. We arrived in the afternoon, the people there having prepared food for us and ours. We made them a present of fifty calico girdles, besides shirts and women's dresses and other small articles. They gave us four pigs and fifteen fowls. We gave returns for these next day, as we wished ours to be a free gift, showing our appreciation of their good-feeling.

In the evening, we had a Magic Lantern display to a crowded house, people having come miles to see it. The pictures were explained, and in that way we hope some heard the gospel who would not attend a service either in church or the open air.

We could not get home, so had to remain all night. We were a party of twenty-two, and slept in the church. We had just settled down comfortably when all sprang to their feet, shouting "yasuk, yasuk" (a rat, a rat!) This, you may be sure, drove all sleep from our eyes, and, like Paul, "we wished for day." In vain I tried to compose myself; my fertile imagination made me apprehensive of rats on every hand. At last I took refuge on the preacher's platform, and although it was only four feet long and railed on three sides, I contrived "to double myself up a wee!" I had some snatches of sleep, now and again awaking to realise where I was, have a look round on my sable companions on the floor below, or listen to hear if William were sleeping or not. We burned a Rowatt lamp, the gift of that generous friend, now no more; and each group of natives had a fire, round which they slept. In the morning I rose refreshed, but poor William had never slept a wink. We got some of the past day's food warmed up, and had a "bite" before we left. We made speedily for home, whither we were soon followed by nearly the whole population, who had intended to escort us, had we not stolen a march upon them by getting away so early in the morning. All that day we held a levee; William being loth to lose so good an opportunity of conversing with them on various and vital subjects. But, alas, we had to pay for it. I had to go to bed with a rending nervous headache, and William was never quite well from that time until he vomited the blood.

In April, there was a triple cold-blooded murder within two miles of our door. Three men, all relations—two of them being father and son—were shot and clubbed to death by relatives, who lived in the same village, and drank kava together nightly in the same house. They were reputed to be takers of nahak, and had given some other cause of offence; so they were summarily dealt with. But as it was like a family quarrel, and nearly all acknowledged that they ought to die, it caused no excitement. The nearest relatives were the murderers. Had others done it, they would have been the avengers of blood. The whole thing has passed away without even being a nine days' wonder. . . .

The "Dayspring" brought me *forty-seven* letters! Wasn't that a feast? But I had to wait a wee before devouring them, as our friends Mr and Mrs Robertson, and our new fellow-labourers Mr and Mrs Charles Murray, had come on shore to see us. Though always glad to entertain visitors, we are specially so when they come as these did, through a rough sea. Mrs Murray was drenched with salt water. It did my heart good to see such a thorough Scotch woman. Though, like ourselves, supported by the Presbyterian Church of New Zealand, and thus in a special sense our fellow-labourers, they will not work on Tanna, but take up the standard on Ambrim, in place of their brother, Mr W. B. Murray, whose failing health has obliged him to leave the field. His case is sad; having studied for long years to specially qualify himself for the work, and then, when almost reaching the goal, to have contracted the disease which has cut off his Mission life ere it was well begun. God's ways are mysterious!

After lunch our friends left, and we sat down to our mental feast. Before midnight I had all my letters devoured, but not without inducing a most excruciating headache. Really, how much pain can be compressed into a small head! Once and again I poured cold water on it, but the relief was only momentary.

However, sleep came to the rescue and soothed the pain. Next day it was nearly gone. . . .

October 20th brought the cry of "Sail oh!" at break of day. But alas, the "Dayspring" is carrying her flag half mast high. This kept us in suspense, wondering what evil tidings she wished to prepare us for. On the boat reaching the shore we heard of the sudden death of Mrs Inglis. In her a mother in Israel has passed away. To us who came here in the somewhat early days of the Mission, her house always looked like home. We also heard that Mr W. B. Murray had entered into his rest. He lay down at night asking for refreshing sleep, being in great distress through shortness of breath. His prayer was heard, for ere day dawned he passed calmly and peacefully away. "So He giveth His beloved sleep."

God's ways are truly very mysterious, for to our minds Mr Murray was peculiarly well fitted for work, and we thought him a great acquisition to our Mission; but the Highest has decided otherwise, for just as he had girded on his armour, the call came to enter into his rest.
. . . By the afternoon all our goods were stored, and after an early cup of tea, William went on board to visit Aniwa, and I read letters till

"The wee short hour ayont the twal."

Next day I had Yamen in to open one of the Foundry Boys' boxes for the precious Hunter's Cough Mixture, to give to a poor little baby that was suffering, and keeping its parents awake as well. Ten drops that night procured sleep to all parties concerned, and in less than a week the cough had disappeared.

On the second day William returned, having been to Aniwa and set up a tank there, then on to Port Resolution and landed a tank there. I fancy that tank did good, for now the people see that we mean to live there. They seemed to look on us as interlopers, coming into their missionary's house and claiming his tank, when really it was more theirs than ours. A few days after that, we went round to Port Resolution by boat. Fortunately, we had a fine day, but even with it all, Nalupas and Naume, my bedroom maids, were both sick. The latter being quite unable to look after her two-year-old baby, I took little Toi in my lap, and with my strong arms round him he was comforted; for this was his first voyage by boat. We got round in good time, and received a very hearty welcome. The following day the people helped us well in getting the tank uphill and into its place. On both Saturday evenings we have had native puddings brought to us for our next day's dinner. On the second Saturday, while some boys and girls stood round, one remarked that it was cooking day; and I said, "Oh, dear me, I forgot to order a pudding for to-morrow." Fancy my amazement and gratitude when a woman brought one at sundown, and on my remarking how opportunely it had come, she replied that her little son had told her to make it, owing to my remarks in the morning. Wasn't it good of him?

You remark in your letters that surely we are never done thatching or whitewashing. Well, note that we did neither during our two last trips to Port Resolution. But we put on the storm-rigging this last visit, and were reminded by the teacher that we will require to re-thatch next year. Oh dear, isn't it trying, and yet what can we do? Through the generosity of friends, we have been able to be much more liberal of late. One and another have got clothing from us. About a month ago, we sent a parcel to an interesting district called "Isumu," where a form of worship has been kept up for a long time, and where Kauraka, a Tannaman, has a grass church, assembling a few people every Sabbath, although he never received any pay from us. He cannot read, and has small knowledge of the "way of life," but still he gropes away. While we were at Epi this year, Narpai (one of our old girls) and Matthew made a runaway marriage, and fled to that district. After being there for a few weeks, of their own accord they took the lead in conducting service—Narpai reading the Scriptures and leading the hymns (for she is a splendid singer), and Matthew addressing the people. God can and does make use of very unworthy means for His own purposes; and we pray that even this dim light may do something to illumine the surrounding darkness. They sent lately for books (you know the Tannese have a great dread of books), and when we sent them we sent also some shirts, women's dresses, and handkerchiefs as turbans. The shirts came out of the Green Street boxes and the handkerchiefs out of the Foundry Boys' box. We feel deeply grateful to Miss Brown and others in Great Hamilton Street Congregation, and our old tried friends the G.F.B.R.S., for sending us such valuable clothing. We are thus reminded that we are not forgotten, and reproved for our lack of faith. While we are plodding along, thinking we are forgotten, kind hearts are planning, and nimble fingers are sewing surprise gifts for us. There was one item in Miss Mackay's parcel specially prized by me, and that was the "Life of General Gordon." In a place like this, where nothing happens, where letters are months old when we get them, and where new books are rarely seen, such a book is worth its weight in gold. . . . What a spice of novelty there was about it! I read it at once, and have enjoyed it very much. If you could only read through my present mail of thirty-five letters, you would find that much of Gordon's experience and many of his sayings have taken a deep hold on my mind. I cannot help feeling that in many ways his experiences and ours are the same, while some of his remarks are so strikingly applicable to our circumstances that I cannot help repeating them.

The Bible says that he who soweth, weepeth; and I believe that invariably the sower has the mournful part to perform, for he must wait and maybe even die ere the reaping time comes. I have been thinking a great deal to-day of that passage of Scripture, "Blessed are the dead which die in the Lord: . . . they rest from their labours; and their works do follow them." I infer that though their works do follow them, they often have not seen the fruit of their labours while on earth. "One soweth and another reapeth," but I can't help envying the man who reaps. We have laboured long, we have spared no pains, we have shrunk from no danger in seeking the salvation of Tanna. Once and again have we hailed a gleam of light, thinking it the dawning of the day; as often have we seen it fade away and the darkness grow more intense.

I fancy we are down in the valley of humiliation just now. Two years ago, and for months before that, we had over one hundred at our principal service, and we had grave thoughts of "letting out" our church to accommodate the increasing numbers. A young lad died; his father believed he was killed by "nahak," and all we could say was of no avail. The father and a band of armed men came down, and, a few yards from our door, riddled with bullets a poor defenceless man. That caused a scattering of the tribes and a thinning of our congregation from which we have not yet recovered. Last year sickness and death were busy, and several who had identified themselves with the gospel were cut off in the prime of life; *that* raised a hatred to the worship which has not yet subsided. This year one of our two male church members fell into sin, and has taken to kava-drinking. This has been the hardest blow of all to me, for while I grieve at seeing the advance moving so slowly, that is as nothing compared to witnessing this going back. I am doubly thankful that Naurita (the other male church member) retains his integrity and proves a true friend to us.

You have all heard of Nahi-abba, our notorious chief. He has always been opposed to the gospel, but nevertheless sent his wife to church. Last year he was at death's door, and begged for medicine, daily visits, and prayer. He recovered; his first act was to perform a heathen rite on his son, shun us in every way, and indeed let us know that we were not wanted. Again he became sick; we again visited and prayed with him, giving him cordials and medicine; once more he has recovered, only to be tenfold more a child of hell than before; and now he has forbidden his wife to come to church, and is doing all he can to prevent others. Thus far he has been successful, for the lads in his village have not been to church since his wife ceased coming. "Render unto Cæsar the things that are Cæsar's" is the Saviour's command, so we always pay him deference as the chief, and give him a small present each time the "Dayspring" comes from the colonies. Though we knew from others of his more decided opposition lately, still we took no notice of the fact, and sent him the usual "custom dues" as I call them. Nancy took the present along—a piece of calico, some biscuits, and a piece of salt meat. He received them graciously, but so far he manifests no softening towards our message. As I have already told you, "an eye for an eye" is the law on Tanna. When any one gets medicine from another he invariably pays for it. As a rule we get something in recognition of the medicine we give, but in Nahi-abba's case we don't even get thanks. Whether, if he were a Christian, his influence for good would be much, I cannot tell; but his influence for evil is very great. "The king's heart is in the hand of the Lord," wherefore I entreat you, my friends, to make him a special subject for prayer.

Oh, for a Pentecostal shower! Nothing but an outpouring of the Holy Spirit can cause the long-sown seed to grow. I want the Foundry Boys *en masse* to pray for Tanna; not in a general way, but that this very year the dawn may come. The Tannese are unique in their long resistance to the gospel. Forty years ago, the good news came to Tanna. They drove Turner and Nisbet away; they withstood the eloquent pleadings with tears of a Paton; they resisted for thirteen years the exhortations of a Neilson; and they have tried to weary us out.

To us, indeed, they are quite respectful; they admire our kindness, nay, more, they say our message is good; but "how can we give up the customs of our fathers?" Again I beseech you, "Pray for them." After the long years of sowing, with the vast amount of Scripture knowledge they have, and the way in which news spreads like wildfire over the island, if we had a revival, you would hear of one of the grandest incomings that have yet been witnessed in the New Hebrides. . . . Whether the reaping time comes in our day or not, we know that we belong to the "Ever Victorious Army," and that sooner or later Tanna will be won for Christ. There is a day coming when both "he that soweth and he that reapeth may rejoice together." . . .

AGNES C. P. WATT.

XIX.

AN ILLUSTRATED LETTER.

GENERAL LETTER, 1886.

In this "general" you will be surprised at my going over the past, but as the circle of readers has enlarged, and many of them know little of us, I think it well to give some account of ourselves and our establishment.

A lady who joined our Mission a few years ago, on becoming intimate with us, told me how surprised she had been to find on her arrival that there were no gray hairs on our heads. On my asking "why?" she said that when she was a little girl in the Sabbath School, she had heard of the New Hebrides and Mr and Mrs Watt of Tanna, so naturally expected to meet two staid, gray-haired people. In the same way, some may wonder what we are like, when told that we have been seventeen years missionaries; and would like to see such lions.

Here is a copy of our photographs, taken by Fergus of Largs in 1879. There are people in the world who think that missionaries should never seek a holiday until worn out. So many of our fellow-labourers have from time to time returned home pale, thin and shattered, that it has become an understood thing that foreign missionaries should appear so. When we visited Sydney a few years ago, one and another said to us, "Why have you come up? you don't look sick." I replied that the climate of the New Hebrides had got such a bad name, and so few would join us, that I had come up to bear witness to the goodness of the climate, and so see if I could induce others to follow me. In the same way, our photographs may encourage some to think seriously of casting in their lot with us. We have the most

un-get-at-able station in the group, being on a weather shore; and many a scare has been experienced in landing here. I fancy so much wind and salt spray must be conducive to health, and, judging from our own experience, would say that this is a healthy station.

The salt spray is not at all pleasant; for it rusts every bit of ironmongery, and keeps us constantly cleaning windows. Every fresh blow sends up clouds of spray which drift inland like steam, and so dims our windows that we cannot see out. It is very destructive also to plants, for after a strong breeze everything has a blasted look. Hence we have only grass in front, with a border of soil round the gravel or coral walks, while our shrubbery is at the back of the house, in the square formed by our dwelling-house, store-rooms and workshops.

What is our house like? It is weather-boarded outside and lathed and plastered inside, with a thatched roof. The weather-boards, studs, flooring, doors and windows are from the colonies. The thatch is New Hebridean, and so is the lath and plaster. The former is made of flexible branches or young saplings; the latter is coral burned. When we first came down in 1869, we got whatever is colonial of two rooms, and by degrees, as we found it necessary, we added thereto until the place stands as you see it. The main house consists of bed-room, dining-room, parlour, and study, with four small "leans-to" on the ends of the verandah, front and back, forming two bath-rooms in the front, and a pantry and box-room at the back. Of the two houses forming the sides of the square, that on the right is the store-room, and that on the left the printing-office, workshop and yam-house; both, as you see, are connected with the main house by passages. The doors and window-frames are all painted inside and out. The annual outside painting is no joke; for so strong is the sun here that in less than a year not a particle of oil is left in the wood; it would therefore spoil if we did not repaint it. The weather-boards outside and the plaster inside are all whitewashed with

KWAMERA CHURCH AND MISSION HOUSE.

coral lime. That too means much labour. Were it not that in employing a lot of people you are bringing them under your influence and providing them with the means of honourably working for clothes and other necessary things, besides teaching them new and useful arts, you would often feel heart-broken at the amount of manual work needed to keep up a station. The thatch roofs alone are a great labour, expense and trouble, and after all, they only last from four to five years at Kwamera, even when there has been no hurricane to damage them. At Port Resolution the one we put on two years ago has already begun to leak. The best thatch, and that which we use, is sugar-cane leaf tied on a reed about four feet long, forming long fringes. These are laid on in rows overlapping each other, and tied severally to the rafters by cinet. On our main house we have as many as two thousand reedsful, and when last we thatched, as many as ninety women were employed making it. Imagine, if you can, the stir; and oh, what a mess! Oh, ye who dwell under slate and other lasting roofs, think of us having our whole house unroofed up to the ridge-pole, time after time, dirty rotten thatch * falling in every direction, while scaffolding and greasy natives crowd up your rooms. Woe betide your bits of treasured furniture or gifts, if down comes a tropical shower!

---

* In some of the northern islands, thatch is much more durable. When well made and put on closely, a roof will last for many years. I have seen thatch which was at least fifty years old, but that was largely due to the preserving action of the smoke and heat from fires inside the house.—T. W. L.

Another constant trouble is the putting on each December, and taking off each April, of the storm-rigging. That consists of poles of wood put on like network, and tied with strong creepers. Under the wood we lay rows of old reed fencing, partly to make it more secure, but chiefly to keep the wood from rotting the thatch. The soil here is so damp that we have found it absolutely necessary to have a new reed fence put round our premises every year, else our place would be overrun with pigs—these creatures being allowed to run about loose. When new the fences look very pretty; they are of light, open basketwork. Some fifteen to twenty women bring about two hundred bunches of reeds, and five or ten men put up the fence. I suppose we will have about four acres enclosed.

All this thatch-making, roofing, reed getting and fencing, cleaning and sweeping, and the knowledge that all has to be paid for in goods—clothing and ironmongery—will lead you to infer that we require some storage room, and can utilise well a box or two of mission goods. Many a time I have wished we could do with less house-room, though indeed we find the house too small when the "Dayspring" sends in a number of people who more than once have been detained by wind or sea. (While I write this, the wind is howling and the sea running high, the poor wee vessel tossing to and fro in sight, but no landing. I sincerely pity those on board.)

Again, when you remember our numerous connections, teachers, helpers, boatmen and general parishioners, who are all dependent on us (for we rarely see a vessel), you will not wonder that we need every nook and cranny in which to store away goods. Besides, we only get supplies twice a year, and have to be prepared for emergencies—shipwreck or hurricane. Our grounds are not too large when you think how numerous our staff is. We have seven grass houses for native accommodation, besides a house for fire-wood—a most necessary thing in wet weather—a fowl-house and goat-house. These latter will commend themselves to you, seeing we are 1200 miles from market; and unless we provide creature comforts we can not have them, and will not live long. So in order to labour we must live. Housekeeping here is no play; for not only must you invent comforts, but with native help you must be at the beginning, middle, and end of everything yourselves.

At present we have, living on our premises, two married couples, four children, two single men, five boys and four girls. There are nineteen entirely dependent on us besides Naurita (the late Yemeitahak's husband, and Paipai his mother). Naurita was an inveterate kava-drinker, a savage and a cannibal. Now he is a consistent church member, and we believe a true and sincere Christian. Paipai too is a church member. Here is a specimen of our girls, and another of our boys. They are fed, clothed, lodged and educated by us, and in return do what they are bid. The girls act the part of table and pantry-maids, sew, and keep each a part of the premises clean. The boys clean knives, brush boots, rake the gravel walks, clean goat and fowl-houses, and feed the fowls.

Houye is our present poultry-man. He is a handy

fellow in the printing-office, and one year he was very proud when he received a sovereign as his year's salary.

YEMEITAHAK AND NANCY (p. 258).

But I hear some say, "Why keep so many on your premises, seeing they involve you in trouble and expense, as doubtless fewer would give you all the help you need?" True, but the absence of appliances to lighten labour, and the many departments needful for life, render more hands indispensable than in civilisation; besides, think of the sweltering heat! However, the main reason is—Tanna is a hard field, and except by taking them into our establishment, we have found it difficult to get any one to wait on regular instruction.

Another "connection" is our boatmen. These are indispensable; for, as a rule, we visit Port Resolution by boat, and on this weatherbound coast a good boat and trusty seamen are required. During the past hot season we have visited Port Resolution by boat six times, and twice overland.

Speaking of our staff, I mentioned *teachers*. Of these, we have six on Aniwa and three on Tanna. The latter are supported by the Glasgow Foundry Boys' Religious Society. Niath is at Port Resolution, Nalvatimi at Meiyahau, and Yamen at Ituko. Narpai and Matthew are at Isumu, but they are not recognised teachers.

June 17th. We have now been ready for the "Dayspring" for a week; and having a breathing time, I devoted it to writing the foregoing. While in the middle of my story, the cry of "Sail oh!" caused me to fling down my pen and rush out to the welcome sight. Welcome to us, snug on shore, but our joy is mixed with grief, seeing the weather is such that the passengers cannot land; and we know from experience that they are in a sorry plight: crowded in a small stuffy cabin, seasick, and knocked about in their bunks with the rolling and pitching of the vessel. Next day, just after breakfast, "Sail oh!" and until twelve o'clock hopes of a landing. Then it began to blow, and the "Dayspring" went further and further away, till four o'clock, when she was out of sight. All my preparations for dining a goodly company were useless, and until a week had elapsed we heard no more of her. On the 24th, she was seen between this and Futuna, and the

GIRLS IN MISSION HOUSE AT KWAMERA (p. 258).

weather was fine. On the 25th, Nahi-abba shot a man, a little to the west of us, in revenge for a friend of his who had died.

We were sure we should see the "Dayspring" on the Sabbath, if all was well, and so were much grieved on the Saturday to see the sea rising again. Just after morning service on Sabbath, we saw the poor wee "Dayspring" off here, with a big sea running and the wind high. I wonder if you can imagine how much our Sabbath rest was broken by thinking of and pitying our friends on board. We rested but little that night. Next morning, it was still blowing hard, but the wind was veering round to the north, and our hopes rose. By mid-day it was well round, and in the afternoon the landing began. Three boats brought all ashore—twelve adults and five children. The single gentlemen occupied our store-room, which was for the time arranged as a "barracks." After the tumblings and tossings at sea, every one was more pleased than another to be on shore, and expressed their joy; so we were a happy company.

Next morning at nine o'clock the Synod meetings began, and by four o'clock Mr Paton left in the "Dayspring" for Noumea, to try and get to Sydney in time for the Federal Assembly. We would all have liked could he have stayed longer, but "time and tide wait for no man." Our company at table now numbered eleven (for we had a separate children's table), and continued so till that day fortnight.

During that time "work, work, work" was the order of the day, from six in the morning till twelve at night. Church bell for native worship at 6.30 a.m.; at 7.15 we met in the parlour for family worship; 7.45, breakfast; and at 9.30 the Synod met and sat till dinner-time, 1 p.m. The afternoons were occupied with committee meetings. Tea at 6 p.m. Then usually all were busy with printing, writing, transcribing, or committee work. Several I rarely saw, save at

TANNA MEN AND BOYS (p. 258).

meal-times. Such a Busy Bee never was, as the one we held here. Mr Murray set up a Primer of twenty-eight pages in the language of Ambrim, and that meant many a weary hour's work for him. William corrected the type, while Mr Lawrie, Houye, and others printed it off and distributed the type again. Mr Robertson and Mr Lawrie also had leaflets printed.

On Thursday, 30th June, baby Gray fell asleep. Next forenoon, we had a service in church, and buried him in a plain deal coffin, made by his father. We felt much for our brother and sister in their trial, but were very glad Mrs Gray had not been left alone at their station. In the afternoon, when the Synod met, we heard reports of stations,—all encouraging. On Emae or Imai, the work is wonderful. Two years ago, all were heathen cannibals, now many are learning to read, and the teachers are much blessed.

Though our Mission is small—and when compared to Africa or China, the New Hebrides are insignificant—still, some of the greatest triumphs of the gospel have been accomplished here. According to their means, our converts will compare favourably in liberality with converts in any other field.

On Sabbath we had a good attendance at church—the Isumu people having come all the way to see the missionaries. In the evening we celebrated the Lord's Supper, Mr Murray preaching, and Mr Laurie dispensing the elements. We had a happy time, although saddened by remembering Mrs Fraser and Mrs Murray, who had been with us at the same feast last year. Later, we held a concert of sacred music; the missionaries singing in English and the Tannese in their own language alternately. All agreed in saying

HOUYE—FROM A PHOTO TAKEN IN MELBOURNE (p. 258).

that the native singing was the best; for the hymns in English were not particularly well known to us all;

while the natives were in full force, knew their hymns well, and sang heartily.

On Friday we held the Bible Society meeting, and at the close several of our people, teachers and helps, contributed. Kaiasi gave ten shillings last year, and the same this year. Very good, I say, seeing a native's salary is only £4! Vahai and Nalvatimi both gave £1 each.

Our boys and girls were sorry, when the others contributed to the Bible Society, that they had no money. Afterwards, when the missionaries gave them presents, instead of buying gay handkerchiefs and beads, they made a thank-offering to the Glasgow Foundry Boys' Society, in most cases of their all. It amounted to 13/. I was much pleased with Nancy's unselfishness. She had got 1/ from two different persons; the others had given 1/ and so had she, but Kiser who cleaned the knives had been overlooked, and so had no money, yet was longing to join in giving. Well, Nancy gave him her other shilling, and enabled him to participate in the pleasure of giving.

As Tanna has long been looked upon as a specially hard field, we asked our friends to join us and pray for a special blessing on this island. We spent the evening of Sabbath 11th thus, each one joining in turn. I liked an expression in Mr Fraser's prayer, that "from henceforth we may not think of Tanna as a hard field, but as a field for which we have prayed." Yes, I fear too many have looked upon Tanna as hard, and so have done nothing for its evangelisation. As of old they say, "Can any good thing come out of Nazareth?" "Can these (dry) bones live?" It requires more faith to preach to dry bones than to living men.

TANNA WOMAN.

On the 15th the "Dayspring" returned from
Noumea, but too late to take off our visitors, so we
spent the evening singing hymns, supposing it to be
our last together. Next day the sea was so rough that
the captain sent word that no one was to come off. In
this way we had another "last evening," but half
expecting to have our friends till Monday. However,
on Saturday morning the wind and sea had fallen, and
H.M.S. "Opal" and the "Dayspring" were both off
here. The captain of the former kindly sent word that
he would take Mr Robertson to Erromanga, Mr
M'Kenzie and Mr Fraser accompanying him. Immediately after breakfast all left except Mr Milne and Mr
Murray, who went off in the last boat. Thus ended the
meeting of 1886, but we trust that the results will
continue to all eternity. *We* enjoyed the society of
kindred spirits immensely, and were gratified by
thinking we had made *them* comfortable. Our helps,
both Aneityumese and Tannese, rose to the occasion,
and there was no hitch in the arrangements. Indeed,
they were far better than colonial servants, who are said
to grumble at visitors. They made common cause of
our meeting, were delighted to exert themselves to
make all comfortable, and expressed great grief when
they left. Mr Murray's loneliness has elicited many
expressions of sympathy. Poor fellow! he will feel
very much alone on Ambrim. Mr Fraser had left his
two wee motherless bairns on Erromanga. What a
sad time he had, when left with an eight-day-old son!
He made a coffin for his wife, and alone, among black
people, laid her in the narrow house. Side by side
she and her infant daughter lie. Jessica had died

shortly before, while Mr Fraser himself had a serious illness.

Seeing we had so enjoyed congenial society, and had such a lot of it all at once, you can imagine the blank we felt, when, after seeing the last safe on board, we re-entered our deserted home.

It was Saturday, and the porker I had got killed for Sunday's dinner had to be divided among our darkies. But alas, ere I had commenced giving my directions, the yells of the people caused me to rush out and away up the banks of the neighbouring stream. There I was reminded that we were still on dark deluded Tanna, and that we needed strength from above and strong faith to face the stern realities of life. Sitting in the stream with a crowd of women around him, was a young lad who a few minutes before had been shot in the left arm near the shoulder. We ran for a dose of laudanum to relieve the lad's distress. Poor boy! when he saw compassion on my face he began to cry. His father carried him home on his back, and he now lies in a precarious state.* This is part of the revenge for the man Nahi-abba shot the Friday before the missionaries arrived. It may interest you to know that the natives took out the broken bones and put a stick in their place.

On Monday we dismantled our barracks, and soon our whole place resumed its wonted look. We are now packing up for a camping-out at Port Resolution. It takes no small thought to remember everything necessary for a five or six weeks' stay in an empty

---

* The lad recovered, and in about six months was again well and strong.

house. The house is in such bad repair that we cannot leave things there, but we have now the promise of an iron roof for it.

After visiting Port Resolution we come back here to await the return of the "Dayspring" from Sydney, when we are appointed to proceed to Malekula as part of a deputation to assist in the settlement of our nephew (T. Leggatt), who is to be known as the "Amy Gertrude Russell" missionary. A Victorian gentleman named Russell supports him in memory of his daughter.

AGNES C. P. WATT.

KWAMERA, July 30th, 1886.

XX.
EXTENDING THE MISSION NORTHWARD.

GENERAL LETTER, 1887.

The hot season of 1886-87 was to Mrs Watt a very trying time. It was less so perhaps among the people than in the mission house, where there was much sickness and anxiety. Mr Morton and myself with our wives being unable to open up our own stations owing to the lateness of the season, remained at Kwamera until April. Acclimation is never a pleasant experience; but when it has to be undergone in the unhealthiest season of the year, together with other illnesses, the result is distressing in the extreme. Mrs Morton had a still-born son in February, and my wife a daughter in March. Both ladies recovered but slowly, and Mrs Watt herself suffered from severe fever and ague with other complications, while Mr Watt was prostrated for a long time with a return of his old complaint, "vomiting of blood." What follows is best told in her own words.

For weeks, nay months, before the vessel came, we rarely, if ever, all met at the table. Always one or two unwell, and oh how I longed for the "Dayspring" to come! We were all a good deal recovered, when on the 26th April the cry of "Sail oh!" greeted our ears. It was like life from the dead. . . .

On Friday 29th, the anniversary of our marriage day, we left Kwamera. We were a good boat-load—four couples and a baby, with quite a number of natives, for we took two as boat's crew, two as house-builders, and Yecrimu to mind the baby. . . .

Wednesday, 8th May. We left Epi for Ambrim at sundown. After tea, we had very vivid lightning, and I remained on deck till late, watching it. The sight was magnificent; there was no wind; all was still and peaceful. Being up late, I slept soundly, and knew no more till, about half-past two in the morning, I was awakened by the captain shouting, " Let go the anchor." I knew something was wrong; for we never anchor save in the daylight. Soon I learned that the current had carried us down on Ambrim, that we were close in to the rocks, and that some of the passengers were dressed, ready to take to the boats. I didn't wish to see our danger, so remained in my bunk. At daylight, I went on deck, but by that time a "kedge" anchor was out, and the boats pulling ahead. How relieved our minds were when we saw that we were slipping from the shore!—a little God-sent breeze gliding us safely off. Just when we were moving, a boat put off from the shore. At first the natives were shy, but when they learned that it was a missionary ship, they came on board. The captain gave them a present, and they returned on shore much pleased. The breeze was now freshening, and carried us along until we reached the anchorage at Mr Murray's station at one p.m.

How much can be crowded into twenty-four hours! During the night we realised that we were in imminent peril; then the rebound of joy when deliverance came;

From Photo by Rev. T. W. Leggatt
BOYS WITH YAMS.

now another sorrow awaited us. Our fellow-labourer from New Zealand was in sore trouble; he had had fever, and looked so ill. The Landels, too, had suffered much; they were but the wrecks of their former selves.

Here, at Ambrim, the Annual Meeting of Synod was held, we going ashore and setting out dinner, while the other meals were served on board, and all being prepared by the "Dayspring's" cook. The "Dayspring" and "Cairndhu" lay here at anchor until Thursday, the 2nd June, when we parted. The object of the "Cairndhu" was to settle Messrs Annand and Landels, and it carried, as a deputation, Messrs Mackenzie, Robertson, Fraser and Murray. With us in the "Dayspring" were Messrs Morton and Leggatt, on their way to be settled, with Messrs Watt and Lawrie as a deputation. The "Cairndhu" sailed for Malo, and we for Sasun Bay, Malekula. We found that the French priests had effected a lodgment there, but their presence only seemed to make the people more anxious for an English missionary. They said, "Man Malekula he no like French missionary, he no got boat, he no got wife, he no got piccanniny, he no got nothing." Their joy was great when they saw that T. W. L. had got all three, or rather all four. They gave him a good site for his house, plenty of good land, with fruit and other trees on it, beside a nice little stream of fresh water. For two weeks the missionaries and their sable assistants wrought late and early, first clearing the land, and then house-building. They left the ship at six a.m., and returned at six p.m., their dinner being sent ashore to them. When beginning the house, it was discovered that there were no nails. What was to be done? We had a few, Mr Morton could spare a few more, but still we were short. Gladly did we remember that Mrs Mackie of Melbourne always sent nails for Aniwa. We got up her box, opened it, and found a splendid parcel of nails. How pleased we were, and how opportune!

On the 20th June, we left them very comfortably settled. That forenoon we visited the nearest native village. We saw an exchange of pigs take place, over which there was a good deal of ceremony. First there was a great beating of native drums, then a conch was blown, and a pig held shoulder-high for some time; another blast of the conch, another pig offered, and so on till all had been presented. Why was this done? Was it an offering to the gods? What more followed we did not see, for they let us know that we were not wanted; but after we left we heard any amount of conch blowing and shouting.

Though we bade Mr Leggatt adieu on the 20th, we were not to sail till the next morning, so we rose before daylight and went ashore to have another peep at him and his wife, then off to breakfast and away to Pangkumu, further up the coast, where we landed the same day and visited a large village. The chief's house here was remarkable, having an immense bird on the wing carved in wood on the ridge pole over the door. The whole village was enclosed by a coral wall, and the chief's house was within a second wall. We wanted much to get seeing through his sanctum, and tried in our best broken English to make him understand, but in vain. At last we discovered the secret; he objected to us ladies going, but willingly took the gentlemen.

The next day was a big day; we searched for a site, visited a village a good way off, saw a magnificent public square, near by which were no fewer than forty-five images painted in green, red, and yellow colours. Each would be from eight to ten feet high, ornamented with a human face. The road to and from the village was level and broad, and I enjoyed the walk. Another day we went to see the young chief, Netinmar, who constituted me his friend, and got several clubs for me. He was such a nice young fellow, and so polite; one of nature's gentlemen. Having got a site for Mr Morton's house, we had to return to Ambrim for the timber, and were one night at sea. Again there was sad news awaiting us. Before our anchor was down we were met by a boat in charge of Mr Norrie, the chief officer of the "Cairndhu," who told us that that vessel had been wrecked on Malo. I have not time to tell of our surmises as the boat approached, of our suspense while Mr Norrie told of the wreck, of the dread lest any lives were lost, or of the sense of relief and the fervent "Thank God!" when we knew there was no loss, save of the ship. Our first impulse was to hasten at once to the rescue, but we were already crowded, and heard that the Malo people, like those of Melita, had showed the shipwrecked people no little kindness.

Monday was a busy day, missionaries and natives all working to the utmost of their strength, and the "Dayspring" people doing their best. Thus we were ready for sea on the next day, and I wish you could have seen our little "Dayspring." So crowded was every inch of room that I hid in my bunk, not wishing to see the confusion. The poop and main deck—every

From Photo by Rev. T. W. Leggatt.

PUBLIC SQUARE, MALEKULA.

corner, indeed—was lumbered up, and I feared lest we should have a night at sea. But God is good; He knew our frames, and so tempered the wind that in a few hours we were again at anchor at Pangkumu. From Wednesday till the Thursday of the next week all wrought late and early. On that day the Mortons' goods were sent ashore, and after dinner we bade them adieu. The wind, however, was towards the bay, and we could not get out; but early next morning we lifted anchor, and were away for Malo. We made Malo early, but the wind falling light, we could not get up to the anchorage. A boat was sent ashore, however, to relieve anxiety with regard to the search-party, for they had been gone so long, and had had a very trying voyage. The wind had been high and the sea rough, and they had been driven hither and thither for three nights at sea. At one place the savages had put off in canoes to come to them, and they had had a shark biting at their oars most persistently, although they fired at him. Truly they deserve great credit for their pluck.

We felt keenly for Captain Eyre when he boarded us. Those who were in the ship when she went ashore speak very highly of his disregard of self in seeking to save the cargo.

We visited the Landels in their new home, and were much pleased with the people of Malo.* These northern islanders seem much less savage and heathenish than those down south. Though the vessel was wrecked,

---

* They do not improve, however, on a longer acquaintance.
—T. W. L.

and might have been looked on as a "God-send" to them, these Malo people stole nothing and treated our people with courtesy.

As soon as possible Mr Annand's goods were got on board, and we, with very lumbered decks, made for Tangoa, Santo. While waiting for the "Dayspring" the deputation had gone by boat; and, rafting over some of the timber, had laid the lower wall plates of Mr Annand's house. On the day of our arrival the studs were set up, and that day week the house was so far finished that we could leave them, which we did on Thursday, the 21st July. They have got by far the finest station of the four new ones, and so nice are the people of Santo that I wished I were being settled there myself. No one could feel nervous among such quiet, docile people. The bad name these people get makes one suspicious of them; but at each settlement we were more and more pleased with our reception. We could hardly realise that they were heathens and cannibals.

We were all night at sea between Tangoa and Malo, where we took on board all the cargo of the "Cairndhu" and her crew. We spent a delightful Sabbath at anchor there, having a service of song in the forenoon and worship in the evening.

From Monday till Friday we were beating up against a headwind. Fortunately I was not sea-sick, and enjoyed life on board. I read much of Dr Parker's "Inner Life of Christ." His way of putting things charms me. . . . At Emai we were again laden to the utmost limit with arrowroot, yams, &c., so that there was not a corner left. I should have mentioned that ten of Mr Mackenzie's people, having heard of the wreck of the "Cairndhu," had come in a boat to Tangoa to look for him. These we had on board, so that, with our own "Dayspring" party, the shipwrecked people, and this boat's crew, we were over fifty in number. Every room, every bunk, every available corner was occupied as sleeping quarters, the very galley and the cabin floor being crammed full. . . . During two tumbling days I read Bishop Hannington's Life. It has a strange fascination for me, and I am intensely interested in his journals. What a bright active Christian he was! Although the Robertsons were only returning home after a long absence, yet they invited us all on shore, and we spent a very happy time. During the night, Korkor, an Aneityumese man who had been with Mr Murray on Ambrim, and who had been taken on shore to die, passed away to his eternal rest. He gave testimony to his faith in Jesus and his hope of eternal life. Now he is among the blessed dead, yea, rather, among the living who have died, whose works do follow them. He did good service in the Master's cause on Ambrim, though he was "only an armour-bearer." His body now rests close by the graves of the martyred Gordons and the sainted Macnair. "Precious in the sight of the Lord is the death of His saints."

We left Erromanga on Thursday, and reached Aniwa on Saturday, the 13th August. We landed about four in the afternoon. Mr and Mrs Lawrie and two children, and Messrs Fraser and Murray kindly accompanying us on shore. We had a busy evening rigging up and extemporising beds for all in the empty house. All were willing to make things pleasant, so everything went smoothly. The natives gave us fowls and yams for Sabbath, and one good friend sent us a big manihot (manioc or cassava) pudding. In the evening we had some fine hymns, and every one seemed happy.

Seeing that the people here get so little attention from missionaries, and have to stand so much alone, we were anxious to get our friends to spend the Sabbath with us. This they did, giving us much pleasure, and I trust profit too. You know how keenly I feel for these poor sheep; do you wonder then that the depths of my heart were stirred when Mr Fraser read his text, "Fear not, little flock"? Mr Murray followed, his text being Isaiah xli. 6, "Be of good courage"; then in the afternoon Mr Lawrie spoke. All three addresses were most appropriate. After dinner we itinerated, visiting the Sabbath schools, and were followed about from place to place by many. We spent a delightful hour that evening. Each of the four missionaries sang a hymn, read a portion of Scripture, and engaged in prayer. The shadows of the parting on the morrow hung dark and heavy over me, and I was glad that no one referred to such events, but directed our thoughts to the cross of Jesus, the love of Christ that passeth knowledge, and the boundless comfort the Lord gives His Church; also to the power of prayer. Such a day and such an evening are "Elims" in our wilderness journey. . . .

AGNES C. P. WATT.

XXI.

TOILING ON.

GENERAL LETTERS, 1887-88.

A missionary's wife once said to me, "It is easy for you to write interesting letters, there is always some exciting event; a great war, or a cold-blooded murder taking place on Tanna, and that gives you something to write about. It is not so with me here, where all goes on in the even tenor of its way, and I find nothing to make a story about." Well, I am happy to tell you that for once I am in the pleasant position of having no sensational news to record. Since I last dropped the thread of my narrative, no war, no murder, no exciting event has disturbed the delightful lull on Tanna. I cannot point to any great advance, but there is a growing dislike to war on the part of our people. Perhaps the last six months have been the happiest we have ever spent on Tanna. We landed on the 26th of August from our northern trip, and were met by an unusually large number of our parishioners. We heard of fewer declensions during our absence, and experienced greater comfort among them. This happy state of matters has continued ever since. Our good reception, after landing, was some compensation to me, as it was very rough; and I did pity those who had to return to the ship in blinding rain, wind, and a heavy sea. It was two days ere they were able to return with the remainder of our goods. On Wednesday we gave a present of salt and soap to all our people, in accordance with the wishes of some friends in New Zealand who had supplied the same. Two days before, we had paid all our helps, and fortunately all were pleased with their pay. Whether that and the subsequent gifts may have had something to do with it, I cannot tell, but on Sabbath two backsliders resumed church-going after an absence of six years. My diary expresses my wishes, "May the incoming begin now!"

The morning of Monday, 5th Sept., was very wet, but on its clearing up we made an early dinner and started for Port Resolution, with a boat's crew and working party of fourteen. Next day we went to Weasisi, where I kept Mrs Gray company while Mr Gray returned to Port Resolution with William, to assist him in roofing. I was anxious about those two gentlemen while keeping "bachelor hall," but I found all my fears had been groundless, as the people had risen to the occasion and kept our band fully supplied. Daily did they contribute yams, puddings, and drinking cocoa-nuts, *gratis*. Indeed, the repairing of this house seems to have been owned of God to further His cause. The people realise our love to them, seeing we have spent so much in making this house habitable. They look on it as our joint property; hence they carried up all the iron, wood, and bricks free of charge, supplied us with daily rations of food, besides making us a present of a pig, fowls and yams. On giving them some fishhooks they expressed amazement, and said they had only done a little towards the good cause.

On Sabbath, 23rd October, the old ship was seen, and on Monday she landed our goods and iron for the roof of our church at Kwamera. This is the year of the Queen's Jubilee, while I call it the "*Iron year*"; for within twelve months William has assisted at no fewer than *six* iron roofs, so he may be called "experienced" in that branch. To show how smartly we do things, I'll tell you this. The iron was landed, as I said, on Monday. That same night, at evening school, all were told to undo the thatch at daybreak. One half of the roof was covered on Tuesday, the other on Wednesday, and the ridge capping put on by Thursday! But that meant working from six in the morning till six at night; the missionary being the head and the centre of all, while his wife, acting as Lady Bountiful, provides and divides meals for all. . . . We eat not the bread of idleness. I can say, like Paul, "in labours more abundant," and as the end of each week comes, I feel that we have not lost a moment. Whether all will stand the fire as pure gold, or only prove to be wood and stubble, *the day* will declare. At least we do all *for the Master;* and He who rewards even the cup of cold water will doubtless accept the offering of our whole energies. I live for Tanna (indeed many think I have Tanna on the brain), and will die for it, if need be. Can you wonder that we love the Tannese? Although they have opposed the gospel till they have become a proverb and a byword, and have by their waywardness sorely tried our faith, yet they are a most affectionate people. Besides, one can never tell how much is being done in a quiet way on Tanna. Could you but hear our hearty singing, and see the people here turning out twice daily to worship, would you not think that seed was being sown? We are strong in hymns on Tanna; we have over seventy; and doubtless our people sing well. " Bright, beautiful home " is an immense favourite with the young folk. The children may not sing skilfully, but they obey the other injunction of the Psalmist and sing " with a loud noise." The iron makes their voices resound clearly, and sometimes we are almost deafened. May they all join in the " Hallelujah Chorus " above !

The early months of this year were dark and gloomy; much sickness prevailed, my hands were too full, and I was prevented from attending to my usual mission work. The later months were bright and cheery; our people were open to instruction. At Port Resolution we have classes three times a day, and much encouragement. At Kwamera several more have resumed church-going, and above all, Tero has decided to refrain from a heathen rite on his son and grandson. We hope for two more. This, if carried out, is a very decided advance. Two of the boys are already clothed (a sign that they are to escape), the other two await our return. In eighteen years we have only rescued *three*. Clothing is a badge of Christianity. When one begins to worship he puts on a garment, and if he becomes disaffected, one of the first acts is to lay aside the cloth.

A little girl, the other day, seeing a picture of the " Holy Family," exclaimed, " Why has the Virgin Mary no garment on her child ? " Some think we put too much importance on clothing, but I cannot imagine Christians going about naked.

1888. 21st April. The "Dayspring" left us on the 21st December, and we were to be alone for over four months. Do I hear you ask, What have you been doing during all these months of uninterrupted quiet? Well, I hardly know how to begin, or how possibly to tell you. Month by month, week by week, and day by day, Tanna alone—its people and its interests—has absorbed our attention. Perhaps the most important part of our season's work has been translating. We have spent a great deal of time over it, but I am happy to say that we have now the whole New Testament gone over for the first time, and are now engaged in revising. We have two pundits, both of them satisfactory; and we hope during this year to get all re-written and ready for the press.

We have also been doing good work with the Glasgow Foundry Boys' Press. The want of paper and binding material has crippled us, however. The number of copies printed was 250, and part of these on coloured paper. We had to use ordinary print cloth for binding. For weeks the missionary stood at the composing-case or at the printing-press, the result being a new edition of our hymn book and catechism in one. We have made additions to our catechism, including the Apostle's Creed, terms of communion, two short prayers, and questions on Bible names similar to those in Willison's Mother's Catechism. We have also added three new hymns, so that our hymnal now contains eighty-two pieces. The Tannese are passionately fond of music, and the demand for new hymns is endless. Ofttimes they listen to us while at worship, and if the tune takes their fancy, they give us no rest till we make a hymn to suit it. Though to some ears the Tannese language may sound harsh, yet I can assure you I feel the power of many of our hymns quite as much when sung in this barbarous tongue as when sung in English; and we hope and pray that the singing of the Gospel will prove a source of glad tidings to many. One of our newest hymns, "Take my life and let it be," is a great favourite, and also "Jesus is mine." The latter is the work of a Tannaman, Kaiasi, and is the first instance we know of a native in this group translating a hymn.

How easily one writes and another reads the words, "we have printed a new edition of our hymn book and catechism," but how few of you can guess what an amount of time and how much labour it costs! We bound up the whole of the edition printed this year, and with the exception of some fifty copies all are now in use. We have also printed and bound a new edition of our Primer.

. . . This year, the dread of books, so common on Tanna, seems to have broken down. It was pleasant to see so many anxious to get a book. At Isumu, Pavenga, the teacher, has forty in constant use. I told you before of the interesting movement at Isumu, under Matthew and Kauraka, and how we got a teacher from Aniwa for them. We settled Pavenga and wife early in January, and have been much encouraged with a school and good church attendance. We spent a very happy night there and had a magic-lantern exhibition. I confess I did not relish the bed all on a slope, for it took all my time to hold on. Of course, I had been sea-sick on the voyage, and after our arrival we spent hours telling them of the good news, and singing hymns. God knows the spirit was willing, although the flesh was weak. Pavenga lives there constantly, and on the first Sabbath of each month we send a deputation from here. We have no drones in our hive; for our cook, herdsmen, &c., all take their turn itinerating. Every Sabbath they conduct service at several villages for miles around, and once a month there is an exchange as far as Isumu. At Port Resolution this is not practicable, so we sent Matthew and Narpai in January, Vahai and Ripa following them in February. They have had encouraging meetings for worship, reading, and singing, on all days of the week. We have also had boarders from Port Resolution and Isumu for some length of time to give them further instruction.

. . . At Kwamera our morning and evening school has been particularly encouraging. Houye left in a labour-vessel and sent back a letter to Naswai, which seemed to give a new impetus to learning, for they saw the advantage of being able to read and write. We have had between thirty and forty present nightly (almost the whole near population). The writing class was the most popular. We gave three whole days each week entirely to the natives. I cut garments on the one, and taught sewing on the other two. We made thirty patchwork counterpanes, and one hundred and twenty-one dresses, besides men's and boy's jumpers. The patchwork quilts they got for the making, and each got a dress for helping to sew the others. I find the cutting heavy work, but I get so much more out of the material than if I entrusted it to them, and we can ill afford to lose any by waste. I often wonder where all the dresses go to ; for although we make so many, the demand far exceeds the supply. A new tribe have, as they express it, " taken the worship," and the cry then for clothing is great. This tribe, the Kapitevemi, has heretofore stood aloof, and as they are reputed to be the chief diseasemakers, they are much dreaded. We cannot say that they have taken a very decided step yet, but they turn out *en masse* to service on Sabbaths, and refrain from work on that day. In this respect they act better than two tribes between this place and theirs, who have long had teachers, and who, knowing what is right, persist in doing what is wrong. . . .

We have had what we call a pleasant season ; no hurricanes, only very slight earthquakes (although they have had very severe ones at Port Resolution), no war, and the general health has been good. . . .

The 1st of January was a Sabbath. On that day we had the Communion. On the previous Friday we baptised five,—Matthew and his two dàughters, Narpai, and an old woman called Kaku. On Sabbath the three grown up people joined with us at the Lord's Supper. Matthew grieved us sorely some years ago by breaking off from the catechumens' class, and falling deeply into sin. Our joy now at his return and decided advance in Christian character is consequently great. He is a most faithful itinerant preacher; and when lately he and our cook went to hold a service inland at a new village, and only saw the backs of the fleeing people, he followed them. Meantime the fugitives had laid a barrier of wood on the way, warning them not to go beyond. When he came to it he gave a look to his neighbour and said, " Let us be strong and go." They removed the obstruction and walked on. When they reached the public square they found all the men gathered inside the kava-house. One entered at one door and the other at the other, and so cut off all way of escape. The fugitives, feeling safe from all interruption, seeing they had laid down the barricade, which they judged sufficient to deter the preachers, had gone into the kava-house to rest and twist their hair. Fancy their amazement when these two men confronted them! Neither party spoke for a considerable time, and the fugitives looked very angry, but Matthew broke the silence by saying, "We are ready to die if you like to kill us, but we are come here to have worship." One, more hardened than the rest, replied, "You cannot have worship here, and hinder us from getting on with twisting our hair. You drove us out of our own village, and now you follow us here." The silence thus broken, Matthew discoursed on the vanity of all earthly things; especially what was purely heathenish. The result was, worship was conducted, although some showed ill-feeling by refusing to close their eyes during prayer. They asked Matthew what he meant by thus hunting them; did he mean to drive them to the other side of the island? It is a common thing on Tanna when you arrive at a village to see numbers vanish into the bush rather than endure worship. An amusing incident occurred lately. A man who lives quite close to us sent a request for a fathom of dungaree for a waist-cloth, to come to church in; his little son having previously joined us. We, of course, gladly gave it, but

three Sabbaths passed and no Taake came. On the
evening of the fourth Saturday we sent Matthew to try
and persuade him, for we know that, if unwilling to
come, our approach would be the signal for him to flee
or hide, whereas Matthew could go round by byways
and through the bush, and so come on him unexpectedly.
When Matthew entered the village, he found that
Taake was still in the public square, so he sat down
and waited patiently for him. One and another offered
to go and tell Taake and not keep him waiting, but
Matthew said No, fearing if Taake knew he was there,
he would not come. At length, just before dark, he
came, and was reminded of his request and promise.
He replied that it was true he had failed, but he
intended to come on the morrow, even if he had not
been reminded of it. After some friendly conversation,
Matthew left, in high hopes of the morrow, but almost
before he had time to deliver his message to us, the
retreating form of Taake was seen in the darkness
wending its way up the hill behind our house; and so
he went away inland to another village, where he
remained till sundown on the following day. He
stated that he feared Matthew would renew his
pleadings on the following morning and he would not
be able to resist him, so he took safety in flight. For
days after that he scanned the path to see that none of
our people were about, before he would venture to pass
our premises. We have little doubt he intended to
come when he first asked for the girdle, but that some
one persuaded him not to join the worshipping party.

    You are aware that the Tannamen believe that they
have the power to do everything by means of sacred

stones called *Nukue nari*. The Bible runs contrary to all such beliefs, and it appears that Nahi-abba and others have been feeling sore at us for saying that God alone has all the power. Nahi-abba has been going far and near to get the sacred men to make a tidal wave to rush specially up the stream near here, and come down carrying our house out to sea. Many of the Tannese were quite excited, and could not sleep for fear of being washed out of their houses during the night. They stared at us in amazement when we and our Christian people said we had nothing to fear, as all was in God's hands and not in man's. We are not certain that they ever went through their ceremonies, as there were some dissenting voices; but as the sea remained particularly moderate about that time, they thought it best to say they had not done so. They are loth to own that they are beaten, even when at their wit's end. . . .

"All work and no play makes Jack a dull boy," and nothing but Tanna and its people tends to make one "cranky," so ofttimes we snatch a wee while for a quiet peep into a book. We are now reading the life of Mrs Prentiss. To me she seems such a *real* woman. *In* the world, fulfilling all its duties, yet not *of* the world. A thousand times have I thanked Mrs James Paton for the book. Lately, I enjoyed exceedingly the memoir of F. L. Mackenzie, also the "Seeking Saviour" by W. P. Mackay. Mr Chalmers tells the story of "Life in New Guinea" well, and the illustrations enhance the value of the work very much. How intensely interested our people are in the pictures! . . .

AGNES C. P. WATT.

P.S.—Ladies proverbially put their most important news in a postscript; hence do not wonder that I have failed to tell you of the change on "terrible Tanna." Lately there have been several severe shocks of earthquake at Port Resolution; and living there, we run the chance of going up in a chariot of fire, for we have now two volcanoes instead of one. On the 20th April there was a tremendous earthquake, and one side of the bay was again uplifted a considerable number of feet. What was once sea-room is now high and dry. We have not seen it, and have only had a very slight shake at Kwamera. Rumours of the change having reached us, we sent a trader to learn the exact truth. He brought a letter from a teacher residing there, who states that the water at the bar of the harbour will now only allow small vessels to anchor. The ground on the west side of Yanikahi was rent and torn in all directions; but although many had narrow escapes, no lives were lost. . . .

Don't we live in exciting times? but how comforting are our Saviour's words, "Let not your heart be troubled."

A. C. P. WATT.

XXII.
"AND THEY WENT FORTH AND PREACHED THAT MEN SHOULD REPENT."

GENERAL LETTER.

December, 1888.

—— I have already told you that there has been a severe earthquake and upheaval at Port Resolution. It seems there had been a second on the 24th of June. The two upheavals have completely changed the harbour; indeed, we might almost say that the harbour has ceased to exist, as only small steamers can now come in with safety. Here at Port Resolution we remained six weeks, then we had to go back to Kwamera to meet the "Dayspring" on her return trip. We had a good deal of encouragement. The Sabbath services were well attended, and at the morning and evening school they were hearty. On moonlight nights we had quite a crowd, and on dark nights as many, nay more than we could reasonably expect, seeing the native paths are crossed and re-crossed with roots, and that the natives have a great fear of ghosts. They bring torches, and it is a fine sight to watch the lights flickering and flashing as the natives wend their way through the bush. In respect of daily attendance at school, the people here far outstrip those at Kwamera.

There, only those boarded with us, or living on our premises, come regularly, but here all within a reasonable distance attend with commendable regularity. Besides teaching and direct Mission work, we had a busy time getting new fences and thatching done. All wrought heartily and with good-will, and we embraced many opportunities of speaking for our Master.

During these weeks we had oft-repeated requests for teachers for two hitherto unoccupied districts; but as we have been sorely tried by the fickleness of the Tannese, we turned a deaf ear to all. At last a special pleader came, and we determined to visit the two districts and people. On Friday, 21st September, accompanied by our cook and his wife, we went to Yakwarur, where we met the entire male population. We enquired as to the sincerity of their requests, and they promised fair to attend school and learn to read. We then went inland to Ikurupu, but not finding the man who is the moving spirit in the desire for teachers there, we retraced our steps. On meeting him and some of his people on the way, we sat down by the road-side and heard his story. As in the last case his promises were fair, so we agreed to try and get teachers for them. We had a lovely day, bright sun but a cool breeze, and I was pleased with my walking powers. I had gone partly as an experiment, for if I stood that walk well, I had a long one in prospect. Often have I walked between Port Resolution and Kwamera, but have been so knocked up, that of late I have always gone by boat. Each voyage the strain on my nerves has been more trying than bodily fatigue. Besides, the people of Isumu had put up a new grass church, and wanted us to go and open it. The landing there is very unsatisfactory, and I was determined not to risk it again, so we planned the bold project of walking to Kwamera and spending a night at Isumu. Accordingly, we started, about a week later, on a Saturday, accompanied by our cook and his wife, who carried sleeping rugs. The morning was dull, but we enjoyed immensely the walk round the bay; I could not help saying what feasts of delight we have in this world. On cool mornings I can think of nothing more inspiriting than the view in this bay. The mountain range in the centre of the island, suggestive of eternity; the calm sparkling water smooth as a sea of glass; the clear deep impenetrable blue of the sky, and the surrounding landscape rich in tropical verdure and gayest colours. After we left the head of the bay we followed a well beaten track, and in due time reached Ikurupu. Here we got three guides, and, passing on to the next village, we met by appointment an old chief named Maruki. He has a son in Queensland who has professed his faith in Christ and been baptised, and has been under instruction with a Mrs Robinson. The old man was very glad to hear about his son, but shook perceptibly at meeting us. His one cry was, "Bring him home! bring him home!" We said, Yes, if you will allow us to settle him as a teacher, and you promise to worship. Oh yes! he would do anything if only we would bring him home. After some further conversation we resumed our walk. The road now lay through a deep natural cutting of rock, something like the entrance to a railway tunnel, and a veritable "Balaam's Pass," suggestive of a terrible squeeze if a severe earthquake should occur while we were there. Soon we emerged at the top, for we were on the slope of a mountain, and I felt relieved when done with our almost subterranean walk. When we reached the summit we should have had a fine view, but the mountains were enveloped in mist. This is very disagreeable in a country where you brush against every plant and shrub; and woe betide your shoes and skirts; for soon you are as wet as can be. So thought I as we marched along our mountain path, but soon found we could be still wetter, for the rain began to descend in earnest; and now all our care was to keep our rugs and changes of clothing dry. By piling bunches of leaves on the top of our basket we hoped to keep the rain out. On we trudged, our three naked darkies dripping from head to foot, and the water making their dark skins shine. Owing to war a great part of the road had become overgrown, and once and again we had to stand while a path was cut through the reeds. Thus in some bodily discomfort we pursued our way. By and by our guides could go no further in safety, and were doing all they could to describe the path, when a voice was heard; so they called, and the speaker came forward. He proved to be a friend, and we were handed over to him, our three guides retracing their steps, while we went down hill to our destination. Coming to the beach I was in a sorry plight with rain and mud, so the first thing I did was to seek out a pool and wash some of my garments; and by wringing and shaking them made all drier than before. Then *hirplin'* along the shore, barefooted, I reached the church which was to be our home till Monday, whither the Missionary had preceded me, who under many difficulties had supplied a change of garments that were at least dry.

On our arrival at Isumu, Pavenga, the teacher, and one or two of his pupils did their utmost for us. The firewood was wet, and it was hard to kindle. By and by, however, we had some water boiling in an old meat tin, and got some tea—tin pannikins doing duty as cups and saucers. Thereafter the cook and his wife started off in the pelting rain for Port Resolution, to conduct the Sabbath services, as Niath, the teacher, had gone on a visit to Aneityum. Several of the people brought native mats and native skirts. With a bundle of the latter we made a pillow, and laying some on our reed bed, we spread our rug and hung up our indispensable mosquito netting. The drenching with rain acted as a soporific, and we awoke next day quite refreshed. Though it still rained, we had a good congregation, and, besides the regular service, we talked and sang hymns the livelong day, being well repaid with such a crowd of eager listeners. We had only tea and sugar with us, but were well supplied with native food, and almost as soon as Monday's sun arose, one friend, of his own accord, brought us a fresh cooked yam for breakfast. After breakfast, morning prayers, and school, we packed up our rugs and resumed our march, accompanied by a band from Isumu. We walked leisurely, and talked to all we saw; visited and prayed with several sick ones on the way, and finally reached Kwamera in time for an early tea. . . .

On the 25th October we went to Imarakak. We

took our boat to Meiyahau, and then walked up hill. We were a large and heavily-laden party. Some were carrying bedding and others garments for the new scholars; others, again, the magic-lantern gear. The people were expecting us, and on our arrival we found all the women engaged cooking. We rigged up our sleeping quarters and then unpacked our gifts. By and by the food began to flow in, and soon we had a pig, a pile of yams and taro, uncooked; and a pig and twenty-five native puddings, cooked. We, on the other hand, gave a shirt to each man, and dresses to all the women and girls. Some of our Isuma friends had come to see the opening of the church.

In the evening we had a most successful magic-lantern exhibition, from which our friends went home by torch-light. We found our reed bed much improved by having taken a cotton quilt with us, which we got from Mrs Anderson, Christchurch, twelve years ago. Next morning all came to school, and we started for home in the afternoon.

We again left Kwamera on 2nd November, called on the way at Yakumaruan, and had a mid-day prayer meeting with the few who attended church there, and gave them a girdle or a dress apiece. It is the first free gift they have ever received from us. Thence we went to Imerakak, staying over night, and had good meetings both at night and in the morning. Thereafter we resumed our journey, accompanied by a numerous band of worshipping people. We took an inland road to visit a village and speak to the people there; and then on to Isumu. As we passed along, we invited all church attenders to meet with us in the school-house that afternoon, when we distributed over *seventy* garments. Each dress I fitted on, and you should have seen the unbounded satisfaction it gave to these daughters of Eve to be thus arrayed in gay print. Pavenga, the teacher, has what I call a school-house up at the principal village, and a church at the sea at Isumu. He is an Aniwan, and is by far our best and most energetic teacher. He is very natty, and had a nice reed bed put up, enclosed on three sides, and hung with pictures from the " Graphic." He has a congregation of *ninety*, and the people are very hearty. Next morning, when all were dressing for church, an appeal was made to me for more men's garments. Kapere, a notorious disease-maker, and a terror to all the people, had come to join our party, also a young man. Not knowing that we had spare shirts, the already worshipping people had rigged them out most comically in women's garments. This Kapere, if won over, will be an acquisition ; for, like Paul of old, he is well known for his opposition to "the way." We had meetings from morning till night. Up hill, down at the sea, and up hill again. The eager crowds and the heartiness of the people prevented us from feeling weary, and it was far on into the night before Bible stories and hymn-singing came to an end.

Next day, after morning school, accompanied by a great band, we took the inland road through villages, and one by one our party bade us adieu as each reached his or her home, only a few remaining as guides, and among these Kapere. We had one heavy hill to climb, but, as usual, my good angels, the Tannese, helped me up. Passing through one or two small villages, we at last reached Yanasirei, a village nestling so beautifully at the foot of the highest range of mountains. Here Kapere made his first speech in favour of the gospel, and told that he intended to renounce the works of the devil. From Yanasirei we continued to rise up a spur of mountain, and, while doing so, Kapere described a tragic murder that had taken place on that road during the past year. Yeru, a man from Meikasaru, had been visiting at Isumu, and was returning home, some friends convoying him, native-like, in single file, each one laden with food or firearms. They went up this way, Yeru leading. But a plot had been laid to kill him in revenge for certain things he was supposed to have done; such as causing the volcano ashes to fall in a certain direction and spoil their yams. He was shot as he reached the summit of the hill, just when he would get the first view of his home in the distance. He ran back a few steps, calling for his son to be brought to him ere he breathed his last. Many of his party fled in terror, but a few remained (Kapere among them) while life ebbed away. They carried him carefully back to Isumu, and buried him with all due respect; for he was interred in the kava-house in the public square. As we trod the path, and were shown each spot, I confess I felt a little "eerie." But now we had a magnificent view. We saw, close by, the coast toward Kwamera, and, beyond the ocean, the island of Aneityum. Before us were the volcano and the harbour of Port Resolution. Looking a little round, we saw Sulphur Bay, Weasisi, and the far point of Tanna, Cape Clear: while across the ocean, in the same direction, lay Erromanga. Now we began gradually to descend, and as we passed through the villages a wondering crowd of savages followed us until we reached Isarkei, where we sat down and waited Maruki's arrival. The public square here is very picturesque, and there is evidently a large population. After some time, our old friend came, and it was interesting to see how changed he was. The first time we met him and told him about his son, he shook with fear; now he welcomed us with open arms, and pointed out a site near the public square where he would build a school-house, were his son to come home. If the son is really a converted lad, what a power he might be at home! but I fear lest the great force of heathenism around should draw him aside, and he relapse into his original state.* Maruki accompanied us to the next village, and from thence we found our way across to Port Resolution in time for tea, that being our first meal since sunrise. We felt cheered by all we had seen, and much encouraged. The great advantage of these journeys is, that we see and talk with people we would otherwise never meet. The more we know of Tanna, the more do we see how closely interlinked the tribes are, and how necessary it is that all should be influenced. I feel somewhat remorseful at the thought that we have not made many more such journeys. The fear of fever and ague, through roughing it, and war, have often deterred us. Besides, we have always had more than enough to do at our principal stations. Kwamera may be called the centre. There all the

---

* The son did not return, and Maruki was shot some years after.

printing, bookbinding, dressmaking, &c., are carried on. This year our New Zealand friends, by sending made dresses, have enabled us to do more for the "regions beyond." . . .

We are having a long tack of drought and no prospect of rain, to procure which our deluded people are using all their enchantments. The supposed rain-makers are being threatened with a violent death if they do not make rain quickly.

I must tell you of another long walk we had to see a famous waterfall called Ifeker. We have heard of the falls for the last twenty years, and were anxious to see them, but as of Canaan of old "an ill report" had been brought up; "the way was long," "we would never reach them," "we would be benighted," "the people through whose land we had to go were cannibals," &c., &c. But, undeterred, we prepared to go, for rarely had there been so long peace among the tribes. We rose at four and started at six a.m., acccompanied by four Christian natives. The morning was dull, and before we had gone very far rain came on, wetting the bush and us too; and, to add to all, we went for half an hour off the road. Returning, we found the footpath and reached a village called Irromanga, where we were expected, and two men volunteered to go with us as guides. Two women and five girls also joined us; thus we numbered fifteen. Our path lay through level country until we came to the foot of the stream, at the head of which were the falls. Not wishing to wet our shoes we were carried across, and began to climb a steep hill. For hours we went on our mountain path, through villages and past plantations, till we reached the last village. Ere then we had made some very steep descents, and my heart sank as I thought of our return journey. Here our friend Naru-Niatengei joined us. Having heard of our passing inland, he set out in search of us an hour and a half after we had left his village. He at once offered himself as my bodyguard, and not even a proverbial Frenchman could have been more gallant than my dusky, painted companion. Now we were down to the level of the stream. We took note of the time as we went on our journey, so as to see how long we might safely stay at the falls. But, alas, we had taken six and a half hours to reach the falls, so there would be no time to spend there at all. We estimated the height of the fall at about eighty feet; and I felt quite recompensed for my long walk by the grandeur of the scene. To sit down for ten minutes was all we could spare ere we retraced our steps. Mr Watt photographed the fall; but had the special correspondent of some paper been nigh with his camera, he would doubtless have secured some comical views worthy of "Punch." At each village a number of gaping, wondering savages had joined our party, until we now numbered fifty. When we got to the foot of the stream our friend and the big crowd left us; and when we reached the nearest village we rested our third ten minutes, drank a cocoa-nut, and then pressed on, as it was already half-past four. Being too tired to walk quickly, we ran down and with an effort reached the head of the bay at seven o'clock, having been thirteen hours on the way, and not forty minutes' rest all day. Weren't we glad to hail our canoe and paddle ourselves home?

Although I have somewhat prolonged this epistle,

still I cannot close without referring to the loss this Mission has sustained in the death of Kaiasi, who for the last ten years has been identified with us. He was one of the few remaining of the tribe Naraimene who received the missionaries fifty years ago, and he was the only one who professed faith in Christ. Nearly all his life he was on the Christian side. He learned to read and write, and gave a helping hand in all mission work, although he was only admitted to the membership of the church two years ago. When the Frasers joined this Mission, and went to Epi, he accompanied them, and Mr Fraser said he was as consistent a Christian as he had seen in the New Hebrides during his three years' service there. After spending a year at home on Tanna, he again went forth to the high places of the field as a helper to Mr Leggatt at Malekula, where he died this year. Poor fellow, he was never robust; but we hoped to have left him during our absence at Port Resolution, and had arranged for his coming home; but the Saviour he loved and served has taken him to a *better* home. Mr Leggatt said that when dying he gave no uncertain indication as to where his trust was placed, and that during his life there, in dealing with a fellow-servant (an Ambrim lad and a heathen), he often put even a missionary to shame by his earnest endeavours to win him over to the Saviour. Though he has passed away far from his home, and no one near who could speak to him in his own tongue, his death has impressed the Malekulans, who say "he was a good man." Nor will he soon be forgotten on Tanna, for he did a unique thing in this Mission; he made a hymn to the tune "Jesus is mine," which has become a great favourite on the island. He lived to receive a copy of our new hymn book, in which his hymn was included. Often I think how his kindly eyes would have sparkled had he been spared to return and hear the eulogies passed on it by his fellow-islanders, and the heartiness with which it is sung everywhere. Thus within twelve months, one of the pioneers at each of the four new stations has died, and the ground has been taken possession of in the Master's name.

Of Kaiasi it could be truthfully said that he loved his Bible. He was a diligent student of those portions which he had; and once and again he contributed ten shillings out of his salary of Five Pounds to the British and Foreign Bible Society.

The "Dayspring" has arrived before all our letters are written, and Mr Robertson has responded most heartily to our request for teachers, and has brought ashore two couples to-day, so that I will be able to tell you of their settlement when next I write. We have a busy season before us, preparing for leaving here next December. Pray for Tanna.

Yours, &c.,

A. C. P. WATT.

XXIII.
CLOUDS AND SUNSHINE.

GENERAL LETTER.

August, 1889.

On the last Sabbath of 1888, along with our teachers and Tannese church members, we commemorated the dying love of our Saviour. We were a small, yet interesting party, for we represented five different languages. Except the Erromangan teachers, who had lately joined us, all were familiar with Tannese, and so could enjoy the services. To say that Tanna is a hard field, is only repeating what you have already heard; how hard it is, none know so well as we; but if even a few souls are saved, have we not cause to thank God and take courage? During the year, we have had no additions to our church membership, but, on the contrary, our losses have been great. Three church members have died within twelve months. . . . The whole of January and February and part of March were taken up principally in printing and binding *one thousand* copies of our catechism and hymn book. William spent hours daily in the printing-office, and I was glad to see it finished; for several times, after close work with the type, he seemed to take an illness like lead poisoning.

While the printing work was under weigh, we had a severe experience. On the 28th of January the sea rose very high, right into our premises, and it was with difficulty we got the boat dragged along into a place of safety. The wind did us comparatively little damage, but we have learned since that it blew down Mr Lawrie's new church at Aname, and also the greater part of Dr Gunn's house on Futuna, as well as his church, school-house, and other buildings.

For the encouragement of the new teachers, and as a stimulus to those only commencing to learn to read, as well as for a break in the printing and other sedentary work at Kwamera, we packed up in the beginning of February for a week's tour among the stations. As we rounded a near point of land it seemed as if the whole of Port Resolution point were on fire. We learned that this was revenge, the people there having been credited with making the late storm. We spent Saturday and Sabbath at Yanatuan, and on Monday went to Yanumarer, where we had afternoon and evening meetings, and slept over night. Next day, after morning worship, we started for Port Resolution. We had great difficulty in getting there as the roads were so blocked with fallen trees and branches, that our progress was slow. Though exhausted with the journey, on reaching Port Resolution we went to see the desolation caused by the fire. Two whole villages had been burnt to ashes, and the plantation fences thrown down. All the people had fled to the Mission premises, and were now herding together in the two villages nearest the Mission house. No lives had been taken, the enemy feeling that a destruction of property would be a fair revenge for the property they had lost by the gale.

Leaving Port Resolution we retraced our steps, visiting Ikurupu and Imerahak by the way, and reached Kwamera exactly a week from the day of starting. Can you imagine what a week of such life involves, in bodily discomfort and mental exercise? Or can you realise the happiness experienced in feeling that we are following the example of Him who went about from village to village and preached the gospel? Unlike Him, we cannot heal the sick, but we can alleviate human suffering as we go along, by prescribing for and praying for the afflicted. Had we only strength of body and means of travelling, I believe the more we mixed among the people the more good we would do.

Nahi-abba, the chief here, who has hindered our work so much, and who has been so opposed to the gospel, had a severe illness last year, and as usual attributed it to *Nahak*, and blamed the neighbouring tribe. He nursed his wrath, and waited patiently for an opportunity of revenge. At last he determined to strike the blow. On the 15th of March he went to a neighbouring village, but left a message with the young men, that they were to shoot the man before sundown, adding, "If you do the deed, it is well; but if not, I will shoot one of you instead of him in the evening." It was Friday, and I was holding my weekly sewing class. We had wrought hard all forenoon, taken a rest at lunch-time, and were about to resume our sewing, when a conch shell was heard. In less time than I take to tell it, the whole population was in a state of intense excitement. The women threw down their seams, and some even left their infants while they ran to save their household goods, for no one knew what would happen next. The man was shot, but the avenger of blood might take revenge on any one, and soon the whole district might be in flames. While every one ran hither and thither I nursed the infants, and, like one of old, sat in the gate to hear the news as the events occurred. For weeks from that day there was nothing but war and suspense. The outlying families flocked into this district, and for many a night few slept. As for me, I spent the first night up to ten o'clock pasting books, and proposed finishing the work the following day; but about midnight I awoke in severe pain, and for six weeks I did no more active work. For five days I neither ate, drank, nor slept in any sense, and for four weeks thereafter the only sleep I got was when under morphia. The poet says:

"They also serve who only stand and wait,"

but the hardest of all service is waiting. This I realised *fully* when laid aside all these weeks. How we longed for friends and medical advice, while at the same time we sang,

"I leave it all to Jesus, for He knows."

By degrees I recovered strength and resumed my duties, and by the time the "Dayspring" arrived on the 7th May, I was fairly well. How late she was! It was 7th May before she reached Kwamera, but she brought us a fat mail-bag and our old friends the Patons. The "Dayspring" had no fewer than eight passengers, and of these three were new missionaries (Rev. T. Smaill, B.A., and Rev. J. and Mrs Gillan), whom we were specially glad to see; for still there is room. We had a pleasant although very short visit from our old and new friends, and were glad to see the Rev. Mr and Mrs Bannerman of Otago. I hope their visit will advance the interests of the Mission as a whole, and encourage the churches to send down deputations to see for themselves what is being done. We are not afraid of the eyes of the world, and feel that the better our churches know the nature and extent of our work, the more help and sympathy will we get.

On the Monday after the "Dayspring" passed here, while we were revising proofs in the evening, about eight o'clock, the cry of "Sail oh!" startled us, and we rushed to the beach and found a boat about to land. This was a party from the U.S.S. Co.'s steamer "Fijian" in search of help. The steamer had run ashore that morning on the other side of Tanna. Poor fellows! they had had twelve hours' hard pulling to get here, and arrived cold and wet, but were cheered by the accommodation we could give them. Next day William accompanied them in his boat, leaving here at seven in the morning and returning about nine p.m. He brought back six passengers: Hon. Mr and Miss Buchanan, Mr Stookes the Captain, and Mrs Groom the stewardess of the wrecked vessel. From October of last year until May of this year no boat had landed; and we felt it might be very awkward for the shipwrecked party (nearly forty) if left here for such a length of time. They were fortunate in their misfortune, however, for on the second day, when we were looking for the rest of them, and were planning where the tents should be placed, a boat came round to tell that a vessel had been spoken to, and that it would take them off. The boat returned to the wreck that day, and it was arranged that the mission boat should follow next morning. During that night the S.S. "Tenterden's" lights were observed, and by means of blue lights her attention was arrested, and she was brought to the rescue. Having taken all on board at the wreck, she came round here and took away those who were with us. Thus on the fourth day after the wreck, help came, and we parted with our shipwrecked friends, who had proved so agreeable, that we were sorry when they left. I am sure they were glad to get away from these hostile shores, for the Tannese stole right and left at the wreck. The more we know of the Tannese, the more we are amazed at the peace we have enjoyed in this terrible land, and the less do we wonder at the little progress made. Like Uriah, we have been set in the forefront of the hottest battle; but the battle is the Lord's, and He will look after His own interests. After the "Fijian" party left, the next big job was the arrowroot. We have made 1044 lbs.; the people working willingly and well. One day we had over a hundred helping. This is the contribution in free labour of the people here.

We had invited the Synod to meet here, and were looking forward to it with some anxiety, as I had been so ill; but our helps did well, and we were all ready for it when the members arrived on June 28th. As previously arranged, our beloved fellow-labourers, Mr and Mrs Gray, came round a week before. The two veteran Tanna missionaries made a boat voyage round the little world of Tanna, leaving their worthy wives to look after affairs at Kwamera. After the "Dayspring"

Revs. A. Morton, J. W. Mackenzie, Dr Paton, J. Landels, F. Smaill, T. W. Leggatt, W. Watt, J. Gillan, O. Michelsen,
J. Bannerman (Otago), and P. Milne.
Mrs Morton, Mrs Mackenzie, Mrs Paton, Rev. W. Gray (Moderator), Mrs Watt, Mrs Gillan, Mrs Gray,
Miss Paton, Mrs Leggatt.

SYNOD OF 1889, HELD AT KWAMERA.

came, we formed a party of twenty adults and four children. Every available place was used as a sleeping apartment; even the storeroom was turned into a barracks with beds for six. We had a busy but very pleasant time, a delightful communion season, and a nice little prayer meeting. It was most enjoyable. Our large party were with us for a fortnight and a day. And oh! it was nice to have the Patons here. But the happiest meetings come to a close, and soon we had to part with our dear friends, who went forth each to his or her own special work. We found the promise true, "As thy days, so shall thy strength be"; and we stood the extra duties well; duties all the heavier, as some of our helps were completely laid up, and others worked on while suffering from influenza. This epidemic came just as the Synod met. As the Grays were going back by boat, we had to wait for suitable weather, and in the meantime we packed up for a visit to Port Resolution and the out-stations. After about ten days we started, getting a fine sea. On our way we landed goods at three stations to await our return overland. The goods were from various parts of the world, but the boxes were the gifts of our never-failing friends, the Sinclairs of Timaru.

We remained over a week at Port Resolution. There, too, we have suffered loss. Navau, Sasairo's wife, has died, leaving an infant a few months old. Sasairo and she have been the most decided among the young people there. She often led the singing; and we sadly missed her sunny face. But we have good hope of her. Among her last words to her mother were, "I am going to leave you and go to heaven."

Since the opening of the new station at Ikurupu, Niath, the Port Resolution teacher, has been there, as the Erromangan teacher could not speak the language, and Sasairo and Braun (another lad) have taken charge of the meeting. May they be kept steadfast! The death also of Yauteki (Braun's father) has been a great loss to our mission, for he was by far the most energetic friend of the gospel at Port Resolution. We trust he, too, has reached the golden shore.

We had arranged to leave Port Resolution on Tuesday (July 30th), but it rained heavily all night, so we waited another day. However, on Wednesday, the Ikurupu girls came to carry our things, and we left. What we dreaded befell us before we had gone far, for the rain came down in torrents, and all our belongings were drenched. Bundles of bedding, changes of clothing, biscuits, &c., were all wet; while we literally swam in our shoes, and were wet to the skin,—rather a cheerless prospect for the night; but there being no help for it, we got up a good fire and dried our clothing. At the two meetings we examined the people in reading and hymn-singing, and were much pleased with the progress made. Already one young man prays in church. As they have no other way of getting clothing, and we were leaving for a long time, we gave each of the forty-one scholars a dress.

Next morning was fine, and we went on to Yanumarer. There the attendance of males and the progress made is very gratifying. Sani and his wife Yecrimu are proving good teachers, and are loved and respected by all their parishioners. There also we distributed dresses, and after staying one night went on to Isumu

(Yanatuan). Pavenga continues to show himself a workman that needeth not to be ashamed, and he has a fine field for his energies. We stayed there three days, and in many ways tried to help the good work. On Sabbath no fewer than six men engaged in prayer in church. Old Kauraka has made wonderful progress in Scripture knowledge, and Kapere, the old sorcerer, made a unique and impressive prayer. That, I think, was one of our happiest days on Tanna.

The people contributed twenty-five fowls to the New Zealand church as a token of love to them. We distributed *seventy* dresses, each individual rewarding us with a smile of delight. On Monday we left them and visited our third new station, Imerakak. The women and girls turn out well, but the men are backward. However, Vahai and his wife Ripa are active teachers, and will devote their whole time to teaching while we are away. Thirty-seven dresses were given here. Amid many expressions of grief at our departure we left, followed by a crowd who accompanied us down the slippery path to the sea. How good the natives are in clearing away every obstacle from our path, and taking our hands at difficult places! It is well that they are so, for in fording one stream, the current was so strong and the water so deep, that without their help we would never have got over. By the help of one on either side I waded safely through.

All our homeward journey was characterised by farewells, and since then one and another band have come to bid us good-bye. The other evening, including the people of Kwamera, we had seventy at

SCHOOL-HOUSE, YANTIAN.

church. About half of these had come as good as ten miles to say farewell. I am in a strait; to leave them is hard, but to carry the New Testament through the press is all important. We are leaving our stations in good working order; our teachers are as efficient as any we have ever had, and Mr Gray has kindly agreed to supervise all. May God greatly bless the people in our absence, and prepare them for the printed Word of Life we hope to bring to them. The revision of the New Testament is complete!

Now about Nahi-abba the chief at Kwamera. The scamp has begun to attend church and school once more, and last Sabbath he brought his little adopted son and heir for the first time; but alas, he shows no signs of accepting the Gospel. Pray for him, that from whatever motive he has come he may get a blessing.

In making arrangements for a prolonged absence from our station, I am struck with the different state of affairs now from what it was ten years ago, when we left the islands. Then we left *one* teacher at one station; now we leave *eight*, some of whom have flourishing schools. Then there were *thirty* books in circulation; now there are at least *three hundred*.

Let us not despise "the day of small things," but pray that "the little one may become a thousand." We have a hard field, and our faith is sorely tried; the Church ought to know this and take its share in the burden of weary waiting.

Why should we be expected to fight against such terrible odds, and yet be expected to write encouraging letters? Let the Church *continue* to help us and uphold our hands by prayer, by Mission boxes, by words of cheer, and so strengthen our hearts. Thus doing, it shall not be said of it by the Angel of the Lord, "Curse ye Meroz, curse ye bitterly the inhabitants thereof; because they came not to the help of the Lord, to the help of the Lord against the mighty."

October 7th. We left Kwamera on the 7th September, and arrived in Sydney on the 4th October. Probably we will leave for Scotland in a fortnight.

AGNES C. P. WATT.

XXIV.
INTO HARNESS AGAIN.

GENERAL LETTER.

December, 1891.

In these days of New Hebridean monthly mails it seems a long time since I sent my last general epistle in June; but after all, this is just the month I would have sent it by the "Dayspring." Our many friends around the world may be thinking that we have forgotten them, while we are having many proofs that we are not forgotten by them. We have had several tangible forms of deep interest in the form of Mission boxes and periodicals. So much for the thoughtfulness of friends; and now for an explanation of my seeming remissness.

Well, you know how we were dragged round the group of islands, owing first to the severe weather, and then,—owing to—well, I won't say what—landed far from our own station. In this way it was long after leaving Sydney before we got back to our station at Kwamera, and even when we did get there it was in our own boat, the gift of the Auckland people, and called the "Aucklander." It did not seem at all like a return from Scotland, landing twenty miles from Kwamera, and then going there by boat. Our people there were

not a little soured at the long delay ; but they were glad
to see us, and a day or two afterwards made us a nice
present of native food. We missed not a few familiar
faces ; for in a little more than twelve months we had
lost four of our small band of church members—four
out of eight. This tells sorely on our Tannese, who,
being very superstitious, think there must be some
fatality connected with church membership.

We were gratified on our return to learn that no
hurricane had done any damage to our premises ; that
those left in charge had been faithful, and kept all in
fair repair, as far as natives can do ; also to find from
the teachers' reports that the attendance at church and
school and at the various places had been good. Thus
in every way we have much cause for gratitude to
God and happiness to ourselves.

The first duty that pressed on us after getting our
goods boated round was to pay those who had done
work during our absence. These were legion ; for in
this land of quick decay things are constantly needing
repairs or renewals. Then we had our annual
contribution of arrowroot made. At this our Kwamera
people worked well, and the result was four casks of
first-class arrowroot. The proceeds are to go to line
the roof of the Kwamera Church, which, as you know,
was built by the same means.

The arrowroot made, bagged, casked, and got
ready for shipment, we came round here (Port
Resolution) for the erection of the "Scotch Church"—
"a memorial of workers and work on Tanna." It
proved a very heavy job, for in this primitive land,
where there is no machinery, and all has to be done by

strength of arm, getting up some parts of the building was no joke. We improvised a derrick by lashing together the masts of the two boats, and with the aid of these and blocks and tackle we got the principal parts into their proper positions; and although carpenters and builders may laugh at it, we heaved a sigh of relief when the last one was secured. Mr Gray and Mr Watt were the only skilled workmen. The others were all inexperienced in such work, being natives of the island. We had them all divided into two relays, who came turn about each alternate day; and I assure you, there are no natives in these islands, or indeed in any land, who would have come more faithfully, or worked more heartily, than these much-abused Tannese. The work went on every day, Sabbaths excepted, from six a.m. till six p.m., for forty days. On ten of these days Mr Gray gave very valuable assistance. In truth, I do not see how we could have done without him. Day by day the women prepared food, the boys pulled drinking cocoa-nuts, and everyone worked willingly, while crowds came and gazed on in wonder as the edifice arose.

Church building may not be considered by some as Mission work, yet we believe that this church erection has been the means of much good to the people, for we have better attendances both on Sabbaths and weekdays than ever we had before. We managed to keep up the daily morning and evening meetings during all the building time, and after the devotional part was over the builders went out, the rest remaining for lessons.

The thing that above all others has given an impetus to our reading classes has been the distribution of the

New Testament. Though in a different language to that spoken at Weasisi, yet Mr Gray uses our books in addition to his own, and the accident of our being landed at his station instead of at either of our own, led to the first New Testaments being given out there. By arrangement, a representative man took them from the missionary and handed them to the people, who seemed much pleased to receive them. Then a boating party being over from Aniwa, they also got a share, to their no small joy, as they have not the complete New Testament in their own language. The Kwamera people were the next recipients. There, Naswai received them from the missionary and handed them round. He had been one of the final pundits, and was thus keenly interested in the book. The last to get their share thus formally were the people here at Port Resolution, but I think they showed more joy at getting them than any of the others, and ever since have plodded diligently to be able to read them. While telling you of the bright side, I must not fail to tell you that at one teacher's station, the young people, at the instigation of the grown-up, refused to take the foreign-made books. Although they use the books printed at Kwamera, and have no fear of them, they dread those printed in a foreign land *—another proof of the dense superstition with which we have to contend. Since then a few copies have been received

---

* Oddly enough, a somewhat opposite superstition prevails on Malekula. A heathen man of rank will not take food that has been cooked on, say, the Missionary's fire on Malekula, but he has no fear of eating biscuits which were cooked in a foreign land where the Malekulan spirits didn't see them.—T. W. L.

in that district. Perhaps you will remember that the dread of books is an old story on Tanna, and it is only lately that the fear has begun to break down.

At present we have some interesting pupils, of whom I hope to tell you more by and by. One of these, called Nirua, alias "Monkey," is a married man, and comes some miles for lessons.

When the building was so far finished that we could safely leave it, we paid a visit to Kwamera. We stayed there about a month, and then came back here prepared for the church opening. On Wednesday, the 28th October, exactly twelve months to a day since we left Liverpool, natives from far and near assembled for the occasion. Mr and Mrs Gray and their two children, Mr Voullaire, a German teacher, and our neighbour Mr Bramwell joined us. We were a somewhat mixed company, speaking a medley of different languages. The building was well filled, but the bigger crowd was gathered outside, for our heathen onlookers were afraid to enter the sacred edifice. We had a nice service, and all seemed happy.

After it was over there was an exchange of gifts. We gave a hundred yards of prints and calicoes, some handkerchiefs, two pots full of cooked rice, a pile of yams and taro, and two pieces of salt beef. Our neighbour gave some print, tins of beef, and rice. The natives gave two cooked pigs, and puddings *ad lib*. These things being divided to the satisfaction of all, we had speeches, when doubtless some good impressions were made. The weather was brilliant, and all passed off satisfactorily. On the next Sabbath we had a good attendance, Mr Gray addressing the people. On the

CHURCH AND PEOPLE—PORT RESOLUTION.

Sabbath following that, we made our first money collection on Tanna. We were much pleased with the hearty way in which the people responded to this the first call to give a free gift to the Lord. One man, whose whole purse was seventeen shillings, gave one shilling himself and one shilling to each of his three sons, so that they might have something to give. Knowing how meanly the Tannese treated the spirits whom they worshipped in heathenism, giving them the scraggiest fish, the poorest bananas and the smallest yams, we were highly pleased with what they contributed. We asked them to give it as a thank-offering for the remarkable exemption from accident during the building of the church, for at times the work was rather dangerous. The result was £3 5s.

During the last month we have been erecting much-needed offices in place of some that threatened to tumble about our heads. In this work, too, the people have done well, and they and we have been very busy. On some days I had to provide food for, and divide it over, no less than forty people. I often think this mission is conducted on wrong lines, and that an industrial mission would suit our people better; for in that way one would get many more opportunities of doing the people good, and putting in a word for the Master. With manual labour on hand at which we can employ them, they are brought more about us, and we can confer more benefits, both spiritual and temporal. Indeed, I sometimes feel that if we were allowed to trade in copra, and had a market for it, we could make our mission self-supporting.

Surely Tanna bulks largely in some minds, though it

is only a small island—a little larger than Arran,—for we have noticed that the "civil war" raging on it was referred to, not only in the Australian papers, but even in a San Francisco paper and the London *Standard*. We have also been receiving letters of condolence from friends who think our lives in danger. Personally the said civil war has not affected us in the slightest, and the Grays, who were in the centre of the scene of action, and who more than once had the bullets whizzing over or around their house, were so assured of their personal safety that Mrs Gray stayed bravely alone with the children, while Mr Gray came up here to assist at our church-building.

Doubtless the kingdom of Christ is coming on this dark island; nevertheless, the devil's kingdom has been powerful during the past two years. Rarely at any time will you not find war raging in some district; but this last year it almost seems to have been wider spread than usual, and certainly the list of "killed and wounded" has been unusually large for Tanna, while the atrocities committed have been worse than we have ever heard of before. Indignities were offered to the dead of both sexes; and in one case, at least, the enemy committed the sin that Elisha said that Hazael would do, and, as in several other cases, the poor woman was left unburied to be eaten by dogs, and would have been completely devoured, had not one of our teachers come on the scene next day, and, unaided, dug a grave and buried her. One instance of the disgusting depravity of these people has shocked me much. A man who attends service in the district where the above-mentioned dreadful affair took place, on seeing the poor mutilated form of the woman, addressed it thus: "If only the Gospel had not reached my village, how I would have enjoyed a feast off you." I cannot tell you how much this has preyed on my mind, or how glad I feel at realising that Jesus is an Almighty Saviour, and can save to the uttermost, else I would despair of these people.

Some have said that the backwardness of the Gospel on Tanna is due to the want of faith on the part of her missionaries; but I agree with our fellow-labourer, Mr Gray, who says it is only those who have *gigantic* faith that could have laboured so many years in Tanna.

I have been suffering for three months with a pain on the instep of my right foot, which has prevented me itinerating, and so William has had to go alone, to the no small disappointment of the women. Lately he visited Yanumarer and Yanatuan, staying from Saturday till Monday at the latter place. Just the day before he arrived a sad accident occurred. A band of women and girls, while bathing, were carried out to sea. All saved had a narrow escape. Two were much exhausted, and one woman, alas, was drowned.

December 17th.—I had written up to this yesterday, and hoped to have to-day printed it on the trypograph. Yesterday we devoted to entertaining the natives, as we would not be here on New-year's-day. We had a religious service in the church, and then distributed the Glasgow Foundry Boys' Religious Society's gifts, reading the texts sent by them, and telling the people here something of the Society. After the meeting was over we had sports in the mission premises, the "tug-of-war" being, as usual, the favourite. We also showed them the dolls sent, and men and women yelled with delight. Many had never seen the like before. While we were in the height of interest over a potato (lemon) race, the cry got up, "There's the steamer!" She was thus more than two days before her time, and consequently we were not ready. To-day I am printing this, and will leave it here for next mail. In a day or two we leave for Kwamera, where we hope to spend the greater part of next three months.

We heard two days ago that there is a great deal of sickness at Kwamera, and as the steamer reported influenza as very prevalent on Aneityum, we fear that that dreaded scourge has at length found its way to this remote island of Tanna.

AGNES C. P. WATT.

TANNA, December 17th, 1891.

XXV.
SICKNESS AND WAR.

GENERAL LETTER.

PORT RESOLUTION, April, 1892.

"Master, we have toiled all the night, and have taken nothing: nevertheless at Thy word I will let down the net." Where is this Christ-honouring faith nowadays? It seems to me that those who cull for religious papers, for foreign mission reports, and for the Christian public generally, pick out the bright things in missionaries' letters and use them as arguments for obeying Christ's command to disciple all nations, as if that were the only way to get people to subscribe for the extension of the Redeemer's kingdom; whereas, the fact that Christ has bid us disciple all nations ought to be enough to make every child of God ready to give for the advancement of His kingdom, whether the fruit be seen or not.

I fear the searchers for encouragements only will find little in this general letter to their taste, for, during the past year, "deep has been calling unto deep" all over the island. Our fellow-labourers, the Grays, have felt this as well as we. Indeed, it seems to me as if it had been the most trying year that they have had on Tanna. I remarked lately in a letter to them, that their letters to us read like a second book of the Lamentations of Jeremiah. Nearly a year ago

Ya-ko-le, one of their most promising natives, was shot, and in the subsequent war their only out-station was broken up, and they were in the centre of the inter-tribal fighting, and had the bullets whizzing round their house, and finally found themselves deserted, as neither side for a time dared to come openly to their premises for fear of the other. The war scare was not well over, when that dread scourge, influenza, laid them and all their parishioners low, and for weeks they were under a heavy cloud. This cleared away, and things seemed brighter when the "Para" brig, a labour vessel, brought back and landed six men and one woman—returned labourers from Queensland. One man and the woman belonged to the west side of the island; but for some reason or other they were landed at Weasisi, some of Mr Gray's parishioners professing to be their friends, and the man assenting thereto. The "Para" left, and the natives scattered to go to their different stations. Mr Gray had resumed the house-building, which had been interrupted by the arrival of the vessel, when a shot was heard. The Tanna lads working with Mr Gray then revealed to his two Aniwan helps the plot that had been laid to kill the man and keep his wife and property, and now asked leave to stop working, which was granted. Mr Gray determined to go and see for himself; so, headed by the two Aniwan helps, he went in the direction of the shot. On the way they saw a Tannaman, who tried to dissuade them from following a certain path; but Mr Gray made signs to the Aniwans to proceed. They had not gone far when the foremost stood still, and pointing over the brae-side, said in Weasisian, "He is there"; and there, a few yards below the path, against the foot of a tree, the man lay dead, stripped of everything but his shirt. Mr Gray went down and examined the body. Putting aside the left arm and tearing open the shirt, he found a large hole, into which the bullet or charge had entered. Mr Gray says he must have been stripped and thrown over the bank before he died, for his right hand was laid over his left breast (the wound was on the left side and near the armpit). He probably laid his hand there as he died. Mr Gray went on to the village and saw Kapakini and Tuman (the latter was the murderer). They still persisted in saying that they were the dead man's friends, and wished Mr Gray to believe that the man was killed by people from the west side of the island. Mr Gray begged leave to bury the body, but could not get it. He even offered them two big axes if they would let him have it, but no. He then gave them a bit of his mind, and for weeks after they showed their resentment at him for condemning this foul deed. Such is Tanna. Two and a half hours after this man was landed he was coolly murdered, his wife and property being confiscated. (The wife, however, has since fled and reached her home.) His body was carried as good as twenty miles, and given to his enemies there, who cooked part and threw part into the sea.

The ill-feeling about this affair was not over when one of Mr Gray's helps gave him a long night of weary watching and talking, trying to pacify an offended husband, who said the Aniwan had acted improperly with his wife, for which cause he went along with an iron "kawas" and a loaded rifle, bent on revenge; and, but that Mr Gray was stronger than he, I suppose the Aniwan's life would have gone. As it was, he had much trouble and a sleepless night. When in Scotland I sometimes heard people complain about needing to pay taxes or police rates. I wonder how they would like to live in a lawless land like this!

My last "general" left just as the influenza was raging at Kwamera and Weasisi, the two principal mission districts. We were sorry we were not at Kwamera, if by any means we could alleviate the sufferings of our people there; but though we were all ready, we were detained by the weather a whole month. During that month the influenza spread from district to district between Kwamera and Port Resolution, and we were daily receiving tidings of its ravages. Husband and wife frequently succumbed; and in one case husband, wife, and grown-up daughter—the whole family—were cut off, the two former being laid in one grave. The much-dreaded scourge came nearer and nearer. Like the disciples of old, "we feared as we entered into the cloud." At length it reached here—Port Resolution— and out of the whole population living around— about 100—we alone escaped, like the messenger who told Job of his calamities (a man and his wife are one, are they not?). Niathuanipciv, the teacher, was on the verge of the grave for days, and many others seemed more like death than life. We went round twice a day with medicine, tea, and biscuit, and our visits seemed to cheer them, besides, we believe, preventing the sickness having the effect it usually has on Tanna, of driving the people away from church.

Here alone, of all our stations, have we none who drew back from church attendance because they had been sick. . . .

Those who have followed the history of mission work on Tanna know that sickness has been the cause of the breaking up of the mission time and again, and you will see that the same superstition still affects the public mind. Here, only one death occurred, and that was due very much to the fact that the poor woman in her weak state got a severe beating, in which some of her ribs were injured.

On January 19th, after nearly a month's waiting, and after our boat's crew had three times walked overland for us (doing as good as fifty miles in all), we got a fair wind and went to Kwamera, taking Niathanipciv, the teacher, with us, as he was too ill to be left. The people there were glad to see us back, but we missed some familiar faces out of church. Five had died. Of these five, one was Yarere, who (as many who read this know) stayed eleven years in our house, and was a good faithful daughter and servant to us. Our loss was her gain; for, though not a member of the visible church, we believe she has joined the church above. These deaths made everything seem sad at Kwamera; but the darkness was not yet passed. Rukweisiari, one of our brightest and best girls, died in very sad circumstances. She had had a daughter who only lived a few days. She said from the first that she would like to follow her baby, but added, "I am trying to say like Jesus, 'not my will, but Thine, be done.'" After the baby died we got her to stay in our premises, and did all we could for her. She was a very pleasant patient, and though often in much pain she never murmured. She trusted in Jesus, and read and sang up to the very last; for she was sensible, and sang a hymn a few minutes before the blood seemed to rise up in her throat and choke her. Her death made a great impression on those around, for they saw that religion gave her pleasure even in death. In Rukweisiari we lost a good scholar, a faithful servant, and an ever-ready help; but we mourn not as those who have no hope, for we believe she has changed the songs of earth for the songs of heaven.

Jehovah reigneth, and all must be well; but in less than nine months we have lost three of our old girls, our best and most promising young women, and our hearts are weak, while the heathen exult and say, "Now, are we not right, the gospel kills, for are not all the Christian girls dying?" These deaths have weakened our hands, and in the meantime none seem willing to run the risk and fill up the blanks caused by death. During the last three years or so we have had no additions to the membership of our little church; but on the other hand, death has carried off more than half. The cause is the Lord's, and the *faithful* servant is commended, not the successful one. Man praises the successful one, though in his success God knows he has sufficient joy without any congratulations. The Lord perfects strength in weakness.

We never seem to get ahead of the manual labour needed. We have been very busy at Kwamera patching up our rotten houses. Galvanized iron, that lasts I know not how long in other places, has quickly rusted, and at the end of five years we have had to renew much of our roof, as the iron was completely gone. Then we printed and bound a new edition of our Primer, and latterly we printed and sent away one hundred copies of a photograph of our "Scotch Church" at Port Resolution. These have been sent to as many friends in Scotland, America, Nova Scotia, New Zealand, and Australia. We hope in this way to show what we did with the money we raised in Scotland, and enable those who so willingly gave it to realise what a nice church we have got. That church is a lasting sermon to this people, and we are pleased to see that it still exercises a good influence over them; for we continue to have good classes in it daily, and good congregations on Sabbaths. We are gratified with the progress they have made during our absence in reading the New Testament, and we labour and pray that the blessed truths may enter their hearts, and the entrance of the Word illumine their darkness. Has God not said that His Word will not return unto Him void?

April 21st. As intended, we came round to Port Resolution a little over a week ago, and found everything satisfactory. . . . We are now on tiptoe expecting the steamer, when we hope to welcome back returning missionaries, and also Dr and Mrs Lamb. We and the Grays would like if they would choose Tanna; for though Tanna is Tanna still, and would doubtless prove a tough piece of work for Dr Lamb, as it has done to many before him, yet nothing but the gospel will heal the sore of this island, and perhaps a medical man will commend its soul-healing properties by healing their bodies.

AGNES C. P. WATT.

XXVI.

THE CARE OF ALL THE CHURCHES.

TO MISS CROIL, MONTREAL, CANADA.

TANNA, NEW HEBRIDES,
July 16th, 1892.

MY DEAR MISS CROIL:

"Duties waiting on the threshold
Will not be denied,
Others, coming round the corner,
Crowding to their side,
How shall I their number master?
How shall I get through?"

These words strikingly describe our circumstances, and express the question constantly on our lips during the first eight or ten months after our return to Tanna from our recent furlough. We were so fully occupied at the two principal stations that it was hard to find time to visit the out-stations. Mr Watt did make one or two trips to all the stations, but evidently the people were disappointed that Missi Bran did not go. Many were the enquiries about the sprained foot, for all had heard of the accident. It almost seemed as if we could not have pressed more work into each day than we did, yet had it not been for said painful foot, doubtless I too would have itinerated.

At length I made up my mind to try and visit one or two places in the part of our district where the native paths are fairly good. Accordingly on Monday morning, May 30th, we started from Port Resolution. The day was fine and the road good. Our destination was Yanatuan, Pavenga's station. The first four or five miles was on comparatively level ground till near our first halting-place; the path then led by a bleak sand hill, on going down which the foot sinks several inches each step taken. Once down the sandy hill-side we were at the sea-beach, and then we wound our way up a gully for some distance and climbed a steep path to the village, which is named Yanumarer. Sane and Yecrimu taught there while we were in Scotland, but owing to certain circumstances we took them away, and now Sane only goes on Sabbaths, or for a spell of a week or two at a time. We intend spending a week there ourselves in a month or so.

We were well received by the few worshipping people, and supplied with luncheon of native roots roasted, and green cocoa-nuts as a beverage, our long walk making us enjoy the simple meal. After that we had a service in the church with the people. I should have said that at Yanumarer we have a nice grass hut of our own, with reed bench for bedstead, &c. Our Aneityumese teachers, Niath and Sane, had been our burden-bearers thus far, but now they turned back, and the Yanumarer people took their places and conveyed us to the next station. Now, however, all the level road was behind, and one hill after another lay before. I did realise very vividly that every hill has its hollow, for it was up and down, up and down, very much like

the switchback railway we saw in the Edinburgh
Exhibition grounds, only more trying to feet and
lungs. I had travelled the same path before, but this

YECRIMU.

time vowed I would never go again so long as I could get
to see our friends by any other road.

On the way we passed through two villages, but, unfortunately, saw no one. As the day was becoming far spent and our attendants had to return home, we trudged on, or as I expressed it, "hirpled," for every step gave me an aching foot, which I set down most gingerly.

At length the last hill was climbed, and we reached Yaneveker. There Yamen has been teaching for a few months, but before he went there the services were conducted by a Tannaman named Rabyiahammer. Yaneveker is the new station that was opened in our absence; it is really a branch from Yanatuan. Here again we were supplied with food, and our burden-bearers were sent back with eatables both cooked and raw. As we had still some distance to go we had no service, but, getting fresh help, we resumed our march. Alas for me, the last descent into the valley and ascent up the opposite side were the worst of all; the path was very steep, and at some places I had to be literally dragged up by a native. At times I felt clean "forfochen," but set a "stout heart to a stey brae," and so reached the top, panting for breath, and drenched with perspiration. But we got a hearty welcome; and when, after tea, we had a wee service in our grass hut with the natives of the village, and heard how heartily they sang, and how fervently two or three prayed, I forgot the long road and the steep climb.

Worship over, we hung up our mosquito netting to keep off lizards, spiders, rats, &c.; laid our cotton mats on the reed bench, the one to do duty as mattress, sheets, &c., the other as a covering, and, with an air pillow for each, we sought rest. We slept well, and

LINE OF MARCH.

rose refreshed. After a breakfast of yams and tea we had service, gave a present of a dress to each individual, and, with many a kind word and look, left Yanatuan and returned to Yaneveker. Along the steep path, however, I would not go, preferring the longer way down to the sea-beach on the one side and up on the other side of the valley. Our burden-bearers had less to carry now, but even when we take only the bare necessaries of life, we require one or two porters, or more generally porteresses; for the women are the burden-bearers on Tanna. At Yaneveker we had a nice service with a hearty people, and then, bidding them good-bye, started to go back to Port Resolution.

On our return journey we took what I call the "mountain path," rising gradually up the spur of the hill. On the one side nothing is to be seen, but on the other you have a splendid view of the mountains towering some 4,000 feet high, while between you and them lies a lovely valley, with magnificent tree ferns waving their most graceful fronds to every passing breeze, and nearer you see some fine fields of taro, yam, and other native crops. By and by we reach a place called Yakuribus, where a splendid stretch of ocean, harbour, hill and valley bursts on the view, with our Workers' Memorial Church distinctly visible as it nestles on the point of land at Port Resolution. This land is known to the natives as the "fish's tail," and indeed, as seen from the high land, it very much resembles the tail of a fish.

Leaving Yakuribus, we had a little of the hill and valley road to encounter, but only a little. A strange custom prevails on this part of the road. Every native, as he passes along, puts a fern or other leaf either on the ground or on the branch of a tree, just as the withered leaves which have been laid down by those who have gone before indicate. We, of course, pay no attention to the custom, but every native does so most faithfully, and gives as a reason that were they to fail, the god or spirit haunting that part of the mountain would hide the path from them and they would lose their way.

A little after passing this place, we began to descend gently, and went through a defile which I have called "Balaam's Pass." It is a deep fissure or chasm, most probably a rent in the earth caused by an earthquake. It is only a foot or two wide at the bottom, and rises at some places twenty or thirty feet. The narrow cutting continues for some distance, and shortly after emerging from it we came to the village of Yakwanemee. There we rested and waited for an old man named Nasueiyu, who had promised to join the worshipping party. He and his old wife came, but the latter drew back in terror when I offered to shake hands with her, and uttered an exclamation of horror when she saw her husband being dressed in a shirt as the outward sign that from henceforth he was going to attend church. I tried all I could to explain that we have to do with God whether we would or not, and that He wishes all of us to worship and love Him. I fear, however, she was not convinced, and since then I have heard of her death. The ceremony of clothing Nasueiyu over, after a little personal dealing with one or two wild-looking fellows, we resumed our walk, and in a short time arrived at the next village, Ikurupu. There we got fresh porteresses, the others returning to Yaneveker, while we plodded homewards. By this time my foot was paining me much, and when a few miles further on we reached the head of Port Resolution Bay, I was very glad to get a sail down in a canoe. Though jaded in body we felt refreshed in mind, for we were encouraged by the attention of the natives at each place; and, have we not the realisation of that blessedness spoken of in Scripture, "Blessed are ye that sow beside all waters"?

About a week after making this tour, in which I limped painfully so much of the way, the inter-island steamer called here on her way to Aneityum, where the Synod meeting was to be held. She had nearly all the missionaries and their wives on board, and we joined the party.

Last year I told you of the dirt and discomfort experienced on board the "Croydon"; and, as the contrast this year was very striking, it is only just to those in command that I should say something on the subject. All that could be done here was done for the comfort of the missionaries. Bedding for shakedowns had been provided, greater cleanliness was everywhere apparent, there was a good table, and, last but not least, there were obliging stewards. To add to our enjoyment we had fine weather, especially on the return trip from Aneityum to Tanna, so that our voyage was a pleasant one, and then how quickly it was done! We lifted anchor in Port Resolution, Tanna, about four a.m., reached Futuna a little after mid-day, taking Dr Gunn and family on board, and finally cast anchor in Anelgauhat Harbour, Aneityum, a little after midnight.

I was fast asleep when we entered the harbour, and would have known nothing about it, but the captain blew his whistle to let Mr Lawrie know of our arrival, and William thought it well to come down and tell me lest I should imagine something was wrong. He simply awoke me saying: "We are at anchor, and the whistle was blown to arouse Mr Lawrie." As nearly every one preferred sleeping on deck, I had the comfort of a cabin, the one occupied by Dr and Mrs Lamb, and hearing we were at anchor, I thought they might want to dress in it for going on shore, so with all speed I rose, and with bag in hand ready to land, went up on deck to announce to the Lambs that their cabin was free. Fancy my discomfiture when one and another took a good laugh at my expense, and I was asked if I was going ashore at two a.m. I did not go ashore, but returned to my bunk and slept till daylight.

We had a very pleasant time on Aneityum. It was so refreshing to be with so many kindred spirits. Owing to Mrs Lawrie's absence, Mr Lawrie had asked me to take charge of the domestic arrangements, which I reluctantly agreed to. My mission daughters helped efficiently, and the natives worked famously, and so all went well, although latterly we were a company of twenty-nine adults and twelve children. We enjoyed the society of the deputation from New South Wales. It consisted of the Rev. Mr Paterson of Pyrmont, and his most amiable wife; Dr Marden, Principal of the Ladies' College, Croydon; and Mr Aitken, law agent of the New South Wales Presbyterian Church. At several meetings we had excellent addresses from the deputies. True, I have not heard all the deputies from year to year (being in Scotland at the time I missed Professor Drummond), but to me it seemed as if Dr Marden's address was the most finely worded composition I had ever heard in the New Hebrides, while the matter thereof was intensely interesting. It was listened to with rapt attention. The subject was the successful, and apparently non-successful parts of the life of John the Baptist. One sentence was particularly soothing to me, seeing we so long have fought against such odds, and can see little advance. He said: "The soldier on the battle-field, though he be cut down and die while the conflict is still doubtful, has done his duty no less than he who, with shouts of acclamation, carries his sword on to victory."

While at Aneityum I consulted Dr Lamb as to the pain in my right foot. He examined the foot and says there is a small tumour on the bone, most probably caused by something having fallen on the part, and that the only cure is to cut it. Unless, however, it becomes absolutely necessary, I will not agree to that.

Just on the eve of leaving Aneityum, it transpired that there was some hitch in the arrangements for next Synod's meeting. The alterations consequent on Mr Lawrie's probable resignation had not been considered. As no one else volunteered to take action in the matter, and as Anelgauhat is the only place where there is sufficient accommodation for a Synod gathering, William and I offered to entertain the Synod next year at Anelgauhat, and allow the usual grant of £40 for Synod expenses, to go towards buying bedding, napery, cutlery, a stove, &c., which would thus become Synod

PARTY AT CRATER, VASHOR.

property, and be seviceable for future meetings. Our offer was accepted.

Returning from Synod, after landing the Gunns, we went to Weasisi. Some fourteen of us spent the night on shore, and next morning a party of twelve started about 5.30 to walk overland to Port Resolution, visiting the volcano *en route*; the rest of us went round by sea in the "Croydon," and had dinner ready for the tired travellers, who had been on the march for eight hours, and were very glad to get a bath and refreshments, but who nevertheless thought the sight of "Yasoor" worth the trouble. After family prayers, conducted by Mr Aitken, of whom we had formed a particularly high opinion, we adjourned to the church, where we had the usual evening worship with the natives. After worship William took the party off to the "Croydon," and we resumed our lonely life. It did seem so lonely after all the excitement of the previous fortnight; but "to the work, to the work!" sounded in our ears, and we were soon up and doing.

After a little more than a week, during which time we were much encouraged by the Port Resolution people turning out well to church and school (old Nasueiyu, who had at least four miles to come, coming regularly on Sabbath), we prepared to visit Kwamera. We purchased the arrowroot (raw material), and sent it round by boat, but we ourselves took the road, as we wanted to settle Kamil and his wife (an Aneityumese couple who had just come from Aneityum), at Ikurupu in place of Sempent, the Erromangan teacher, who had died during our absence. During the vacancy, Nirua (Monkey), a Tannaman, had been conducting meetings here.

On Friday, 1st July, we left Port Resolution, accompanied by three Aneityumese teachers and their wives all laden with goods, for we were going to give presents at Ikurupu. The people there had the mission ground in good order; a new fence had been made all round, and our own grass hut had been repaired and aired for our reception.

Calling all the worshippers together into church, William formally inducted Kamil, after which we gave over thirty garments out of a box sent by the North Belt Church, Christchurch, and which had arrived by the "Croydon" just in the nick of time. The natives had cooked a nice supper of fowl and bananas, and to this we did ample justice. We then held an evening meeting, at which prayer was offered by several, and hymn after hymn sung.

We had got a great heat on the road, and perhaps caught cold; be that as it may, we rose from our reed bed next day far from refreshed, but after breakfast and morning worship with the people, we resumed our travels past Yakwanemi, through Balaam's Pass, over the mountain path to Yakuribus, and down to Yaneveker. There we had a reed bench put up for us in the church, and so spent the night. Alas! we rose next morning more tired than when we lay down. We had, however, good and hearty meetings in the forenoon, and after mid-day we went on to Yanatuan, where, that afternoon, evening, and next morning, we had most pleasant services. My very lungs felt sore with the hard benches, so we made up our minds to go on to Kwamera, staying only an hour or two at Imerakak, a station where Vahai goes to conduct service on Sabbath, and of which Weesep, a Tannaman, has charge during the week. I would like to have told you of the road between Yanatuan and Imerakak, first round a stony beach, over rocks and boulders, where a native on each side took my hand and helped me along; then up one steep hill and down another; over a running stream, and then up another hill; of the meeting we had with the heathen in the public square; of the difficulties they see to accepting the Gospel; of the good repast the worshippers gave us; of the steep path down to the shore; of the clambering over rocks, through sinking sand, round rocky points, &c. At last we reached Kwamera, where, alas! no welcome awaited us, for the people were shy, being busy reviving an abominable practice that had been in abeyance for nearly twenty years. We felt that had we no field but Kwamera, we would either die or leave in despair. One by one our best people there have died. Nearly all my old girls are dead, and the people who are left are "wishy washy." Nahi-abba, our chief, has been an enemy to the Gospel, and a thorn in our side for many years, and we believe he is the moving spirit in all this sin and heathenism. . . .

Perhaps some one may ask what kind of buildings we have for churches at these out-stations. Well, they are simply grass huts, European-shaped, having doorways but no doors, and windows but no glass. In the one at Yaneveker, which on this trip had to do duty as church, school, reception-room, and bedroom, there is a single doorway and ten windows, and through these numerous openings the wind blew rather strong to be agreeable, and may have had more to do with our wearied bones than the hard benches. We are having grass huts for bedrooms put up both at Imerakak and Yaneveker.

I have failed to mention that on our arrival at Aneityum we had ocular proof that the labour traffic had been resumed by Queensland, as we found the "May" lying there at anchor ready to start on her legalised, but nefarious search for natives. Sir S. Griffiths may think he can frame laws to prevent abuses, but many of these laws must simply be so many dead letters, as no Government agent, however well intentioned, can carry them out. Who, for example, is to know whether the man accompanying a woman on board is really her husband? He may be, but the probability is that he is not.

I am told that without these natives Queensland cannot prosper. I believe the curse of God will rest on Queensland until she washes her hands clean of this matter.

Yours very sincerely,

AGNES C. P. WATT.

XXVII.

A COOL SEASON'S WORK.

GENERAL LETTER.

TANNA, NEW HEBRIDES,
December 5th, 1892.

My last general epistle was made up on July 16th. We were then in the middle of our annual arrowroot making; of which I told you. . . .

Early in August we went to the opening of a new church at Itaku. There was the usual exchange of gifts on both sides. We had an encouraging prayer meeting, at which, from the prayers of some, I was convinced that the kingdom of light was beginning to penetrate the dense darkness.

Friday, August 5th. Began to retrace our steps Port Resolutionwards, again walking overland. Went to Ukwarep, where we halted, and had a prayer meeting and gave gifts. At Imerakak we also gave rewards for regularity and progress. Rain came down heavily all the afternoon and evening, so that the Magic-Lantern Exhibition was poorly attended. We occupied our new grass cottage for the first time, and overheard Kawa and Naba singing a hymn; went out and called on them afterwards, and found they had family worship daily. This was a glad surprise to us, for this is one of the darkest spots in our district. (Have since heard that both Kawa and Naba are dead.)

Saturday 6th. After such a night of rain, the prospect of travelling was far from pleasant, but go we must; for all along the line we were expected. So with Nisap and Toi's help I got down the steep hill-side to the bed of the stream, which we found in flood. Here we both had to prepare for wading. I laughed, as I wondered what a comical-looking photograph could have been taken of us, as, shoeless and stockingless, first the missionary and then his wife were helped across the rapid torrent by two strong young men, now springing from rock to rock, now wading, and all the while holding my arms with firm grasp. Safe across, and foot-gear again adopted, we laboriously climbed up the other side of the gully. The rain again began to fall heavier than ever. The native paths were miniature streams, and we literally swam in our shoes. The natives were sorely distressed about us, and begged us to take shelter under a tree, which we did for a little. I again thought of the camera and a photograph of nine or ten "drookit craws" trying in vain to find a dry spot even under the big tree. No hope of it clearing up, so down the steepest and most slippery path of all we descended with difficulty; one of the women cutting foot-holes for me in the path, while my two good angels held me up, till at length we reached the sea-beach. Our path lay along the shore for two miles, and then, after going up another hill-side, we reached Yanatuan, where we got such changes of raiment as we could.

Sabbath 7th. Kauraka-asori and his wife Kuau, and

Nanawivau, were baptised, and thereafter we had Communion; the teachers, the three new members, and ourselves, making a company of eight. This is the first time our Tanna Communion service has been used; and this is the first Communion ever celebrated in this district; though for years Kauraka has taken a decided stand on the side of the Gospel. Our little love-feast was a happy one.

Monday 8th. Kauraka's son and namesake was married in church before an interested audience. The bride and bridegroom were both rigged out by us. At sundown there was a wedding supper, which consisted of two good-sized porkers, with other things on a like liberal scale. Had a splendid turn-out at the Magic-Lantern Exhibition. The visitors were treated to part of the marriage supper. This was the first Christian marriage ever celebrated in the district. In honour thereof, we had a live pig given to us, which will be carried from village to village by willing helpers until it reaches Port Resolution.

Tuesday 9th. Went to Yaneveker; Maui, a girl, accompanying us for medical treatment. Great exchange of cooked food, and a substantial supper given to the crowds who came to see the Magic Lantern. Slept in our new grass hut, which is rather green and damp, but a great improvement on the many-apertured church in which we slept on our last visit.

Wednesday 10th. Maui coughed so much that we got no sleep. I fear she is too far gone in consumption to recover, but she is anxious to follow me. Reached Ikurupu. Old grass house very grimy. Quite a large number have joined the school. Large Magic-Lantern

Meeting in the evening; the church was too small, so we met in the open air, and here, as at other places, many heard the story of Jesus for the first time. May this seed sown by the wayside find good soil. The crowd gazed and listened most attentively.

Thursday 11th. Emerged at Port Resolution, having been six nights on the way. Though very tired and lame, yet we were very happy; for we had tokens of encouragement all the way, and felt sure more good had been done than we could see. The day will declare.

Again, on the 15th, we made a journey to Yanumarer, staying one night and giving a Magic-Lantern Exhibition. As the district is much broken up by gullies, it is hard to get the people to meet daily, so we proposed that Kapere-maur should build a school-house on his side of the main gully, to which he heartily agreed.

Several friends in writing make reference to my "generals," remarking how sad they have been of late, and suggesting that I must have been "depressed," "low-spirited," "not very well, &c. Only one, who had lived for many years on Tanna, understood all, and wrote: "We particularly sympathise with you in your own trials"; and again, "On reading your letter I felt how much I could put between the lines." Yes! we had sad times in the end of last year and the beginning of this, and in telling even half the truth, our epistles would be sad; but as you see, I have fewer trials to tell of this time. The records of the cool seasons, one of which is just closing, are always more cheering than those of the hot seasons, when we suffer more from heat, have generally more earthquakes, are in terror of hurricanes, and the consequent quarrelling among the tribes. In the good (?) old times when the "Dayspring" left us early in December, and we knew we should be isolated for at least four months from the outside world, with all the may-be's which might happen during these long lonely weeks, I used to say I was like one entering a long dark tunnel, and felt clammy and creepy at the thought. When we got beyond the middle of the time, the hope of the return of the "Dayspring" was like a ray of light dimly gleaming in the far distance, which day by day became brighter, till the vessel came back laden with letters, messages, and tokens of love from home and friends.

This dark tunnel has been greatly illuminated by the monthly visits of the inter-island steamer, which never failed once to call on us during last hot season; and if the stopping of the New South Wales Government subsidy leads to the steam service ceasing, and we have to return to a sailing vessel, and two mails a year, I fear we will not take kindly to the change.

On the 22nd August we went on board the S.S. "Croydon," for a trip round the group on account of some mission business. We had lovely weather nearly all the time, and enjoyed our voyage much. The vessel was so clean, and every one from the Captain downwards was courteous and kind; thus things were in every respect a great contrast to what they had been twelve months before. We called at nearly every mission station, saw Dr and Mrs Lamb still enjoying tent life; had a peep at not a few copra stations, met a good many of the island traders, and formed our opinions of each. I do not wish, however, to express these opinions, for I have seen how true the poet's words often are, "things are not what they seem," and people making a hurried visit and getting a cursory glance, seldom come to right conclusions.

While at Aulua, Malekula, Tukoru, an Efatese teacher, caught a fine turtle, and next morning Mr Leggatt and we took it on board. Mr Leggatt shouted to the Captain that he was bringing off a fish for his breakfast. Fancy the Captain's surprise when the gift weighed 280 lbs. We had many a breakfast off it, and when enjoying the cutlets, stew, or soup therefrom, we thought of the proverbial London alderman whose mouth is said to water at the sight of the delicious soup or morsels of green fat. We spent about a week in Fila waiting for the "Rockton," and were much impressed with the march of civilisation there; if the presence of four steamers in one day, besides other craft, imply that. . . .

November 4th. Celebrated the anniversary of our church opening by giving every individual in this district some article of clothing: also strings of beads and Jews' harps as rewards for regular attendance at school. We put up ropes on either side of the church, and hung the gifts on these, instead of a Christmas tree. Each gift had the recipient's name pinned on it. We had a prayer meeting, and distributed them at the close. We met again in the afternoon, when I made up nearly one hundred portions of food, consisting of a quantity of rice, a piece of salt meat and a biscuit. Every man, woman and child had a share, and went home glad. We had a grand Magic-Lantern display in the evening to a crowded house, many heathen coming for the occasion.

I think no one can call this a sad record, seeing we can report three new church members, three Christian marriages, a new station opened, some encouraging tours among our out-stations, and the renewal of an old station. But I have still another encouraging fact to note.—Many of you will remember that our people gave their first collection last year in money. This year they have given in all *eleven* bags of copra, which realised £4 4s. That has been duly sent to the Treasurer of the Presbyterian Church of New Zealand.

November 5th. Kapere-maur having built the school-house as we proposed, we went to-day to the opening ceremony, at which we had a prayer meeting and a native feast. We gave presents out of a parcel sent by the Sydney Ladies' Association. This new station is called Iresban, and is our eighth out-station. Here Kapere and his little daughter will conduct a daily or even twice a day meeting, singing hymns, praying, teaching the alphabet, and repeating by rote.

We have now six Tannese helpers, men who, in the absence of a teacher, call their fellow-villagers to prayer. Their qualifications are few, their lives far from what they ought to be; but they are superior to their fellows, and it is a decided advance on Tanna for these men to take the position they do. They are all eloquent in prayer, and one or two of them seem very much in earnest. We have given them £1 each this year in recognition of their services. We hope they will soon be worthy of the place of teachers, and get full salary.

November 30th. Kwamera. It is not quite a fortnight since we came here by boat, accompanied by

Mr and Mrs Gray and two children. In that time, the missionaries have made a tour to the west side of Tanna, coming back by boat. That over, they printed two books in Weasisian. At these they worked very hard; some days they were eighteen hours in the printing-office; but this could not be avoided, as a week was lost through weather, and our time was limited, seeing we must be back in Port Resolution to catch the steamer. The wind and sea are now high, so the next move seems to be to walk overland.

December 5th. Left Kwamera on the 2nd, and slept that night at Yaneveker. Mr Gray had his Aneroid Barometer with an altitude scale, and by it Yaneveker was found to be 450 feet above sea-level. Next day we came on here, taking the highest road, and the highest point we reached was 870 feet. We had good weather; and having chosen the easiest paths, we accomplished the journey in comparative comfort, though very tired.

I often remark how good the Tannese are in helping us along. This time we were a goodly band, and needed many carriers from district to district. Besides ourselves, Mr and Mrs Gray and the two children, we had a goat which caused us no little amusement by the way, as well as toil. Many saw a goat for the first time, and she pulled and dragged on her rope every way but that in which she was wanted to go. The children were carried a good deal in the first part of the way, but as we neared Port Resolution and got to the smooth level road, they trotted along merrily.

AGNES C. P. WATT.

XXVIII.

"FAINT, YET PURSUING."

GENERAL LETTER.

Port Resolution, Tanna,
12th June, 1893.

In my last journal, written in January, I referred to the remarks of some who thought certain letters of mine had been written when I was despondent. I suggested that probably the journals, written as we commenced the hot season, were darker-tinted because of the prospect of all the may-be's of that usually trying time of the year. On the other hand, the cool season letters ought to be bright and cheery; for our life then is usually very enjoyable. The weather is cool, there is no fear of hurricane, and we usually see some visitors. I have often said that April and May are my happiest months, as all the season lies before me; and with regard to things earthly, I find more enjoyment in anticipation than in realisation.

Well, at present, I am as happy as the day is long; but, that you may keep pace with me, I must go back to January. Shortly after writing that month's mail, we left Port Resolution and went overland to Kwamera. Never before did I feel so unwilling to undertake the journey, and never before did I accomplish it in such weakness. We spent five nights on the way, and day by day we became more miserable in body, though happy in mind, for the people were kindness itself, and we were on the path of duty; but on the last day William fairly broke down, and had to lie for hours under a tree on the beach, or in a native hut. When somewhat rested we resumed the last stage of our journey, and crawled home in time for tea.

We were so glad to be at Kwamera again, and away from Port Resolution house, which, being some distance from the sea and surrounded by dense vegetation, is very hot, while Kwamera being on the ocean beach, we knew that there we would get any breeze that was going. Thus we entered hopefully on our work there; but alas! the people seem twice dead; nay, plucked up by the roots. True, there was much sickness, and many were ill, but that alone did not account for the thin congregations and the small classes, which grieved us from day to day. About that time I read a story about the "Lone Star Mission," and I felt that if Kwamera were the only parish we had, I would call this the "Lone Mission without the Star." Many things have led to this state of affairs. In 1889 several of our lads were taken away to Queensland in a labour vessel; then death took away a goodly number of our best people. Since our return from furlough in 1890, the mortality has been striking among our girls and young men. Of a Sabbath Morning Bible Class I had before 1889, nearly all are dead or away in Queensland; and in January last, two of my three remaining girls emigrated to Queensland; one accompanying her husband, the other eloping with a young man, though she was a grass widow, her husband being already in Queensland. The young boys who are left are turned against school. They are told, "Look how all the young people of the Mission have died." Whether if we had kept our health and been able to go out more among the people, things would have improved, I cannot tell; but from being miserable and only able to crawl through our duties, we were laid completely aside. William had been out of sorts for months, but on February 8th he became alarmingly ill. For ten days he was very weak, and had all the symptoms of remittent fever. Then he began to recover, but oh, how slowly! Fortunately I was able to nurse him; but I did long for civilisation with all its comforts, and for friends with all their help and sympathy. He was only one week well, when I took ill; and for a whole month I was confined to bed or sofa. The nausea was continuous; I was brought very low, and had to be waited on like a child.

Having two head stations, we cannot keep flocks of goats at each, and so we had only two milk goats at Kwamera. One of them was giving a good pint a day while William was ill, but alas! she died suddenly one day, apparently of poison, and so our milk supply ceased. Milk diet was the best for us, and to me it was a real trial to be without it. How I did loathe *milkless* gruel, *milkless* arrowroot, and *milkless* sago, or, for a change, *tinned* beef tea. Nor dare I take more solid food even if I had had the appetite, which was awanting. In the beginning of April I was brought round here, to Port Resolution, on a mattress in the stern of the boat. It was a risky thing, as I had not been out of bed for a month, but we had a fair passage, and the change acted like magic. In a few days I was able to move about, and recovered much faster than William had done. Health returning, we did not repine, although here, too, we are reduced to a milkless diet, the trader's dog having worried the one milk goat, and the other being strangled a short time after by its tether.

Many a time when we were ill, and often since then, we have said, "What a blessing we were not both ill together, else there might have been no one left to tell the tale." I, especially, was helplessness itself. While native Christians do very well when there is some one to superintend and suggest, they rarely do anything of their own accord. I have known of traders, men living alone in grass huts, being five days without seeing a human being, and quite unable to help themselves. So you see the Old Book is right in this matter, "Two are better than one."

We were informed by the last mail from the "Croydon" that a vessel of some kind would leave Sydney in April with stores and mails for the Mission. It is now the 14th of May, but we have seen nothing of the expected vessel. A sailing vessel is a very uncertain visitor; she is so dependent on weather. I, for one, will mourn all my days in the New Hebrides if we have to return to the good (?) old days of the "Dayspring." The "Croydon" came to anchor every four weeks in this bay, where I could go on board, if I wished, in smooth water. This made life much more pleasant than when, as of yore, the "Dayspring" lay miles off, and when I had to go on board, my tongue literally clove to the roof of my mouth, as reeling and staggering through a heavy sea our little boat ploughed her way to the "Dayspring"; and then, who can describe the scene at the ship's side!

Notwithstanding all our sickness at Kwamera, we managed to get seven new hymns printed, bringing our hymnal up to *ninety-five*. We added them to our hymn books, and bound about two hundred and fifty copies; but we were never able to teach these. Since coming here we have introduced four of the new hymns, accompanied by our baby organ, and the effect has been very encouraging. Without doubt our Tannese have an ear for music, and under training would prove good pupils. "Go, sound the trump on India's shore," they sing with great gusto, and a paraphrase of our Saviour's words as recorded in Matthew v. 43-48, sung to the tune "Barrow," has proved a great favourite. But the greatest favourite of all is a translation of "Thou did'st leave Thy throne," sung to the tune to which it is set in "Songs and Solos." We practise morning and evening, and we pray that the saving truths thus committed to memory may prove good seed sown on a good soil.

Here, unlike Kwamera, we have excellent meetings daily, and on Sabbaths all the population, with the exception of one man and two women, attend the services. Much Scripture knowledge is being acquired; and we earnestly desire an outpouring of the Holy Spirit to quicken their hearts and apply the truth to them; for although they thus fear the Lord, they serve other gods, and cling to their heathen customs with a tenacity worthy of a better cause. Many heathen customs have been given up, and the grosser heathen ceremonies are things of the past; but there is still much to be undone before real progress in Christianity can be reported.

The past hot season has been exceptionally wet, and, so far, the cool season is keeping up this peculiarity; but I am pleased to say we have had no earthquakes, no hurricanes, and no war.

On Tuesday, May 11th, the schooner "Sovereign" called at Weasisi, and we received a mail by her which had been landed at Efate by the "Rockton" about a fortnight before. By her, we heard from Dr Lamb that Ambrim was a desolation, and that their infant twin sons had died. We also heard that two of Dr Gunn's family had died on Futuna; and, heaviest of all, that Mrs Mackenzie of Efate had died of dysentery. In her death, our Mission has lost one of the bravest and noblest of its women; and our hearts bleed for brother Mackenzie, left alone at his station, and the four young people in the colonies left motherless. Doubtless she is now realising the hundredfold reward promised to those who leave all for Christ's sake.

We learned from the "Sovereign" that the "Lark" was the vessel chartered to do the Mission work, and that she might soon be expected here; but her arrival was to be of little consequence to us, as the band of brethren and "sistern" returning from furlough, whom we expected to see in passing, had already arrived in Efate by the "Rockton." Thus all hope of seeing kindred spirits was cut off. We also learned that there was to be no Synod this year.

On the 24th May the "Lark" cast anchor in the

Bay. She brought the appalling news from Dr Gunn, that, besides his two children who had died, Ruth, the youngest, had been at death's door, and he himself had been very ill. The sickness was dysentery, and it has cut off 130 people in Futuna, out of a population of 480.

At this season of the year there is usually a great amount of feasting and dancing on Tanna. Generally a Tannese feast is accompanied with dancing, and a Tanna dance by feasting. When we speak of a Tannese feast we mean what is called here a "Niari," which might be described a "Fair," only that the food is exchanged in presents, and not bought and sold. Dancing we use as the equivalent of the Tannese "Nakwiari." At the Nakwiari, cooked food and live pigs are exchanged, but dancing is the principal thing.

In our neighbourhood there was a "Niari." Our church-goers gave the yams to a heathen tribe, who in return killed and gave them fourteen pigs. We estimated there would be about five or six tons of yams given. Whole bunches of yams were hung from a scaffolding built round the sides of the public square ; single yams were hung by creepers from the branches of the overspreading banyan tree, each draped in green leaves. A pile of yams was raised in the middle of the square like an immense sugar loaf. It measured about twenty-four feet round the base, and was about ten feet high. We were pleased with the dress and demeanour of our parishioners, who, by the absence of paint and other signs of heathenism, and the presence of clothing, testified to their profession of Christianity.

A small schooner, the "Harold" of Sydney, was lying

in the Bay, and the party on board were interested witnesses of the above feast. The various hues and designs of paint on several faces caused one to remark, " If I had a girl like that (pointing to one) on exhibition, I would make my fortune." Said girl had on scarlet, yellow and black paint in abundance, and evidently thought she was a beauty.

The day following the feast there was a Nakwiari at an inland village. To a heathen Tannese the Nakwiari in his village is the event of the year. Special dances and special music are got up for the occasion, and for months these are practised almost daily. During these preparatory weeks both men and women fast to a certain extent in order to look slim and neat for the dance; but when all is over excess of every kind is indulged in, as well as obscene practices.

How isolated our life is this year! what a contrast to the previous years when we had a monthly mail! We are both feeling dragged down and in need of a change, but that is next to impossible this year. . . .

AGNES C. P. WATT.

XXIX.
WAITING.

THE LAST GENERAL LETTER.

PORT RESOLUTION, TANNA,
NEW HEBRIDES,
November 18th, 1893.

The chief characteristic of this season has been *rain*, and here it never rains but it pours. To the natives the incoming year threatens to be one of scarcity—they say, famine; but then we know that natives exaggerate at times. During twenty years' life on Tanna we never saw the native gardens so far back; at Kwamera only one is finished, all the rest are barely begun, as the incessant rain prevents the work being done, and in fact causes the bush to grow as fast as it is cut down. As the Tannese believe that they have power over the elements, one and another is credited with making this rain. In some cases pigs have been given as bribes to have it removed; in other cases threats of murder have been made for the same purpose; but alas! from the Tannamen's point of view bribes and threats have alike been in vain, and it is still rain, rain, rain.

As rain is the special feature in the physical world here, so *waiting* has formed a large part of our service, and the grace of patience has been much called into exercise. We have had a long wait for health, weary waits for an erratic maritime service, trying waits for favourable winds to enable us to go between our two principal stations, and a continual wait, looking for the " early and latter rain " on our work.

Although our lives are eminently busy ones, yet in another sense they are wholly made up of waiting— waiting like the husbandman for the precious fruits, which require long patience. During this year of isolation I have felt the waiting much. I was deeply impressed with an article which came to us last mail, and as it expresses exactly our experience, I will quote a part of it : " Every old soldier knows that the hardest thing in connection with a battle is the waiting under fire for the orders to move. To push forward in the fight is exciting work, so exciting as to call out the energies of a man and keep his mind full with thoughts of that which he has to do for the moment. He has no time then to think of danger, or to speculate upon chances. But when a man has to stand or lie in line with the bullets whistling about his ears, and nothing to do in the nature of action or effort, he is sure to be thinking of danger and fearing the results of delay, and to be suffering from the strain upon his nerves, which is all the more intense because there is nothing for his muscles to do. As it is with the soldier in physical warfare, so is it with the soldier in life's battle. Waiting under fire is harder than moving forward in the thick of the fight; yet waiting is a large part of man's duty in life, when he would fain be actively doing something. . . . A city business man, who had not indulged in the luxury of vacations, was induced to take a holiday in the country. It did not suit his active mind, and when he was asked by a friend how it seemed to him, he answered, 'I feel all the time as if I was waiting at the corner of the street for a car to come along.' Many another man can appreciate that state of mental strain. . . . Yet just because waiting is so hard, waiting is the one duty of the hour to be endured bravely and in hope, when there is nothing to do but to wait. Patience is the endurance in waiting at the call of God, and such patience is enjoined and commended as a Christian duty and a Christian virtue." The apostle says, " Ye have need of patience"; and our Lord says, " In your patience ye shall win your souls."

Our illnesses of February and March had so pulled down our strength that it was August before we attempted any itinerating. In August, however, we had a twelve days' mission in the bush. We spent two nights each at Yanumarer and Yanatuan, and seven at Yaneveker. At the last place we superintended the erection of a new grass school-house. The old one was taken down on the Monday; the new one commenced on the Tuesday and finished on Friday. Many hands made light work, and we had over forty assisting. Some were gathering material, some were building, and others cooking. Saturday was the feast day over it; the inaugural dinner, so to speak. Two pigs were cooked, and native puddings *ad libitum* were prepared. As at home the minister's wife frequently provides a table at the annual soiree or debt extinction social, so here we did our part by giving dresses or girdles to all.

As some one wisely remarks, " A minister must teach the poorest of his flock that he is something more than a superior relieving officer, although he must bear in mind that it is often in this capacity that he is able first to reach their hearts. Christ not only taught, but fed the multitudes that followed Him, and the proclamation of the Gospel has ever been accompanied by deeds of charity. Sympathy and silver are among the most certain ways to popularity." Believing in the above sentiments, we gave out about a hundred garments on this tour, and feel that all will tend to the furtherance of the Gospel; for these love-gifts from Christians enable our simple-minded people the better to understand the love that led Christ to give Himself. Among the heathen a pure gift is unknown. A gift only means an exchange of goods, and often some article is given with the expectation that the giver will receive far more than its value.

On Sabbath the united congregations of Yanatuan and Yaneveker met in the new church; and being clad in their new "braws," looked very well. We had Communion, but of the Tannese, only Kauraka communicated, as both Kuan and Kauawan were lying very ill. Thus our company only numbered seven; but is not the presence of Jesus promised to the two or three?

Often I feel sure that the smoke and din of battle keep us from seeing the victory that is being won; for doubtless the Tanna of to-day is not the Tanna of ten years ago. We were most hospitably entertained by the people, and in that alone we have a proof of the great change effected on them. Lately, an old fellow living near us at Port Resolution tried to incite us to give presents indiscriminately, by telling us how the first missionaries did, making the gospel a lucrative profession to the Tannaman. Unfortunately for our greedy friend, we were able to remind him of the other side, better known to us, how three missionaries had been robbed, their houses broken into, their teachers maltreated, and even killed; and they themselves at last obliged to flee for their lives. Now the tables are completely turned, for not only are we fed and cared for while in their villages, but on leaving Yaneveker we had three splendid porkers given us; one preceded us by a few days, and one followed a few days after, but the third headed the procession as we returned. The comicality of our line of march excited my risibilities. Of course we will give them return presents; but even double or treble their value would not induce an unfriendly or heathen person to give them to us. The sight of us returning, laden with gifts, and followed by an affectionate band of church-goers, impresses the heathen with the idea that there may be something in our message after all. Notwithstanding our long walks and life in grass huts, we were much benefited by our bush residence, and our hearts were cheered with tokens of advance.

On the 12th September, the "Lark" called with our much-longed-for mail, and had on board Mrs Gillan and Miss Jessie Mackenzie; the former on her way to Malekula to rejoin her husband and resume her work; the latter to join her father at Erakor. I had thus the rare pleasure of seeing a white woman's face. I had parted with Mrs Gray in December 1892, and from that till September 1893 I saw nought of my own sex save the sable beauties of Tanna. I felt so excited with joy that I fear I failed to show them much attention. That night we read and wrote letters till two a.m., and were up and at it before six next morning, this being the only chance of getting a mail away for at least three months.

Since our illnesses we have longed for a change, but with the present maritime service, any change off the island is next to impossible, so we made up our minds to make a visit to the Grays suffice. We spent a very pleasant fortnight under their hospitable roof. How I luxuriated in the freedom from household duties and cares after more than a year of daily toil, save a month on a sick bed! and how pleasant we felt it to be with kindred spirits! We went and returned in our boat. The going down was lovely; the sky bright blue and the ocean calm as a millpond. But coming back it was just on the eve of a gale; the sea was dark and lumpy and the sky black as ink. We left Weasisi in rain, but got little by the way. For more than a week we were detained by high winds and heavy seas. On the 11th October a boat's crew, who were here from Aneityum, took us round to Kwamera. Both wind and sea were still high, so to save what is usually the worst part of the voyage I walked over a neck of land to Kwanaris, and the boat met me there. I was prepared to walk to Kwamera if the sea had been too rough, but William persuaded me to go by boat. We did have a spin through the water; we surged and raced along like a race-yacht, taking in a spray now and again. Having a very heavy load of corrugated iron on board, I felt no fear of a capsize; but I felt sure we would sink like lead if we took a sea on board, such as we had done some nine years, ago when we barely escaped being swamped. I am not ashamed to say I was nervous, but I had to hide it, as Watonia* shook like an aspen leaf; and though it took me all my time to keep a calm exterior, I did my best to still her fears. I believe a year of life and hard work is not so wearing to me as an hour in the boat in such weather; and yet this year I have travelled sixty miles of open sea, round a coral-bound coast, and generally we have had rough trips. It is very awkward having two principal stations and only one boat; for while the Tannamen are willing boatmen, they cannot walk overland for fear of other tribes. After all, we were very fortunate in our run round to Kwamera, for we got no rain, and our unexpected arrival on such an unpropitious day helped to bespeak an unusually hearty welcome for us. No sooner were we and our perishables safe up at the house, than down came the rain, and it fell in torrents all afternoon; yet one and another came through the wet to shake hands with us. Truly, Nahi-abba's death † has cleared the atmosphere, and we have greater liberty.

We had an important meeting the day after our arrival, and persuaded the men to resume church attendance. It was gratifying to see many, who had turned their backs on all services for many years,

---

* A trader's child she had taken charge of.

† Wednesday, 5th July. Awakened last night about twelve by our dog "Rockton" barking, and heard crying. On William asking what it was, we were told, "Nahi-abbi is dead." Could not believe it, but the daylight revealed it. "How are the mighty fallen and the warriors laid low!" Crowds came to wail. He was buried at sundown.—*Extract from Diary.*

WATERFALL AT KWAMERA.

returning on the following Sabbath. During the three weeks we spent there, we were much encouraged by their attitude to the gospel, and their demeanour toward us. I long to see the Tannese embrace the gospel, and pray that the Lord would seal them for His own.

We spent exactly three weeks at Kwamera, and they were remarkably busy ones, especially to the now grey-whiskered missionary, who worked like a tradesman, or rather a slave, putting corrugated iron on our outhouses instead of thatch. He had willing helpers in one teacher and the Tannamen, but much had to be done by the missionary himself; and I was often sorry as I saw him crawling over the iron roof either in the broiling sun or pelting rain; for such work in this climate is no child's play. The sad thing about such roofs at Kwamera is that they last so short a time, owing to exposure to the salt spray. Can any one suggest a preventive? We are at endless labour and no little expense, but see no help for it. Even painting the iron does not suffice. This roof-damaging exposure to the sea air has its compensations. How cool we feel there! and now that all the men have resumed church attendance and the lads come to school, we intend to spend most of the ensuing hot season at this, our ocean-beach station.

While at Kwamera we heard with deep sorrow that war had broken out near Ikurupu. An old veteran heathen had been shot in the bush as he was returning home from a neighbouring village. His body lay all night where he fell; but next day his friends carried it home and buried it. A few hours after, his friends sought revenge. They went stealthily to the village of another tribe, but their approach being discovered by a young woman, her life must go. Poor lassie, all unsuspecting, she had gone a few yards from her own door to cut some firewood, when the mean assassins aimed at her. There were three shots fired; two missed, but the third took fatal effect. I cannot tell you how unwilling I was to believe the report, but alas! it was too true.

My ever-willing lassie! she who was one of our regular carriers between the bush stations, who was ever ready to obey our wishes, who was our best scholar at Ikurupu, and who gave good help at teaching, has suffered for the sins of others. The dreadful deed was done about sundown, and one of the last acts of Yauikau's life was reading some of the New Testament just before going out.

The war has led to the partial suspension of work at Ikurupu. Kamil (the teacher) and his wife have come down here for the present, as the people are all too excited to attend school. He goes up on Sabbaths and conducts service. Not long ago he was late in going up, and on his arrival found that two young Tannamen, supposing he was not coming, had conducted a prayer meeting instead.

The gospel on Tanna is like a plant on a foreign soil, and yet there is here and there a fair show of leaves and a promise of fruit. As you already know, the New Testament has given an impetus to the work. Here at Port Resolution all are learning to read, and a few can do so fluently. We have four Scripture readers who take their turn and read the chapter for the day at the Sabbath services. To encourage good reading, we are offering prizes to the value of 2/6 and 5/ each to those who will either read a chapter at first sight or commit a portion to memory.

I must tell you about Ka-u. He is a young man at Itaku who never had lessons from us, but who learned the alphabet and small words through the teacher. Last year he was laid up for months with diseased feet. He whiled away the hours of weariness deciphering the New Testament. When we were at Kwamera he came to see us, and in course of conversation asked why Take (another man) had not got a New Testament. I said, "Perhaps because he was ill when they were distributed, or else he has just been forgotten." "Well," he said, "it is good you give me one for him now; I sit beside him in the church, and I can point the place for him with my pointer." I gave him a New Testament, and I was amazed and gratified to see him open it at random, and commence to read the first chapter of 2nd Thessalonians. He told me of another lad who spends hours poring over the precious book, and when surprise was expressed at his diligence, he said, "The words in this book are not like the words of man; they are good."

I have always had great faith in the word of God pure and simple, knowing that "The entrance of His word giveth light," and would hail the day when every one could read; but, as many know, the Tannese are a book-dreading people, and we have to keep dunning at them to attend school.

I must not fail to mention that we have got tangible and valuable help in our work from various parts of the world in the shape of made dresses. As far as I know the donors, I have written thanking them for their timely aid. The natives marvel at the love that incites such gifts, and many a talk they have about the good women who, out of pure love, cut and make garments for them.

After the "Lark" calls, about December 1st, till next April, we have the prospect of what I call solitary confinement with hard labour and great heat. This we understand to be the last call of the "Lark," and what we shall have next year we do not know. We hope it will be better. It could hardly be worse. The present prospects are—*nothing* till April at the earliest. Truly the "tunnel" looks longer and darker than usual; but with good health and God's grace "All will be well." *

People wonder what we get to do down here. I sometimes wonder myself; yet from day to day we have more than enough. We have innumerable calls on our time in the way of medicine. Many a day we have as many patients as if we were "medicals," while in the matter of medical comforts (tea and tilts) the calls are even more numerous.

Although it may seem rather premature, I wish you all a Happy New Year!

"Is the path difficult? Jesus directs thee;
Is the path dangerous? Jesus protects thee.
Fear not and falter not, let the word cheer thee,
All through the coming year He will be near thee."

AGNES C. P. WATT.

---

* This "general" was sent by the "Lark," but before she had left Port Resolution the s.s. "Croydon" arrived there on her way to Fila to resume the inter-island steam service.—W. W.

Appendix.

MEMORIAL MINUTES, ETC.

1. FOREIGN MISSION COMMITTEE OF THE PRESBYTERIAN CHURCH OF NEW ZEALAND.

The Committee desires to express its sorrow at the sad intelligence of the death of Mrs Watt, which took place at Port Resolution on April 26th, 1894. Mrs Watt for twenty-five years has been the untiring helpmeet of her husband in his efforts for the evangelisation of the darkened people of Tanna, and her own efforts for the salvation of the natives were constant and untiring, and she was much beloved by all the natives who were favourably disposed towards Christianity. Mrs Watt was well known to the members of our Church through general letters, which, notwithstanding the pressing claims of the work on Tanna, she found time to write; and by all who had met her personally she was highly esteemed and beloved, not only for her work's sake, but also on account of her beautiful and Christ-like character; so that the sorrow caused by the news of her death is deep and widespread. It was not her privilege to see many sheaves gathered upon Tanna, but amidst the more difficult and trying labours of the long sowing she was sustained by an unshaken faith in the goodness and purpose of God, "who will have all men to be saved, and to come to the knowledge of the truth." Now she rests from her labours until He comes, who shall cause the sower and the reaper to rejoice together, rewarding each as his work has been. To Mr Watt we desire to convey our heartfelt sympathy in his unspeakable loss, while we pray that in his sad bereavement he may be sustained by the Blessed Master, whom he, and she for whom he mourns, so diligently and faithfully served.

WILLIAM GRANT, Leeston,
Interim Convener, Foreign Mission Committee.

2. MINUTE OF THE PRESBYTERY OF AUCKLAND.

St. Andrew's Church, Auckland,
Tuesday, 5th June, 1894.

Which day the Presbytery of Auckland met and was constituted. Inter alia:—On the motion of the Rev. R. F. Macnicol, seconded by the Rev. Thos. Norrie, it was unanimously resolved, "That the Presbytery record their deep sense of the loss which the Presbyterian Church of New Zealand has sustained by the death of Mrs Watt, the devoted wife of our much esteemed senior missionary, Rev. W. Watt. The Presbytery have, from the beginning of Mr and Mrs Watt's labours on Tanna, entertained a high estimate of Mrs Watt's adaptation to the arduous and important position she was called upon to occupy, and the devoted and efficient services which she rendered to the cause of Christ in that difficult field. They instruct the Rev. G. B. Munro, the Assembly's corresponding member of the Foreign Mission Committee, to convey to Mr Watt their sincere Christian sympathy with him in his sore bereavement."

3. RESOLUTION OF THE PRESBYTERY OF WELLINGTON.

The Presbytery of Wellington have heard with deep regret of the death of Mrs Watt, wife of the Rev. Wm. Watt, the church's esteemed missionary on Tanna, and they desire to put on record their high appreciation of her excellent Christian character, and of her valuable services to the Mission. Closely associated as she was with her husband, not only in their home life, but also in his missionary life, she devoted herself entirely to her duties in the home and in the work of the mission, and thus proved herself in every way a true helpmate, and a valuable coadjutor in the service of their common Lord. Her kindly genial manner and high-toned Christian character endeared her to all who came into intimate acquaintance with her, and her energy and devotion, combined with tact, judgment and sympathy, made her influence felt in the work of the mission, and in commending that work to the Church. Those who knew her intimately feel that they have lost a warm-hearted and sympathetic friend, and cannot but regard her death as a loss to themselves as well as to the Church. The Presbytery desire to express their sympathy with Mr Watt in his sore bereavement; and they pray that the Divine Master, whom he has so long and so faithfully served, may be with him in his loneliness and in his work, consoling and strengthening him, and that this sad event may be made the means of blessing to the native population of Tanna, among whom he has so long lived and laboured.

4. LETTER FROM THE REV. DR GOOLD, EDINBURGH, CONVEYING SYMPATHY OF THE DIRECTORS OF THE NATIONAL BIBLE SOCIETY OF SCOTLAND.

My immediate object in writing to you at present is to fulfil a request of the Directors of the National Bible Society. At a meeting of the Board this week they requested me to convey to you an assurance of their deep sympathy with you, and of their sincere respect for the memory of your late wife. Some of them knew her personally, such as Mr Gardiner of Pollokshaws; most of them knew her by report; and all of them knew how much the cause of the Bible is indebted to you. A tribute of respect for her memory from some thirty gentlemen is of some value, all the more that the chief ground on which it rests is not private friendship, but the public usefulness of the deceased to the cause of Christ. It could have been no ordinary woman who, after long service in a remote corner, evokes the grateful recognition of her worth from a Board sitting at the opposite end of the earth.

5. MEMORIAL MINUTE OF THE NEW HEBRIDES MISSION SYNOD.

ANELGAUHAT, ANEITYUM, NEW HEBRIDES,
May 2nd, 1895.

Which time and place the New Hebrides Mission Synod met and was duly constituted. Inter alia:—

"When on the eve of meeting as a Mission Synod, we have been called upon to mourn the loss sustained by the sudden and unexpected death of Mrs Watt, the wife of the Rev. W. Watt, Tanna. During a period of twenty-five years she was permitted to go out and in among the people of Tanna, whose eternal welfare lay upon her heart. Being possessed of wonderful tact and energy, she became all things unto all classes, that she might save some. She was ever devising new schemes or improving old ones, that Christ might be glorified in their lives. Humanly speaking, we should have expected her amongst us for many years to come, but God, whose she was and whom she served, has called her to higher service, and our loss is great. To her bereaved husband and relatives we offer our deepest sympathy, and pray that the God of all consolation may heal their wounded hearts."

www.ingramcontent.com/pod-product-compliance
Lightning Source LLC
Chambersburg PA
CBHW030408230426
43664CB00007BB/790